READING PHILIP ROTH

Reading Philip Roth

Edited by

ASHER Z. MILBAUER

Associate Professor of English
Florida International University

and

DONALD G. WATSON

Associate Professor of English
Florida International University

St. Martin's Press   New York

First published in the United States of America in 1988

Printed in Hong Kong

ISBN 0–312–00934–8

Library of Congress Cataloging-in-Publication Data
Reading Philip Roth.
Bibliography: p.
Includes index.
1. Roth, Philip—Criticism and interpretation.
I. Milbauer, Asher Z.   II. Watson, Donald G.
PS3568.0855Z85 1987   813'.54   87–9838
ISBN 0–312–00934–8

For our wives and parents

Luba, Tzviya and Yishayahu

Nancy, Louise and Garner

Contents

Preface

By presenting our readers with the thirteen essays especially written for this anthology,* we hope to extend the critical understanding of Philip Roth's fiction and to clarify some fundamental misunderstandings of his intentions and meanings.

After having reviewed both the academic and journalistic critical responses to Roth's canon, we realise that while some of them are solid and helpful, many are permeated by a constant confusion of tale and teller, a confusion that defeats the very essence of literary criticism – to lead the reader *to* the text rather than *away* from it. In fact, this is exactly what Nathan Zuckerman, Roth's protagonist-author and frequently his mouthpiece as well, requires of the critic of his own fiction: 'It's one thing to think you're pretending to your students when you tell them there's a difference between the characters and the author, if that's the way you see it these days – but to strip the book of its tone, the plot of its circumstances, the action of its momentum, to disregard totally the context that gives to a theme its spirit, its flavor, its life –.' Although out of breath and too exasperated to complete his sentence, Zuckerman manages to convey a clear message to his critics: to perceive the book's tone, to follow its plot, to discern the spirit of its theme the text must be read.

Indeed, this obsessive urge to read attentively and to respond reflexively emerges not only as a recurrent motif in Philip Roth's fiction but also as a key to understanding it. One cannot help but notice that all of Roth's main fictional characters are constantly reading and responding to their readings. Whether they read, interpret (or misinterpret) Shakespeare or Chekhov, Flaubert or Mann, James or Babel, Kafka or Tolstoy, or themselves, as Zuckerman's own case testifies, they remind Roth's own readers of the notion that literature matters, that it may be a means to know the world and bring meaning to an 'unhallowed existence'. All this, however, can be achieved only if the writer's work is read. And there is hardly anything wrong, maintains Roth in his interview with us, if it is then misread, provided 'what's meant [by

---

* Milan Kundera's essay is based upon two pieces published in French but rewritten for this volume. The editors are responsible for the translations.

misreadings] isn't [a] reading that's shallow and stupid, but that's
fixed in its course by the reader's background, ideology, sensibility,
etc.'.

In editing this collection of essays we never asked of our
contributors anything more than to reread Roth's books and to
suggest fresh ways of looking at his corpus of fiction. This they have
done with much discretion, skill, and talent. We are grateful to
them.

A.Z.M.
D.G.W.

Acknowledgements

While editing this anthology we accumulated a number of debts. We want to thank David Reif for his assistance in translating from French and Richard Schwartz for his helpful comments on several of the essays.

Our special thanks go to Elaine Dillashaw and Vilma Valdes for preparing the manuscript for publication and patiently responding to our many demands.

Finally, we should like to thank Philip Roth for being accommodating and generous with his time.

Permission to quote from *Zuckerman Bound* published by Farrar, Straus & Giroux is gratefully acknowledged.

Notes on the Contributors

Aharon Appelfeld is Professor of Literature at Beersheva University and a leading Israeli novelist. His books include such celebrated novels as *Badenheim 1939, Tzili, The Age of Wonders* and *To the Land of the Cattails*.

Jonathan Brent, Professor of English at Northwestern University, is the editor of *Best of TriQuarterly* and *A John Cage Reader*. He is the Director and editor-in-chief of Northwestern University Press and editor of *Formations* magazine.

Estelle Gershgoren Novak, poet and essayist, teaches at the University of California, Los Angeles; for the last twenty years she has published widely in a variety of journals and anthologies.

Sam B. Girgus, Director of American Studies at the University of Oregon is the author of *The Law of the Heart: Individualism and the Modern Self in American Literature, The New Covenant: Jewish Writers and the American Idea*, and editor of *The American Self: Myth, Ideology and Popular Culture*.

Martin Green, Professor of English at Tufts University, is the author of *Children of the Sun, Cities of Light and Sons of the Morning*, and *Dreams of Adventure, Deeds of Empire*. He is the editor of *A Philip Roth Reader*.

Donald Kartiganer is Professor of English at the University of Washington. He is the author of *The Fragile Thread: The Meaning of Form in Faulkner's Novels* and editor of *Theories of American Literature*.

Milan Kundera is a Czech novelist currently residing in Paris; formerly a professor at the Prague Institute for Advanced Cinematographic Studies, he is now a faculty member at the Practical School of Advanced Studies in Paris. Among his publications are such widely acclaimed books as *The Joke, The Book of Laughter and Forgetting, Life is Elsewhere*. His most recent novel is *The Unbearable Lightness of Being*.

Asher Z. Milbauer, Professor of English at Florida International University, is the author of *Transcending Exile: Conrad, Nabokov, I. B. Singer*. He has recently completed a soon-to-be-published study on 'The Image of Eastern Europe in American–Jewish Literature'.

Patrick O'Donnell, Professor of English and Director of Undergraduate Studies at the University of Arizona, is the author of *John Hawks* and *Passionate Doubts: Designs of Interpretation in Contemporary Fiction*.

Clive Sinclair is a British novelist, short-story writer and essayist. His most recently published book is *Blood Libels*. He is the book editor of *The Jewish Chronicle*.

Martin Tucker, Professor of English at Long Island University, is the author of *Africa in Modern Literature* and *Joseph Conrad* and editor of more than fifteen volumes of literary encyclopedias. He is the editor of *Confrontation* magazine, as well as a widely published poet.

Donald G. Watson is Professor of English at Florida International University. He has published essays on the writings of Shakespeare, Boccaccio, Erasmus and is the author of a book about Shakespeare's early history plays.

Hana Wirth-Nesher, Professor of English and Chair of the English Department at Tel Aviv University, is the author of numerous essays and studies on American, British and Jewish fictions. She is the author of a book on urban fiction entitled *Legible Cities*.

1

An Interview with Philip Roth

ASHER Z. MILBAUER and DONALD G. WATSON

Many critics and reviewers persist in writing about Roth rather than his fiction. Why this persistence after all these years?

If that's so, it may have to do with the intensity with which my fiction has focused upon the self-revealing dilemmas of a single, central character whose biography, in certain obvious details, overlaps with mine, and who is then assumed 'to be' me.

The Ghost Writer was automatically described in the press as 'autobiographical' – which means about Roth's personal history – because the narrator, Nathan Zuckerman, is an American–Jewish writer, my age, born in·Newark, whose earliest writing elicits a protest from some Jewish readers. But as a matter of fact, that about constitutes the similarity between my history and Zuckerman's in that book. The unsettling opposition from his father that young Zuckerman confronts and that propels the moral plot of *The Ghost Writer*, I happen to have been spared; the intelligent, fatherly interest taken in his work by a renowned, older writer whose New England houseguest he's lucky enough to be at twenty-three, resembles no experience of mine starting out in the fifties; nor have I ever met a woman to whom I have been romantically drawn because she resembled Anne Frank, or whom I mentally transformed into Anne Frank and endowed with her status in order to try to clear myself of Jewish charges of self-hatred and anti-Semitism.
charges of self-hatred and anti-Semitism.

Though some readers may have trouble disentangling my life from Zuckerman's, *The Ghost Writer* – along with the rest of *Zuckerman Bound* and *The Counterlife* – is an imaginary biography, an invention stimulated by themes in my experience to which I've given considerable thought, but the result of a writing process a long way from the methods, let alone the purposes of autobiography. If an avowed autobiographer transformed *his* personal themes into a

1

detailed narrative embodying a reality distinct and independent from his own day-to-day history, peopled with imaginary characters conversing in words he'd never heard spoken, given meaning by a sequence of events that had never taken place, we wouldn't be surprised if he was charged with representing as his real life what was an outright lie.

May I quote John Updike? Asked about my Zuckerman books, he said to an interviewer 'Roth's inventing what looks like a *roman-à-clef* but is not'.

But if your books are misread, other than by John Updike, isn't that more or less the fate of most good writing? Don't you expect to be misread?

That novelists serve readers in ways that they can't anticipate or take into account while writing doesn't come as news to someone who spent eight years with *Zuckerman Bound*. That's the story told on nearly every one of its 800 pages, from the opening scene, when Nathan the budding writer enters Lonoff's living-room seeking absolution from sins committed in his juvenilia against his family's self-esteem, to its conclusion on the day that, as an established writer in his forties, he is forced to surrender to the Prague police the wholly harmless Yiddish stories that they've decided to impound as subversive.

The only reading resembling the ideal reading that a writer sometimes yearns for is the writer's reading of himself. Every other reading is something of a surprise – to use your word, a 'misreading', if what's meant isn't reading that's shallow and stupid but that's fixed in its course by the reader's background, ideology, sensibility, etc.

To be misread in any way that bears thinking about, however, a writer has to be *read* as well. But *those* misreadings, conferred by skilful, cultivated, highly imaginative, widely read misreaders, can be instructive, even when quite bizarre – witness Lawrence's misreadings of American literature; or Freud's, the all-time influential misreader of imaginative literature. So are those misreaders, the censors, influential, though for other reasons. And *are* the Soviet censors necessarily misreading, in Solzhenitsyn's fiction, his political aims? Though censors may appear to be the most narrow-minded and perverse of all misreaders, at times they may be more discerning about the socially injurious implications of a book than the most tolerantly open-minded audience.

Serious misreading has little to do with a text's impenetrability –

geniuses misread nursery rhymes; all that's required is for the genius to have his own fish to fry.

In the light of this, what about an audience? Do you think you have one, and, if so, what does it mean to you?

I've had two audiences, a general audience and a Jewish audience. I have virtually no sense of my impact upon the general audience, nor do I really know who these people are. By a general audience I don't refer, by the way, to anything vast. Despite the popularity of *Portnoy's Complaint*, the number of Americans who have read, with any real attention, half of my books – as opposed to those who may have read one or two – can't number more than 50,000, if that. I don't think anymore about them when I'm at work than they think about me when they're at work. They're as remote as the onlookers are to a chess player concentrating on the board and his opponent's game – I feel no more deprived or lonely than he does because people aren't lined up around the block to discuss his every move. Yet an unknowable audience of 50,000 judicious readers (or inventive misreaders) whose serious, silent attention I freely command is a great satisfaction. The enigmatic interchange between a silent book and a silent reader has struck me, ever since childhood, as a unique transaction, and, as far as I'm concerned, it's what the public side of the novelist's vocation has to come down to.

Counterbalancing the general audience has been a Jewish audience affording me, really, the best of both worlds. With my Jewish audience I feel intensely their expectations, disdain, delight, criticism, their wounded self-love, their healthy curiosity – what I imagine the writer's awareness of an audience is in the capital of a small country where culture is thought to mean as much as politics, where culture *is* politics: some little nation perpetually engaged in evaluating its purpose, contemplating its meaning, joking away its shame, and sensing itself imperilled, one way or another.

Why do you irritate Jews so much?

Do I any longer? Certainly 'so much' must be an exaggeration by now, though one that I've helped unintentionally to perpetuate because of the writer's predicament in *Zuckerman Bound*. After fifteen books I myself have become much less irritating than the Zuckerman I've depicted, largely because the Jewish generation that didn't go for me is by now less influential and the rest are no longer ashamed, if they ever were, of how Jews behave in my fiction.

Because it *was* shame – theirs – that had a lot to do with that conflict. But now that everybody's more confident about the right of Jews to have sexual thoughts and to be known to engage in authorised and unauthorised erotic practices, I think that stuff is over. On the whole Jewish readers aren't quite so responsive to other people's ideas (real or imaginary) of what constitutes socially acceptable Jewish behaviour, and don't appear to be obsessively worried that damaging perceptions of them can be indelibly imprinted on the public mind through a work of fiction, and that these will set off an anti-Semitic reaction. American Jews are less intimidated by Gentiles than they were when I began publishing in the 1950s, they are more sophisticated about anti-Semitism and its causes, and altogether less hedged-in by suffocating concepts of normalcy.

This isn't because they have been socially blinded by the illusory gains of assimilation, but because they are not so preoccupied as they once were with the problematical nature of assimilation, and are justifiably less troubled by ethnic disparities in the new American society of the last fifteen years – a society created by a massive influx of over twenty million people far less assimilable than themselves, about eighty-five per cent of them non-Europeans, whose visible presence has re-established polygenesis as a glaring and unalterable fact of our national life. When the cream of Miami is the Cuban bourgeoisie, and the best students at M.I.T. are Chinese, and not a candidate can stand before a Democratic presidential convention without flashing his racial or ethnic credentials – when *everybody* sticks out and doesn't seem to mind, perhaps Jews are less likely to worry too much about *their* sticking out; less likely, in fact, *to* stick out.

In addition to the shame I fomented there was the menace I was said to pose by confirming the beliefs of the committed Jew-hater and mobilising the anti-Semitism latent in the Gentile population generally. Years ago, the eminent scholar of Jewish mysticism, Gershom Sholem, published an attack upon *Portnoy's Complaint* in an Israeli newspaper, predicting that not I but the Jews would pay the price for that book's imprudence. I learned about Sholem's article only recently in Israel – a university professor from Tel Aviv summarised Sholem's argument for me and asked what I thought of it. I said that history had obviously proved Sholem wrong: more than fifteen years had passed since the publication of *Portnoy's Complaint* and not a single Jew had paid anything for the book, other than the few dollars it cost in the bookstore. His reply? 'Not yet,' he said; 'but the Gentiles will make use of it when the time is right.'

The Jews I still irritate, who angrily disapprove of me and my work, are for the most part like the Israeli professor: for them the danger of abetting anti-Semitism overrides nearly every other consideration.

Of course there must be many Jews as well as many Gentiles who don't care for my books because they don't think that I know how to write fiction. Nothing wrong with that. I'm pointing rather to a psychological or ideological orientation, a view of politics and history that *had* to make *Portnoy's Complaint* anathema to a certain group of Jewish readers. Though the example of the Israeli professor might seem to suggest otherwise, this particular Jewish orientation seems to me to be disappearing just *because* of the existence of Israel and its effect upon Jewish self-consciousness and self-confidence in America.

I'm not referring to the pride that may be inspired in American Jews by Israeli military victories or military might – it's not images of Israel triumphant or naive notions of Israeli moral infallibility that have signalled to American Jews that they needn't any longer be too tightly constrained by protective self-censorship, but just the opposite, their awareness of Israel as an openly discordant, divisive, society with conflicting political goals and a self-questioning conscience, a Jewish society that makes no effort to conceal its imperfections from itself and that couldn't conceal them from the world even if it wanted to. The tremendous publicity to which Israeli Jews are exposed – and to which they're not unaddicted – has many causes, not all of them always benign, but certainly one effect of unashamed, aggressive Israeli self-divulging has been to lead American Jews to associate a whole spectrum of behaviour with which they themselves may have preferred not to be publicly identified, with people perceived as nothing if *not* Jews.

To move to a more general subject, do you think of fiction as a way of knowing the world or of changing the world?

As a way of knowing the world as it's not otherwise known. Clearly a lot can be known about the world without the help of fiction, but nothing else engenders fiction's kind of knowing because nothing else makes the world *into* fiction. What you know from Flaubert or Beckett or Dostoyevsky is never a great deal more than you knew before about adultery or loneliness or murder – what you know is

Madame Bovary, Molloy, and *Crime and Punishment.* Fiction derives from the unique mode of scrutiny called imagination, and its wisdom is inseparable from the imagination itself. The intelligence of even the most intelligent novelist is often debased, and at the least distorted, when it's isolated from the novel that embodies it; without ever intending to, it addresses the mind alone rather than suffusing a wider consciousness, and however much prestige it may be accorded as 'thought', ceases to be a way of knowing the world as it's not otherwise known. Detached from the fiction a novelist's wisdom is often just mere talk.

Novels *do* influence action, shape opinion, alter conduct – a book can, of course, change somebody's life – but that's because of a choice made by the reader to use the fiction for purposes of his own (purposes that might appal the novelist) and not because the novel is incomplete without the reader taking action. The 1967 conference near Prague, organised by Czech intellectuals around themes in Kafka, turned out to be a political stepping-stone to Dubček's reform government and the Prague Spring of 1968; none the less it was not something that Kafka invited, could have foreseen, or would necessarily have enjoyed. Ways of knowing the world that he entitled *The Trial* and *The Castle* – which to most people still look like no way of knowing anything – were exploited by these Czech intellectuals as a means of organising a perception of *their* world persuasive enough to augment a political movement already underway to loosen the bonds of Soviet totalitarianism.

You sound as though you really prefer that fiction should change nothing.

Everything changes everything – nobody argues with that. My point is that whatever changes fiction may appear to inspire have usually to do with the agenda of the reader and not the writer.

There is something that writers do have the power to change and that they work to change every day, and that's writing. A writer's first responsibility is to the integrity of his own kind of discourse.

Do you feel that the importance, if not even the integrity, of fictional discourse, is threatened by rivals like film and television and the headlines, which propose entirely different ways of knowing the world? Haven't the popular media all but usurped the scrutinising function that you attribute to the literary imagination?

Fiction which has a scrutinising function isn't merely threatened, it's been swept away in America as a serious way of knowing the world, almost as much within the country's small cultural élite as among the tens of millions for whom television is the only source of knowing anything. Had I been away twenty years on a desert island perhaps the change in intelligent society that would have astonished me most upon my return is the animated talk about second-rate movies by first-rate people which has almost displaced discussion of any comparable length or intensity about a book, second-rate, first-rate, or tenth-rate. Talking about movies in the relaxed, impressionistic way that movies invite being talked about is not only the unliterate man's literary life, it's become the literary life of the literate as well. It appears to be easier for even the best-educated people to articulate how they know the world from a pictured story than for them to confidently tell you what they make of a narrative encoded in words – which goes some way to explaining why what the verbal narrative knows has itself become less knowable. It requires a kind of concentrated thought that has become either too difficult or too boring or both.

The popular media have indeed usurped literature's scrutinising function – usurped it and trivialised it. The momentum of the American mass media is towards the trivialisation of everything, a process presided over and munificently abetted during the last six years by the Great Trivialiser himself. The trivialisation of everything is of no less importance for Americans than their repression is for the Eastern Europeans, and if the problem does not seem to have achieved the same notoriety at the PEN Club as political repression, it's because it flows out of political *freedom*. The threat to a civilised America isn't the censorship of this or that book in some atypical school district somewhere; it's not the government's attempt to suppress or falsify this or that piece of information; it's the *superabundance* of information, the circuits *burgeoning* with information – it's the censorship of *nothing*. The trivialisation of everything results from exactly what they do *not* have in Eastern Europe or the Soviet Union – the freedom to say anything and to sell anything however one chooses.

There are now writers in the West tempted to think that it might really be better for their work if they were oppressed in Moscow or Warsaw rather than twittering away free as the birds in London, New York or Paris. There's a perverse undercurrent of persecution-envy around, an envy of oppression and the compression of freedom. It's as though without an authoritarian environment imaginative possibilities are curtailed and one's literary seriousness is open to question. Well, unfortunately for writers who may be afflicted with such longings, the intellectual situation for thinking Americans in no telling way mirrors, parallels, or resembles what is horrifying for thoughtful people in the Soviet orbit. There is, however, a looming American menace that evokes its own forms of deprivation and suffering, and that's the creeping trivialisation of everything in a society where freedom of expression is anything but compressed.

The Czech writer Josef Skvorecky, who now lives in Toronto, has said, 'To be a bad writer in Eastern Europe, you *really* have to be bad.' He means that in those countries the political origins of their suffering are plainly visible in everyday life and the predicament is constantly staring them in the face; personal misfortune is inevitably coloured by politics and history, and no individual drama is seemingly without social implications. What Skvorecky wryly suggests is that there is almost a chemical affinity between the consequences of oppression and the genre of the novel; what I'm saying is that in the unlikely, less graspable consequences of our unprecedented Western freedom, there may well be a subject for imaginative scrutiny of no less gravity, even if it doesn't light up and flash 'Serious! Significant!' and 'Suffering! Suffering!' in everybody's face. Our society doesn't lack for imaginative possibilities just because it isn't plagued by the secret police. That it isn't always as easy to be interesting in our part of the world as it is in Skvorecky's occupied country, may only mean that to be a good writer in the West and of the West, you have to be very, very good.

Was it not a problem for your generation of writers to establish the seriousness of your fiction without resorting to or falling back upon the established conventions of seriousness, be they the realism of James or the modernism of Joyce?

That's a problem for every generation. Ambitious young writers are always tempted to imitate those verified by authority; the influence of an established writer upon a beginning writer has almost entirely to do with the search for credentials. However, finding a voice and a subject of one's own entails making fiction that may well prompt the writer's first readers to think, 'But he can't be serious', as opposed to, 'Ah, this is very serious indeed'. The lesson of modernism isn't encapsulated in a technique that's 'Joycean' or a vision that's 'Kafkaesque' – it originates in the revolutionary sense of seriousness that's exemplified in the fiction of Joyce, Kafka, Beckett, Céline –

even of Proust – fiction which to an unknowing reader probably bears the earmark less of seriousness than of high eccentricity and antic obsession. By now the methods of these outlandish writers have themselves become the conventions of seriousness, but that in no way dilutes their message, which isn't 'Make it new', but 'Make it serious in the least likely way'.

Has the 'least likely way' for you been your kind of comedy?

Comedy for me has been the most likely way. I could do it no other way, though it did require time to work up confidence to take my instinct for comedy seriously, to let it contend with my earnest sobriety and finally take charge. It's not that I don't trust my uncomic side or that I don't have one; it's that the uncomic side more or less resembles everyone else's, and a novelist's qualities have to have their own distinctive force. Through the expressive gradations of comedy I can best imagine what I know.

Yet isn't Zuckerman, in The Anatomy Lesson, *afraid that he is not 'serious' enough, afraid that for all his physical ailments he is not 'suffering' sufficiently? Isn't that why he wants to enrol in medical school, and, in* The Prague Orgy, *travels to Eastern Europe?*

Yes. His comic predicament results from the repeated attempts to escape his comic predicament. Comedy is what Zuckerman is bound by – what's laughable in *Zuckerman Bound* is his insatiable desire to be a serious man taken seriously by all the other serious men like his father and his brother and Milton Appel. A stage direction that appears in *The Prague Orgy* could easily have been the trilogy's title: *Enter Zuckerman, a serious person.* Coming to terms with the profane realities of what he had assumed to be one of the world's leading sacred professions is for him a terrific ordeal – his superseriousness is what the comedy's *about.*

Zuckerman Bound opens with a pilgrimage to the patron saint of seriousness, E. I. Lonoff; it ends, as you point out, at the shrine of suffering, Kafka's occupied Prague. Imagining himself married to Anne Frank is the earliest escape that he attempts to contrive from the seriousness that first challenges his youthful illusions about a dignified role in the world. Judge Leopold Wapter, Alvin Pepler, the Czech secret police, a crippling and unexplained pain in the neck – all are representatives of impious life irreverently encroaching upon that seriousness he had once believed inherent to his high calling. But what most successfully subverts the high calling's esteem is his sizeable talent for depicting impious life: it's Zuckerman who gives his dignity the most trouble.

The denouement of the trilogy begins midway through the third volume, when, on the way to Chicago to become a doctor – for those American Jews who most disapprove of him, the supreme embodiment of professional seriousness – Zuckerman adopts the disguise of a pornographer and, abandoning whatever claim he believes he still has to be taken seriously, transforms himself into a vessel of the profane (in every sense of the word). Well, it's a long way from pretending to be the husband of Anne Frank in E. I. Lonoff's sanctum sanctorum, to proclaiming himself a vice king, at one with the polluted, as publisher of *Lickety Spit*. Like a good modernist writer, Zuckerman the pornographer imagines at last the least likely way to dramatise the serious lesson taught him by the chastening ordeal of unhallowed existence.

I realize that this sort of ordeal, especially as suffered by the high-minded, looks a little like an old, obsessional theme if you think of Gabe Wallach in *Letting Go* or of David Kepesh in *The Breast* and *The Professor of Desire*. The ordeal of an unhallowed existence is really what Portnoy's complaining about, too.

Are you complaining about it – is that why it's an old, obsessional theme?

Obsessional themes evolve from astonishment as much as from enduring grievance – a writer is not so much beset by the theme as by his underlying *naïveté* in the face of it. The novelist suffers from serious ignorance of his obsessional theme. He lays siege to it time and again because the obsessional theme is the one he least understands – he knows it so well that he knows how little he knows.

My answer to the question is no: no complaint from me about unhallowed existence – it's all you get and I'm not so refined as to feel defiled by it. Of course you come here to be insulted. It's what they put on the tombstones – *He Came Here To Be Insulted*, carved in letters three inches deep. Lowly life, however, so long as it doesn't tumble over into misery and horror, can still be entertaining, and, for all its grittiness, strangely uplifting. As young Zuckerman discovers in *The Ghost Writer*, what makes ours a species of moving creatures isn't the high purposes but the humble needs and cravings. Yet there *are* those high purposes, and inappropriate as they may be to an unhallowed existence, they have been provided for some odd reason and just won't seem to go away. My obsessional theme is calculating what it costs a creature of humble needs and cravings to be saddled with a high purpose as well.

We realize that you are reluctant to appear to be explicating a book prior to its publication. However, without 'explaining' it away, can you comment generally on the unusual form for The Counterlife, *which is certainly unlike anything you've done before?*

Normally there is a contract between the author and the reader that only gets torn up at the end of the book. In this book the contract gets torn up at the end of each chapter: a character who is dead and buried is suddenly alive, a character who is assumed to be alive is, in fact, dead, and so on. This is not the ordinary Aristotelian narrative that readers are accustomed to reading or that I am accustomed to writing. It isn't that it lacks a beginning, middle, and ending; there are too *many* beginnings, middles, and endings. It is a book where you never get to the bottom of things – rather than concluding with all the questions answered, at the end everything is suddenly open to question. Because one's original reading is always being challenged and the book progressively undermines its own fictional assumptions, the reader is constantly cannibalising his own reactions.

In many ways it's everything that people don't want in a novel. Primarily what they want is a story in which they can be made to believe; otherwise they don't want to be bothered. They agree, in accordance with the standard author–reader contract, to believe in the story they are being told – and then in *The Counterlife* they are being told a contradictory story. 'I'm interested in what's going on,' says the reader, '– only now, suddenly, there are two things going on, three things going on. Which is real and which is false? Which are you asking me to believe in? Why do you bother me like this!'

Which is real and which is false? All are equally real or equally false.

Which are you asking me to believe in? All/none.

Why do you bother me like this? In part because there really is nothing unusual about somebody changing his story. People constantly change their story – one runs into that every day. 'But last time you told me –'. 'Well, that was last time – this is this time. What happened was . . .' There is nothing 'modernist', 'postmodernist' or the least bit avant-garde about the technique. We are all writing fictitious versions of our lives all the time, contradictory but mutually entangling stories that, however subtly or grossly falsified, constitute our hold on reality and are the closest thing we have to the truth.

Why do I bother you like this? Because life doesn't necessarily have a course, a simple sequence, a predictable pattern. The bothersome form is intended to dramatise that very obvious fact. The narratives are all awry but they have a unity; it is expressed in the title – the idea of a counterlife, counterlives, counterliving. Life, like the novelist, has a powerful transforming urge.

2

The Artist as a Jewish Writer

AHARON APPELFELD

The label 'Jewish writer', it seems to me, has never been loved by
any Jewish writer. This label has always conveyed a sense of
poverty, neglect, and provincialism. The Jewish writer has
preferred to be recognised as an international writer. Even the
Yiddish authors, whom this label fitted best, were not happy to be
called Jewish writers. Moreover, the writer who writes in Hebrew
prefers to be called an Israeli writer. As years went by, it goes
without saying, things got worse. As a result of this, now no one
labels a Jewish writer a Jewish writer; only those writers of the past –
those remembered and those forgotten – are 'Jewish' writers. Today
a Jewish writer asks to be called simply a writer, and if a label must
be attached, he prefers that it be 'American' or 'Israeli'. 'Jewish
writer' goes beyond mockery; it is an insult.

Many quills were broken over the definition of 'Jewish art'. Every
now and then a small tumult arises around this problem and is
promptly forgotten. Apparently there is a spiritual need for some
kind of definition, but any definition is hard and slippery and gives
rise to many arguments in favour of or opposed to the definition. I
will neither correct nor hide nor add to all that has already been said
about this problem, because of a simple reason: I do not believe in
the usefulness of any definition.

Philip Roth, in my opinion, is a Jewish writer, not because he
considers himself to be a Jewish writer or because others regard him
as a Jewish writer, but because he writes about people called
Zuckerman, Epstein, Kepesh, and their mothers, about their lives
and their lives' upheavals, in a manner a novelist relates things he
knows intimately. As a result, he knows about both the recognisable
and the hidden movements of his characters. Whenever possible,
he observes them with a scrutinising attention and without
interfering in their lives. He has never idealised the Jew. He has

never elevated him to sainthood, never created him faceless; rather he speaks of him as if he is flesh and blood, about his human successes and his human defeats. I use 'flesh and blood' because I have not found a better concept to single out the bare essence of human existence. In Philip Roth's fiction there is hardly any Jewish philosophy, Jewish tradition, mysticism, or religion, and there is no discussion of who is a Jew or what is a Jew. There are those who are proud of their Judaism and parade it whether there is a need for it or not. And then there are those who are ashamed of it and those for whom Judaism has no importance at all. Roth's Jews are Jews without Judaism.

Because his works do not discuss and make reference to 'typical' characteristics of the Jewish spirit, let alone events in Jewish history, Philip Roth is often perceived as a very American writer; although the Jew is found in his fiction, he is there because of biographical accident rather than philosophical commitment. The writer is primarily interested in everyday existence and not in raising – to use Jungian terminology – the collective consciousness of the chosen people. Certainly, this point of view can be reinforced by rereadings. To reiterate, Philip Roth's works have no Talmud, no Jewish philosophy, no mysticism, no religion. His literary production does not reveal Jewish sources in the same way as Orthodox Christianity is found in Dostoyevsky's and Tolstoy's novels. If this is so, why then are Roth's novels Jewish? I still maintain that Roth is a Jewish writer because all the experiences in his fiction, from *Goodbye, Columbus* to his last novel, reflect the facial expressions, words, intonations, the mannerisms of the eye's language of stares and grimaces, with which the Jews are so generously endowed. Add to this the humour and the grotesqueness, and you are faced with works of art that remind you of a family relatedness to such writers as Saul Bellow and I. B. Singer on the one hand and Franz Kafka on the other. I am mentioning these writers because Philip Roth's affinity with them surpasses mere literary kinship.

What is the nature of the Jews in Philip Roth's books? They are descendants of the children of the decendants of the Eastern European Jewish tribe who in the beginning of the century were threatened by evil forces, both from within and from without, that dispersed them to the four corners of the world. Some came to America. In this dispersion the tribe lost many of its ancient beliefs and teachings as well as characteristics of its traditional lifestyle but not its ways of responding to reality and its patterns of behaviour. These responses and modes of behaviour lengthened its life even after the basic beliefs had faded.

These are the Jews who have apparently forgotten their Jewishness while at the same time replenishing it. In formal terms, this forgetfulness is immense, yet it contains miraculous exceptions and gaps: the reflexes are Jewish and often very Jewish. These contemporary Jews have neither a Jewish prayer nor knowledge of Judaism, yet they have both. They do not live any longer in overcrowded ghettoes but nevertheless they are immersed in the ghetto existence: the ways in which they live with, speak to, and attach themselves to each other, or the ways in which they leave each other alone express an ancient mentality, as does the manner in which they relate to strangers by being attracted to as well as being alienated from them. Philip Roth has observed the stranger closely; in fact, the stranger brings out the Jew in Roth. However, what he knows most intimately and comprehensively is the Jewish family: the love, the closeness, the burden, and all the entanglements of mother, father, and sons who chase one another as if one of them were going to be kidnapped. The warm nest called the Jewish family is sometimes a nest of lepers. Roth thoroughly knows the texture of such a family that receives its sustenance from the ancient Jewish ghetto; he is also well in tune with their desires and fears. Regardless of anything, they continue to stick to each other as if they still belonged to a tribe under the shadow of an all-encompassing covenant. Roth consistently follows the waves that revitalise the tribe's spirit. I say a tribe because this concept not only points to an extended family but also to a group of people with a secret, the secret of the past that unknowingly feeds the present.

There is no American writer whose works have generated as much tribal fermentation as Roth's have. Jewish readers suspect that the artist who is addressing them is describing the Jews from intimate experience and is raising from the depths some hidden tribal essence, not exactly what the majority would have liked him to raise. This controversy – that is, this complete misunderstanding between the tribe and the artist who threatens its good name – has reached an intensity which had not been known since Shalom Asch published his book on Jesus of Nazareth. All the tribe's intelligentsia – the rabbis, the leaders, the scholars – rose up against the betrayer of Israel, Philip Roth, in order to sever him from his Jewish roots, his identity within the tribe. In this struggle, the most important thing was forgotten: Philip Roth the writer, who has been following the lives of the great and the small, the quiet and the violent, with much understanding. In their hearts, the prosecutors are aware that Roth knows his characters intimately, and his writing reflects not a rootless tale but rather a world well anchored in the contemporary Jewish existence. The prosecutors knew this, but in spite of their knowledge they rose against him with passionate anger that brings to mind the ancient excommunicators.

The fight forgot the writer. Today no one points an accusing finger at Roth as betrayer of Israel, but the sediments this controversy generated have not yet disappeared. There are few writers today considered to be Jewish writers; Philip Roth is one of them. To underscore this fact, I would like to say that Roth has a spiritual homeland whose roots are in the Jewish Newark. From there they spread. It is obvious that he did not remain bound by his locale; he distanced himself from it, as did Saul Bellow and Bernard Malamud. Yet Roth's devotion to roots made possible his flights of imagination and success as a novelist.

It is a pity that his works have had to stumble over so many misunderstandings, especially misunderstandings with his Jewish brethren. The one small consolation – and one which is not very convincing – is that most of the tribe's writers, and often the very best ones, have never harvested too much joy from their tribe.

Translated from the Hebrew by the editors.

3

From Newark to Prague: Roth's Place in the American-Jewish Literary Tradition

HANA WIRTH-NESHER

In *The Anatomy Lesson*, the central character of Philip Roth's trilogy *Zuckerman Bound* comes into his inheritance. Right after his mother's death of a brain tumour, her neurologist hands Nathan Zuckerman a white piece of paper on which one word appears in his mother's handwriting, her response to the doctor's request that she write her own name. The word is 'Holocaust', and Nathan notices that it is perfectly spelled.

> This was in Miami Beach in 1970, inscribed by a woman whose writings otherwise consisted of recipes on index cards, several thousand thank-you notes, and a voluminous file of knitting instructions. Zuckerman was pretty sure that before that morning she'd never even spoken the word aloud. (p. 477)[1]

As the neurologist is uneasy about throwing it away, he passes it on to Nathan who cannot discard it either. It is a legacy alien to his experience and incomprehensible; a scrap of paper both portentous and incidental. His compelling need to preserve it serves as an emblem both of Roth's relationship to his Jewish tradition and of a significant portion of what has come to be called Jewish–American literature.

Definitions of Jewish-American literature abound, beginning with Malin and Stark's landmark essay in 1964 in which the Jew is seen to be an existential hero and therefore a modern Everyman.[2] In a thesis that rapidly became a trend, the Jew is singled out, because of his victimisation, uprootedness, and history of suffering, as the

17

most apt symbol for humanity in the twentieth century.[3] Jewish-American fiction, argued Malin and Stark, tends to be about seeking home (as a result of mass immigration), about the conflict between fathers and sons (cast in terms of generation conflict brought on by immigration), about coming to terms with history (caused by the awesome scope of the Jewish past), about dualities (chosen by God and rejected by the Gentiles), about the heart (suffering as initiation into humanity), and about transcendence (through humanity not God). Since all literature of the West tends to be about the longing for 'home', the conflict between parents and children, the individual in the face of history, duality, suffering, and transcendence, the only conclusion that one can draw about Malin and Stark's formula is that of Shylock, 'If you prick us, do we not bleed?' If Jews are men, and all men are Jews, there seems to be little point in discussing American-Jewish literature.

Several years later, Malin pursued the implications of his definition in a theological approach to the subject. Jewish-American writers, he argued, 'are made crusaders hoping for a transcendent ideal'. Malin continued to see Jewish literature in a religious perspective, 'Only when a Jewish writer, moved by religious tensions shows "ultimate concern" in creating a new structure of belief, can he be said to create "Jewish literature".'[4] It would seem for Malin that a religious impulse linked with individualism and anti-traditionalism make for Jewishness. Continuity through discontinuity.

While not everyone agreed with Malin's stress on religion, other critics sought the Jewish elements in universal terms as well. Theodore Solotareff, for example, defined Jewish-American writing in a thematic and moralistic framework. In Malamud, Roth, and Bellow, Solotareff identified the theme of suffering leading to purification: 'There is the similar conversion into the essential Jew, achieved by acts of striving, sacrificing, and suffering for the sake of some fundamental goodness and truth in one's self that has been lost and buried.'[5] As it would be problematic to argue that the ennobling of suffering is a Jewish concept, or that 'the moral role and power of the human heart' are attributes distinguishing Judaism from other moral systems, the moral approach is hardly more enlightening than the religious one.

As early as 1964, when the sanctity of the melting pot was being replaced by pluralistic and ethnic ideals of American culture, Donald Daiches doubted whether American-Jewish writing really amounted to a movement. 'The American-Jewish writer has been liberated to use his Jewishness in a great variety of ways, to use it not aggressively or apologetically, but imaginatively as a writer probing the human condition', but he denied that extreme sensitivity was enough to qualify as a criterion for distinguishing Jewish-American literature from any other corpus.[6] That same year Allen Guttmann limited Jewish-American literature to a transient social and historical phenomenon, to documenting the immigrant Jews' conversion to other passions – Communism, capitalism, and secularisation. Assimilation, he argued, was inevitable and imminent.[7]

The most vociferous and sensible objection to existing definitions of Jewish-American literature has been that of Robert Alter: 'It is by no means clear what sense is to be made of the Jewishness of a writer who neither uses a uniquely Jewish language, nor describes a distinctively Jewish milieu, nor draws upon literary traditions that are recognizably Jewish.' For Alter, unless a writer's imagination is impelled by a consciousness of Jewish history, such as that of Kafka, there is no case for labelling him as Jewish. Admitting that there is 'something presumptuously proprietary about the whole idea of sorting out writers according to national, ethnic, or religious origins', Alter sees Jewish-American literature as one that informs the reader 'of the precarious, though stubborn, experiment in the possibilities of historical continuity, when most of the grounds for continuity have been cut away'.[8]

'Tradition as discontinuity', Irving Howe's summation of what constitutes the Jewish-American novel, turns Alter's observation into a dictum. Howe's corpus for this genre has been the literature of immigration, and as he has tended to see immigrant neighbourhoods as a kind of region, Jewish-American literature is for him a 'regional literature' focusing on one locale, displaying curious and exotic customs, and coming as a burst of literary consciousness resulting from the encounter between an alien group racing toward assimilation and half-persuaded that it is unassimilable. Drawing a parallel with American Southern writing, Howe has noted that a 'subculture finds its voice and its passion at exactly the moment that it faces disintegration'.[9]

By the time Jewish-American fiction was legitimised to the extent that a full chapter was reserved for it in *The Harvard Guide to Contemporary Writing* (in an ill-conceived project that distinguishes among Black Literature, Women's Literature, Experimental Fiction, and Drama), Marc Shechner had abandoned any attempt at defining what he went on to describe under the title of 'Jewish Writers'. Cautiously and defensively, Shechner admits that 'neither "Jewish writer" nor "Jewish fiction" is an obvious or self-justifying subdivision of literature, any more than Jewishness itself is now a self-evident cultural identity'. Nevertheless, Shechner chronicles a 'historical fact' – that many American novelists happen to be Jews – and he invokes the Jewish writer as a 'convenient shorthand for a feature of the literary consensus that we want to examine but are not yet prepared to define'.[10]

Jewish-American literature, then, has emerged as a recognisable corpus of work in the American literary tradition, although criteria for admission into this canon remain problematic, as recalcitrant as criteria for determining definitions of Jewishness itself. Where is Philip Roth in a tradition as tenuous and difficult to pin down as this one? For a large number of his Jewish readers, Roth started out as an *enfant terrible* and matured into an informer. His writings have been called vulgar, vicious, and stereotypical of anti-Semitic lore. He has been accused of unfocused hostility and self-hatred. In his repeated self-defences, Roth has portrayed himself as a victim of incompetent readers, philistines, impervious to irony and artistry. In his zeal for self-justification, declaring that he never received a thank-you note from an anti-Semitic organisation or that his stories were not likely to start a pogrom, he occasionally became as single-minded about the processes of culture formation as his readers had been about the status of art. With implicit analogues to Joyce, Roth has depicted himself as an artist rebel, unfettered by social restraints and collective anxieties. The task for the Jewish novelist, he has argued, 'has not been to go forth to forge in the smithy of his soul the *uncreated* conscience of his race, but to find inspiration in a conscience that has been created and undone a hundred times over in this century alone'.[11] Despite his resistance to the label of Jewish-American writer, he has reviewed his own work in relation to other authors regularly included in that corpus. For example, he linked *Portnoy's Complaint* with Bellow's *The Victim* and Malamud's *The Assistant* as 'nightmares about bondage'. The novelistic enterprise in such books, he explained, 'might itself be described as imagining Jews *being* imagined, by themselves and by others'. In 'Writing about Jews', Roth recorded what was 'once a statement out of which a man might begin to construct an identity for himself: *Jews are people who are not what anti-Semites say they are*'.[12] From which one can deduce that Roth would see Jewish writing as literature that is *not* what American Jews say it is, namely that renunciation, being Jewish, must be the inevitable subject of any Jewish literature.

Roth's early works, before he embarked on the long journey from Newark to Prague, are records of the last stages of the immigrant's assimilation into American life. From *Goodbye, Columbus* to *Portnoy's Complaint*, much of his writing documents the second and third generation of Jewish-Americans, well ensconced in the suburbs, the university, the army, and other American institutions, yet haunted by a tradition they do not understand and cannot abandon. 'Defender of the Faith', set in the American army, is exemplary for measuring the distance between Jewish literature of the immigrants and that of their sons and grandsons. Jewish immigrants from Eastern Europe would have regarded the army as does one of Sholem Aleichem's characters, Shalom Shachnah, in the comic story 'On Account of a Hat'. Borrowing from the tall tales of the Chelm repertoire, Sholem Aleichem describes a rattlebrained Jew on his way home for Passover who takes a nap in a railway station and upon awakening accidentally grabs the hat of a high-ranking army official instead of his own. When the conductor escorts him to third class, he reads his obeisance as mockery, as no Jew could be expected to be treated so deferentially. Only when he catches a glimpse of himself in the mirror does he realise what happened – the peasant boy he paid to wake him, he reasons, must have wakened the army officer instead! The story is spun around the shtetl Jew's anxiety at being mistaken for a Gentile and the impossibility of reconciling the army attire with Jewish identity. It brilliantly embodies the total separation of Shachnah's life from that of the Russian culture around him, the very unimaginability of assimilation.

In marked contrast, 'Defender of the Faith', removed by several generations and set in America, records the anxiety of a Jewish army officer about being singled out as a Jew in the American army. One of Sergeant Nathan Marx's Jewish privates, Sheldon Grossbart, blatantly exploits his Jewishness to weasel out of his responsibilities in the army. As a result, Marx is caught between the expectations of Grossbart that he will abide by the collective loyalties of a minority and not betray him, and the expectations of his equally obnoxious superior Captain Barrett, who, in an anti-Semitic diatribe, praises Marx for his assimilation and loyalty to the army. When Grossbart invokes the persecution of the Jews and the invidious complicity of self-hating brethren in order to plead for a weekend pass on religious grounds, Marx relents. But when Grossbart brings back a Chinese eggroll from what was to have been a Passover seder, Marx has Grossbart's sole exemption from the Pacific deployment revoked. Nathan Marx is 'Defender of the Faith', but which faith? Did he defend the faith from the abuse of religious charlatans like Grossbart? As Grossbart and Barrett are equally reprehensible, Marx finds himself in a position of dual loyalty, and although one can argue that he sought a just position regardless of American or Jewish allegiance, it would not be interpreted as such by either Barrett or Grossbart, and the vindictiveness of his action, the exaggeration of his response to Grossbart's misdemeanour, is indicative of how excruciating it is for him to be on the cutting edge of these conflicting loyalties.

In 'Eli the Fanatic', the smooth assimilation of second- and third-generation Jews into the upper-middle-class suburb of Woodenton is threatened by the infiltration of obtrusive orthodox immigrants, including a yeshiva for orphaned refugees from the displaced persons camps after the Second World War. Eli Peck, appointed to represent the community in its campaign to keep this blight from their sanitised idyll, offers his tweed business suit to one of the black-garbed newcomers so offensive to Woodenton. Finding those black garments deposited at his doorstep, he cannot resist wearing them himself. Loping across the manicured lawns of his neighbours' on his way to the hospital to see his first born son, he vows that he will pass the same black garments on to the next generation. Treated like a madman by the hospital attendants, Eli screams 'I'm the father!', an affirmation of both his familial role to the newborn and his role as purveyor of the ancestral line. But the response of suburban America to so far reaching an outcry is to tear off the troublesome jacket and administer a sedative. 'The drug calmed his soul but did not touch it down where the blackness had reached.'[13]

These two early stories embody the Jewish elements in his fiction up to the publication of *Portnoy's Complaint*: they are both chronicles of the drama of assimilation several generations removed from immigration, and also tales of near-pathological allegiance to a collective past that has no meaning for Roth's protagonists other than an emotional knee-jerk brought on by any reference to Jewish persecution, particularly the Holocaust. Both 'Defender of the Faith' and 'Eli the Fanatic' concern the Second World War, and each of these protagonists assumes extreme behaviour to protect his only connection with the Jewish people, identification with their suffering. With the publication of *Portnoy* and Alexander Portnoy's endless and outrageously comic complaint about the crippling effects of Jewish psychic baggage on his sex life, Roth finally turned the 'nice Jewish boy' into a pathological joke. 'I am the son in the Jewish joke – only it ain't no joke! . . . who made us so morbid and hysterical and weak? . . . Is this the Jewish suffering I used to hear about?' By depicting narcissistic Portnoy, intent on blaming all of Jewish history, of which he is mostly ignorant, for his inability to lead a life of pure pleasure, Roth made himself vulnerable to moralistic attacks on his alleged self-hatred and vulgarity. The outburst of rage occasioned by the publication of *Portnoy* was a turning point in Roth's career. From then on, Roth's art began to turn inward so that the drama between the Jewish writer bent on freely expressing his desires in his art and his moralistic readers bent on denouncing him becomes the central subject of his fiction. And when his art begins to turn in upon itself, it also moves toward a more complex identification with Jewish life. Roth has himself admitted that this is the case. 'Part of me wishes the misreading had never happened, but I also know that it's been my good luck; that the opposition has allowed me to become the strongest writer I could possibly have been. In fact my Jewish detractors insisted on my being a Jewish writer by their opposition.'[14]

How is this translated into his work? Roth has always been a comic writer with a moralistic streak, preoccupied with the relation between the carnal and the spiritual. Nathan Zuckerman, the writer-protagonist of Roth's most recent works, the *Zuckerman Bound* trilogy, is a comic author experiencing writer's block, exacerbated by his mother's legacy to him, the scrap of paper with the word 'Holocaust' on it. Symptomatic of the relation of the Jewish-American writer to recent Jewish history, it has a grip on the writer's consciousness disproportionate to its meagre presence in his own life. One word on a scrap of paper invokes guilt and anxiety powerful enough to further paralyse Zuckerman. The Jewishness in Roth's more recent writing goes beyond chronicling the last stages of assimilation (as in *Goodbye, Columbus*), by taking the form of a vaguely felt duty to identify with the most recent Jewish past, namely the Holocaust. Roth's work is marked by the discomfort of the American Jew who has never suffered as a result of his Jewishness, but is heir to a tradition that, from his point of view, is characterised by suffering. While he had already explored this theme in earlier works such as 'Defender of the Faith' and 'Eli the

Fanatic', his more recent fiction has an additional dimension, the discomfort of the Jewish-American author, particularly the comic writer, committed both to his art and to some identification with the suffering of his fellow Jews.

Roth's artistic strategy for dealing with his dilemma begins to become evident in 1973 with 'I Always Wanted You to Admire My Fasting; Or Looking at Kafka'. It is a daring essay in which he first documents Kafka's life, largely from the point of view of his 'habit of obedience and renunciation', and then writes an imaginative life of Kafka as the road not taken, of Franz Kafka not dead of tuberculosis and enshrined as a world-wide synonym for modernism, but surviving the war as an unknown Hebrew-school teacher in New Jersey, underpaid, and still practising renunciation. It is told as a reminiscence from the point of view of the child who remembers him as the Czech refugee with the formal bow who courts his spinster Aunt Rhoda, but never marries her. When the courtship comes to a tearful end after a weekend trip to Atlantic City, the narrator's brother explains that his aunt's tears have something to do with sex. The story closes with a stormy confrontation between the adolescent narrator and his father, paralleling the reverse of Kafka's relation with his father: 'Others are crushed by paternal criticism – I find myself oppressed by his high opinion of me!' Having left home, he receives a letter from his mother with Kafka's obituary thoughtfully enclosed that describes him as 'a refugee from the Nazis' with no survivors, who died at the age of 70 in the Deborah Heart and Lung Center in Browns Mills, New Jersey. 'No,' reflects the narrator, 'it is simply not in the cards for Kafka ever to become *the* Kafka – why, that would be stranger even than a man turning into an insect. No one would believe it, Kafka least of all.'[15]

In this *tour de force*, Roth attempts to do what he strains for in all of his recent work, to strike a balance between the Jewish writer's moral impulse to draw on themes from his people's recent suffering, and the artist's insistence on creating in his own terms, in this case his comic mode; and furthermore, while he does draw on his own experience as an American Jew for his fiction, he also draws on the more compelling drama of his fellow Jews in Europe which naturally overshadows his miseries, always threatening to belittle his own life and to render it pitifully inauthentic. One of his strategies is to bring that history closer to home, to rescue Kafka and place him on his own turf in New Jersey, thereby domesticating and deflating what is awesome in its own context. In one respect, this denial of the Holocaust, which always acts as a standard by which to measure

American-Jewish history of the same period, restores to the protagonist the legitimacy of his own family dramas and sexual problems. But by beginning his text with the actual recounting of Kafka's life, he insists on the fictionality of his comic alternate history which is drawn from a background similar to his own and which pales beside the narrative of the 'real' Kafka. In the juxtaposition of the two texts, 'Looking at Kafka' elegantly sets forth the moral and artistic quandary of the comic Jewish writer in America.

Moreover, as the immigration experience ceased to be the Jewish element in his works, and his audiences began to blame him for betraying Jewish experience with his ribald comedy, Roth has continued to seek the artistic means to remain a Jewish writer without admitting to the charges levelled against him. To do so, he has had to see himself as part of a Jewish literary tradition. Without the benefit of writing in Hebrew or Yiddish, so that the language itself would be a purveyor of a literary tradition, he has identified in Kafka a literary father, his European *alter ego,* the writer who bridges both Jewishness and Western modernism and who is locked into a battle with his father that takes on mystical and mythic proportions in his art. But the real Kafka is an overwhelming father-figure both in terms of the drama of his own life and the place he now occupies in the post-Holocaust view of that life and art. So Roth can claim him as a literary father and then minimise that threat by making Kafka an unpublished author, a pathetic elderly man with comic elements, the subject of mockery by his Hebrew school pupils. This leaves room for Roth's life and art, while also diminishing it.

Roth repeats this strategy several years later in *The Ghost Writer,* when he brings Anne Frank to New England, the road not taken had she not walked down that road to Bergen-Belsen. In *The Ghost Writer,* the first book in the trilogy *Zuckerman Bound,* Nathan Zuckerman's fantasies about a young woman named Amy Bellette as the real Anne Frank made up a story within the story, and those fantasies contribute to the self-referential theme of the young artist who must vindicate his life and art before his family and community. Nathan's two fantasies are:

1. That Anne Frank, learning of her father's survival and the publication of her diary by a chance reading of *Time,* chooses not to be reunited with him because she is convinced that knowledge of her survival would diminish the power of her art and the message it brings to the world. She has drawn this

conclusion from sitting in the midst of a weeping matinée crowd at a Broadway performance of *The Diary of Anne Frank.*

2. That Amy alias Anne falls in love with Nathan, making it possible for Nathan to be vindicated spectacularly by his family. 'I'd like you to meet my wife, the former Anne Frank.'

The Ghost Writer, then, is a sophisticated and richly structured response to Roth's critics who accuse him of betrayal in that he poses questions about the nature of American-Jewish identity through a tale about the nature of art and life. Just as Roth has deliberately projected his own problems onto Nathan, Nathan has projected his own wishes and identity onto Anne/Amy. Nathan imagines that Amy is Anne in order to be reconciled with his own father. But he also identifies with Anne for she is an artist who has willingly sacrificed her own bond with her father for the sake of her art. Thus, Amy is the paragon of both Jewish suffering and of renunciation at the holy altar of art. She is both artist and Jewish saint. If Nathan married her, he would become an accomplice in her secret scheme to preserve the memory of the Holocaust for readers like his own parents, while they, ironically, could still consider him a traitor to the Jewish community. Both Nathan and Anne, in his fantasy, are artists sacrificing personal happiness for their art, except that Anne's art is seen as holy in his community and his as profane.

As in 'Looking at Kafka', the implications of Anne Frank's life for the Jewish-American comic writer are neutralised by bringing her to the American scene and turning her into a college girl infatuated with her professor, and as in the Kafka story, it has the opposite effect of dramatically contrasting the world of Roth's fiction with recent Jewish history, turning the Jewish-American writer's problem into the central issue of the fiction. Roth raises the very complex issue of the morality of using the Holocaust, a symbol of collective trauma, as a social tool, to bludgeon the Jewish artist into restraining his imagination for the sake of 'the common good', or as an artistic tool to invoke sympathy from a critical audience by offering up one of its most sacred subjects.[16]

In *The Anatomy Lesson* and *The Prague Orgy*, the third novel and epilogue of his latest work, *Zuckerman Bound*, the search for a literary father in the context of being a Jewish-American writer is developed even further as Nathan Zuckerman inherits that scrap of paper with the word 'Holocaust' on it. In *The Anatomy Lesson*, Nathan

Zuckerman is incapable of writing any more fiction, as he is suffering from severe pain of a mysterious origin. His sole quest in that work is relief from his paralysing and undiagnosed ailment. Life under the influence of this disease is a parody of wish-fulfilment: confined to a mat on the floor, Nathan is catered to and entertained by a variety of beautiful women. Nathan begins to believe that his agony is self-inflicted, the product of his guilt about his writings, 'penance for the popularity of *Carnovsky* . . . for the family portrait the whole country had assumed to be his, for the tastelessness that had affronted millions and the shamelessness that had enraged his tribe. . . . Who else could have written so blasphemously of Jewish moral suffocation, but a self-suffocating Jew like Nathan?' (p. 440).

Nathan Zuckerman comes to the conclusion that he can no longer write because he has lost his subject: 'A first-generation American father possessed by the Jewish demons, a second-generation American son possessed by their exorcism: that was his whole story' (p. 446). In this summation, Roth has located his own movement away from the subject of Jewish-American fiction that marked some of this own earlier work. Having left behind the fiction of immigration, he takes up the subject of the reception of that fiction, turning the drama between writer and audience into the moral dilemma of the Jewish writer in America, suspecting the legitimacy of his own private anguish when contrasted to that of his fellow Jews. Confronting the issue directly, Roth parodies Zuckerman's suffering while underscoring its debilitating effects. For a while Nathan considers basing his next fiction on the past suffering of his Slavic lover, Jaga (in a manner similar to *Sophie's Choice* in which American writer Styron invents a Slavic World War II victim in order to write about experiences alien to his own life).

But he couldn't get anywhere. Though people are weeping in every corner of the earth from torture and ruin and cruelty and loss, that didn't mean that he could make their stories his, no matter how passionate and powerful they seemed beside his trivialities. One can be overcome by a story the way a reader is, but a reader isn't a writer. . . . Besides, if Zuckerman wrote about what he didn't know, who then would write about what he did know? Only what did he know? The story he could dominate and to which his feelings had been enslaved had ended. Her stories weren't his stories and his stories were no longer his stories either.   (p. 544)

To do penance and to bring about his own healing, he decides to abandon his writing career and become a healer himself. Viewed by the same audience that roundly condemned his writing, Nathan Zuckerman's desire to become a Jewish doctor would be supremely ironic and a posthumous victory for his parents, whose son's literary successes earned him what he believes to have been a deathbed curse from his father, and what surely would have been a blessing had he been a penitent medical student years before. But Roth does not give Zuckerman's community that satisfaction. On his way to medical school, Nathan launches what is first a practical joke and then an obsession – he presents himself to strangers as Milton Appel, pornographer. As Appel is the critic who has been most vociferous and persistent in his moral diatribes against the writer (Zuckerman's Irving Howe), Nathan can take revenge by the same tactic, public shaming. Nathan soon warms to the prank, however, and begins to identify with Milton Appel the pornographer, so that by the end of the book he is suspended between the two extreme identities that his community and family have forced upon him all along: the good doctor and the evil pornographer. Even a medical degree will not erase his having been the author of *Carnovsky*, nor is that necessarily what he wants.

The Anatomy Lesson ends with Nathan as a patient, not for the mysterious pain in his shoulder, but from the injuries incurred attacking a friend's father as the old man laments the end of his line because his adopted hippie grandson is 'everything we are *not*, everything we are *against*'. Zuckerman accosts Freytag with 'What do you see in your head? Genes with JEW sewed on them? Is that all you see in that lunatic mind, the unstained natural virtue of Jews' (p. 668). His own father dead, Nathan lunges at Freytag, 'the last of the fathers demanding to be pleased', intending to kill him. 'Freytag! Forbidder! Now I murder *you*!' (p. 669). Suffering takes on a different dimension for Nathan when he is recuperating in the hospital, for among the other patients he comes face to face with genuine physical pain and the disfigurement of disease. Zuckerman's craving for a real enemy and for a therapeutic mission peaks in what he perceives to be the universality and very literalness of disease – and he'd given his fanatical devotion 'to sitting with a typewriter alone in a room!' (p. 697). Yet the book ends without that resounding conviction, for Zuckerman roams the hospital corridors, 'as though he still believed that he could unchain himself from a future as a man apart and escape the corpus that was his' (p. 697).

Zuckerman can escape neither the corpus of his own ageing body, Yeats's spirit chained to a 'dying animal', nor the corpus of his fiction, the testimony of his having set himself apart and undoubtedly a cause of his pain.

In Roth's fiction, the Jewish-American writer cannot alleviate the anxiety provoked by his inheritance of that scrap of paper with the awesome word on it by relocating and neutralising the Jewish past on his own territory ('Looking at Kafka' or *The Ghost Writer*), or by avoiding art altogether and redirecting his passion into the art of medicine. He will have to relocate himself, and since he cannot return to the past, he can only travel to the scene of that past, which for Roth is embodied in the city of Prague. This he does in the Epilogue to the trilogy, *The Prague Orgy*, although he had already made this journey in search of Kafka earlier in *Professor of Desire*. In the Epilogue Nathan Zuckerman returns to a first person account of his experiences as was the case in *The Ghost Writer*, and he travels to Prague on a mission to retrieve the Yiddish stories of a Jewish author allegedly killed by the Nazis. The Epilogue is both a finale to the Zuckerman trilogy and a coming together of Roth's central motifs. The goal of retrieving the fiction of a Jewish writer from anonymity and seeing to their publication is a most appropriate action for a Jewish-American author anxious about his link to the Jewish history of loss and to Jewish literary fathers. It is also parallel to Roth's own goal of publishing the work of Eastern European writers in his 'Other Europe' series.

A major effect of his helping to reconstruct a lost literary tradition is that it may provide a literary father for Zuckerman/Roth. The Epilogue is haunted by three literary fathers – Kafka, Roth's literary *alter ego* whose uncertain identification with his own Jewishness and comic treatment of alienation is most compatible with Roth's sensibility; Henry James, Roth's American predecessor, whose self-consciousness about the place of the artist and preoccupation with the interpretation and misinterpretation of fictional texts influenced Roth's exploration of the same motif; Sisovsky, the lost Yiddish writer (in this case a fabrication of Roth's), whose absence haunts the post-Holocaust Jewish writer. The Jamesian influence in Roth's work is evident in his allusions to *The Middle Years* in *The Ghost Writer* and to the variation on the *The Aspern Papers* in *The Prague Orgy*. In neither James's nor Roth's tales about literary retrieval do the literary narrators actually get hold of the papers they are after, and in each case they court a woman in order to procure the manuscripts. But Roth's version is a reversal of James's, for in *The Aspern Papers* the woman rebuffs the narrator and destroys the papers; in *The Prague Orgy*, the woman propositions the narrator who rebuffs her, while she hands over the papers only to have them confiscated by the Czech police. In Roth's version, then, political forces come into play. Moreover, in James's version, the papers are letters and the narrator is a literary critic prying into the life of a poet, while in Roth's version, the papers are works of fiction and the narrator is a writer himself, torn loose from the kind of clear literary tradition that James enjoyed.

The epilogue also draws on another of Roth's central motifs, that of trading places with another. In a new twist, Sisovsky remains in America and Zuckerman actually goes off to Prague to wrest the papers from the hands of the Czech author's wife, Olga. In an especially telling reversal of Roth's own fiction, Zuckerman contemplates making love to Olga as a means toward retrieving a bit of Jewish literary history, as opposed to Jewish history acting as a psychic obstruction when it comes to the goal of unrestrained sexuality. Sisovsky and Zuckerman both share the frustration of scandalous receptions of their books, and Sisovsky insists that the weight of stupidity, in the case of Zuckerman's readers, is heavier than the weight of banning. Zuckerman disagrees.

When the Jewish-American writer trades places with the Jewish-Czech writer in search of a literary father, he must finally skirt real danger. Apprehended by the Minister of Culture and deported as 'Zuckerman the Zionist agent', Zuckerman is forced to turn over the shoe box full of manuscripts – 'Another Jewish writer who might have been is not going to be; his imagination won't leave even the faintest imprint' (p. 782). Each of the several crimes which Zuckerman is accused of committing is punishable by sentences of up to twenty years. For a moment, Zuckerman can feel what it might mean to have historical and political forces shape his life, but he is no martyr, and he only meant to trade places temporarily. While Roth explores the road not taken in America for Jewish figures like Kafka and Anne Frank, Nathan Zuckerman walks the road not taken only up to a hint of real danger. Like Bellow, who made his journey to Israel to record the drama and the price of Jewish continuity in *To Jerusalem and Back* without ever sharing the vulnerability he describes, it was time to go back. But back to where? Back to what he calls the 'national industry of the Jewish homeland, if not the sole means of production (if not the sole source of satisfaction), the construction of narrative out of the exertions of survival' (p. 761).

By the beginning of the twentieth century American literature was reflecting a change in national consciousness in its stories of returning East rather than heading westward. Philip Roth's long odyssey from Newark to Prague is also a turning point in the Jewish-American literary tradition, for it marks the passage from a literature of immigration and assimilation into a literature of retrieval, of the desire to be part of a Jewish literary legacy alongside the European and American literary traditions. Roth's strategy for locating his fiction in such a tradition is to turn the denial of his work by many Jewish readers into his theme, to trace his own moral dilemma as a Jewish-American writer compelled to treat recent Jewish history in his fiction (often by trading places), and to carve out a literary tradition by drawing on Eastern European predecessors. At the end of the *Zuckerman Bound* Epilogue, Nathan is left without a real or literary father, without a family, and without a home. Roth's intensifying preoccupation with the self-reflexive theme of his work's reception and with his own identity as a Jewish writer is narcissism turned moralism. These last works face the plight of the Jewish writer cut loose, as he is, from linguistic, religious, or cultural continuities, but seeking a literary tradition. They also signify, often elegantly, the impossibility of Philip Roth's *not* being a Jewish writer, given his need to document imaginatively every comic and tragic nuance of his own displacement.

NOTES

1. Philip Roth, *Zuckerman Bound* (New York: Farrar, Straus & Giroux, 1985); subsequent references to this work will appear in the text.
2. Irving Malin and Irwin Stark, 'Introduction', *Breakthrough: A Treasury of Contemporary American Jewish Literature* (New York: McGraw-Hill, 1964); reprinted in *Jewish-American Literature: An Anthology of Fiction, Poetry, Autobiography, and Criticism*, ed. Abraham Chapman (New York: New American Library, 1974) pp. 665–90.
3. See Jeremy Larmer, 'The Conversion of the Jews', *Partisan Review*, 27 (1960) pp. 760–8.
4. Irving Malin, 'Introduction' to *Contemporary American-Jewish Literature* (Bloomington: Indiana University Press, 1973) p. 7.
5. Theodore Solotareff, 'Philip Roth and the Jewish Moralists', *Chicago Review*, 8 (1959); reprinted in Malin, 'Introduction', pp. 13–30 (the quote is from p. 20).

6. Donald Daiches, 'Breakthrough', *Commentary* (August 1964); reprinted in Malin, 'Introduction', pp. 39–57 (the quote is from p. 37).
7. Allen Guttman, 'The Conversion of the Jews', *Wisconsin Studies in Contemporary Literature*, 6 (1965); reprinted in Malin, 'Introduction', pp. 39–57.
8. Robert Alter, 'Jewish Dreams and Nightmares', in his *After the Tradition* (New York: Dutton, 1961); reprinted in Malin, 'Introduction', pp. 58–77 (the quotations are from pp. 58–9).
9. Irving Howe, *World of Our Fathers* (New York: Harcourt Brace Jovanovich, 1976) p. 586.
10. Marc Shechner, in *Harvard Guide to Contemporary American Writing*, ed. Daniel Hoffman (Cambridge, Mass.: Harvard University Press, 1979) pp. 191–240 (the quotations are from p. 191).
11. Philip Roth, 'Imagining Jews', in *Reading Myself and Others* (New York: Bantam, 1977) p. 221.
12. Ibid., pp. 221, 150.
13. Philip Roth, *Goodbye, Columbus* (New York: Houghton Mifflin, 1959) p. 216.
14. Quoted in Clive Sinclair's 'Why Philip Roth Says Goodbye to Columbus', *The London Jewish Chronicle*.
15. Roth, *Reading Myself*, pp. 243–4.
16. See Hana Wirth-Nesher, 'The Artist Tales of Philip Roth', *Prooftests: A Journal of Jewish Literary History*, 3 (1983) pp. 263–72.

4

The Shape of Exile in Philip Roth, or the Part is Always Apart

MARTIN TUCKER

Recently I took my mother to one of several doctors she is now obliged to visit because of a serious illness. This physician, an eye doctor examining her for damage caused as a result of her diabetic condition, asked her to 'have a good look' at him. She said, 'Why, are you good-looking?' Her wit broke him up (and surprised me, who had always regarded everything about her as heavy-handed and fingering), and he smiled. She went on to ask him, 'Are you married, doctor?' When he said yes, the next question was inevitable, though she delayed it for several catches of breath. With as little trace of significance to innuendo as she could muster, she asked, 'Are you Jewish, doctor?'

'Why, don't I look Jewish? What do you think?', the doctor replied.

Now it was my mother's turn to smile.

This incident is characteristic of any number of Jewish-American writers, but the presence of a profoundly invidious mother (and father) in the story-telling is indissolubly (and indissoulably) Rothian. As Joycean and Freudian as he can be (without being either, ultimately, but only himself searching for the whole of himself), Roth includes a mother and father in practically every novel he writes, and the abiding love/hate, difficulties/sustenance the hero has in the course of his encounters with them. (I am excluding his two novels where the central character is a heroine, and where the *modus vivendi* is essentially atypical of Roth. Significantly the heroines in both these cases are Gentiles, and the Jewish motifs of guilt and affection in their peculiar guises are absent from the two works. Again, significantly, these are the only two novels of Roth that are called 'serious' or at least not customarily

33

referred to as 'comic'. Apparently Jewish filial situations have attained the distinction of irreverent comic binding, while Gentile difficulties are treated as serious rupture, divorce and alienation within the populist tradition.)

Terms of reference, like terms of endearment particularly among family members, are easily obvious and clearly misunderstood in some contexts. I believe Roth to be dealing with exile as his major theme, not because he states it explicitly but because his house of characters and situations is divided into unequal parts of conflicting tensions, and out of the division come his anguish and his journey to resolution and the closing of the broken circle. It is easy and obvious (though not false) to psychologise Roth; he bares his soul in his work, like any great writer, and the soul is brought to heal by the discerning reader. Thus, it can be seen that Roth has been working since his first published work with the motif of contraries, either in the form of two characters in conflict with each other or in the shape of a divided one. He plays off the civilised man against the natural ape, the good boy, the thoughtful considerate Scout against the anarchic and self-centred bohemian; the assimilated worldly Jew against the romantic bearded Hasidic or ecstatic fanatic. He does all these things very well, and he does them better with each new work, for his latest works are openly honest and compassionate. Indeed, in his latest works, there is a humility that seems the mirror of an ingrown need to apologise for his talent. Roth, and his heroes, cannot stop apologising; not even achievement can relieve him and his self-styled heroes of the doubt that his and their success is a mistake due to hazardous luck or to the Cossacks in their midst, quiescent for the moment and not noticing the village in which Roth and his characters ply their magic trade to success and rewards.

A long time ago Roth learned some modernist tricks. He ends his work (or more accurately infects the whole of it) with ambiguity and unknowingness, for that is the condition (I believe as he sees it) of modern man. Yet, like Joyce and others, he returns to the scenes of his achievements for further probing. Thus each work is another step along the way to knowledge; each work is but one passage, completed in time, before the next book is started on the same but always new and enriching mysteries.

Consider the reappearance in name as well as identity of spirit of Nathan Zuckerman and David Kepesh. As Roth grows in understanding them, he brings them back on stage. He is, like many writers, an autobiographic fabulator, someone who puts on view his visionary veils of imagery and his nude bodies of painful, persistent, fantastic thought. The parallels between his early and later heroes are obvious, but perhaps not always apparent in their metaphysical boundaries. Zuckerman is a well-known writer, rich and famous largely because he exposed a young man's Oedipal appetites and his sense of guilt and anxiety over his ensuing success. David Kepesh is a more gentle soul, but just as driven and divided. Kepesh is suffering from the trauma of his divorce, of a failed relationship for which he feels some sense of responsibility (and guilt over his own judgement of irresponsibility).

Kepesh's sentence of guilt is his period of becoming (and remaining, the book implies) a breast; the shame he fears is not unlike the fear of Roth's earlier heroes about their emotional withholdings. Indeed Roth's heroes are consistently concerned about their public images. Like good Jewish boys they fear the consequences of acting out of turn. Flaunting is an acceptable act (as is the acting-out of it), but firm admission of difference shall not be conditioned within the tribe nor forgotten by the elders.

Yet Roth also suggests that his heroes must go through their trials, and expose themselves. Unlike some Jewish writers who may be compassionate about the temptations of lust and blasphemy but who come down on the side of obedience to the Law, Roth inevitably sends his heroes into hell, but tries to bring them back to a new circle. His most significant works have the same kind of ending: a new beginning, even if the beginning is not yet shaped. Consider the ending of *Portnoy's Complaint*, so famous it has become a cliché – the psychiatrist telling the analysand-hero: 'So. Now vee may perhaps to begin. Yes' (p. 274).

It is also significant that Roth's tone in all these endings is mock-ironic. In *Portnoy* the analyst is clearly an ironic and paradoxically lovely portrait of a venerable Viennese father-figure, old-fashioned beyond belief but the impatient patient, Portnoy, is now desperately trying to reach the analyst's calm.

Or the ending of *The Breast*, which consists of a poem by Rilke concluding with the line 'You must change your life' (p. 78). Kepesh has been fleshed literally (Roth makes the point many times in the novella) to a breast; this is no mental delusion on the hero's part, and the parallel for the reader is that the novel is not to be conveniently filed away as a symbolist joke. Roth wants the reader to literally feel the pain of Kepesh who is being punished for his excessive masturbation, his excessive sexual bouts with women without a corresponding emotional uprising in his daily spiritual state. The crime Kepesh has committed for which he is being punished is the sin of somehow not joining into the tribe, or the family, or even a relationship. And there is a second crime, a crime he shares with Nathan Zuckerman, a sense that he has exploited his family and not played fair with them.

Kepesh wants 'in' and forgiveness; he who flaunted the family and tribal laws, who did not continually recognise the realities of those laws, is now reduced to a blubbering breast. Worse, he is at the mercy of any passer-by because his breast is unduly sensitive to the touch of others over whom he has no control. Is then the impotence of enclosure into the breast a fitting judgement on Kepesh's earlier insensitivity?

The suggested resolution in *The Breast* is for change, just as Portnoy's analyst called for movement. For whatever varied reasons, Roth's fiction urges on its characters the necessity to move on to a beginning. The irony is that each new work (and the parallel of each new day for his characters) is an outgrowth of the past. Nothing new can happen without the acceptance of the old and its reference points. If the past is not forgotten, it wreaks its presence. If the past is forgotten, it makes a new return on those who have forgotten its relevance.

This desire for relief from the unbearable sense of guilt about the past allies Roth with many modern writers, particularly Jewish-American writers, and among them the great father-love of his life, Bernard Malamud. But the profoundest identity is with Kafka. Roth has made no attempt to hide this bond. His periodic journeys to Czechoslovakia are his way of signifying the pilgrimage to a holy place. (Curiously, Roth, critic of religion in his early days, has made pilgrimages throughout his life: first to Henry James and the golden bowl of language, and later to Kafka, the source of freedom through the admission of guilt.) The parallels, as stated before, are obvious but not always apparent. Both Kafka and Roth punish their heroes for no overt crime but for the greater one of not acting on one's profoundest needs. Both Kafka and Roth send their heroes into hell – or rather show that hell is the awareness of eternal loneliness after the opportunity to overcome it has gone by. Parallel to this sense of psychic separation – or what I call exile of the spirit – is the guilt over masturbation. Roth's heroes are often jaunty about their masturbation in the same way teenagers fabulate their meetings with members of the opposite sex. His heroes, however, are whistling in the dark and ultimately cry out for some light.

Roth's choice of masturbation as provocation, an identifying reference of rebellion and isolation, is a part of his larger concern with exile. He is not unaware of the tribal injunctions against masturbation, the seed going to waste: it is the root of loneliness because it continues aloneness; the punishment for it, in Roth and Kafka, is the perverse Dantesque one of eternal, enormous isolation from one's fellow people. Just as Kafka's Gregor Samsa is recognised for a roach and exposed in his shell, so Roth's Kepesh is a sucker of breasts, but the breast no longer succours him; this is what he must learn. Kepesh must accept woman not as mother; he must accept his mother as a woman.

Roth's use of the exilic sense – the invidious stream of apartness from others, the self as fortress *a priori* and *a fortiori* the incidence of wounds and charred wonder – may be seen in his work from *Goodbye, Columbus* onward. The hero in that brilliant first novella lets the girl go (though he finds rationalisations for saying she gave him up); in any case, each is relieved at the separation. The avoidance of union is inevitable, good for both parties, but loss is still there beneath all the reasons for the worthiness of a separation reasonable enough in materialistic, socially mobilic terms. In his long short stories and particularly in 'The Conversion of the Jews' and 'Eli the Fanatic', the theme of apartness for the hero is more clearly delineated. In both these fictions the hero, a secular Jew, experiences the profound need for a religious fulfilment. In 'The Conversion of the Jews', his rebellion takes a perverse air as he climbs the stairways to a heavenly rooftop and refuses to descend till his Jewish suppliants, eager for his safety, mouth words of conversion to Jesus. Many strands of literary allusion and moral complexity are at work in the story. Roth's hero does not have to wait as long as Marvell's Coy Mistress was told she would have to wait for the conversion of the Jews (and to which delay her impregnable virtue is compared). One strand seems rock bottom, floating from story to story, a plea rooted in the base of his eternal longing: *make me a part of the whole, obliterate from me the presence of emptiness*. Roth is, of course, expressing a yearning in a character and by means of the characterisation illuminating the condition of modern man. But the yearning, the ever-present *cri de coeur*, is a constant in his work, and it therefore seems valid to posit that Roth's subject is the Exile of the Jews, exile in its sense of having lost a place, whether that place is a house, a childhood, a memory of warmth that no one else remembers but the memoirist and that everyone else can contradict until their mouths go to waste spewing out words the memoirist refuses to eat.

In 'Eli the Fanatic' the desperate yearning for communion is less cloaked than in Roth's previous works. Here is an elegant young man, bright, charming, full of worldly promise, who succumbs to the fundamentalism of black-frocked and iron-curled Jews dancing and chanting their heads off. It is an attraction more widely advertised in popular newspapers in the current generation in images of bearded fanatics in India, chadors in Iran, spit-iron curls in Rastafarian Jamaica, and perhaps in the fatigue-uniforms of Latin-American soldiers – all expressing the need for physical, material, outward group identification. The list can be multiplied but the division is stable – the gulf between those who opt for the liberation (as they see it) of rationalism and those who need the ecstasy of a constant religious experience. In 'Eli the Fanatic' the hero is presented in a double bind – or double loss – for the reader does not know if Eli has attained to a satisfaction of his needs or if he will be further excommunicated from the western family of man by his decision to reveal himself as a naked human being crying out to wear the uniform of an ancient tribe.

Roth's fiction has continued in this divide between the mad angels and the sane devils, the fools who demand what is ridiculous in the eyes of rational man and those who take what man provides and deal with God behind closed doors. His *vision* is not unique – the Jewish-American novel is replete with the fools of naïvete and the conmen of rationalism, but he is unusual in that he does not seem to move closer to his own resolution of the eternal conflict. The paradox is not that he chooses when nothing but his own peace of mind will be gained by choice, but that he goes on recording the pain of irresolution and the fascination of that painful growth to understanding, an understanding which ultimately can only be summed up as mystery.

A comparison with Roth's writer-hero may show the difference between the two kinds of writers and their visions. Roth's portrait of Lonoff in *The Ghost Writer* is now accepted (though not legally verified) as that of Bernard Malamud. It is an affecting and compassionate portrait of a writer who must wrestle with the demands of daily life – family, friends, human meetings – and those of his craft, the priestly vocation of writing. Roth's young hero Nathan Zuckerman, on his way up the literary ladder but still a naïf in the byzantine ways of worldly success, is astonished by the problems of a man whom he had set up as a guru. The tale is largely one of disillusionment – the ways by which we accept our human gods as mortal men – and then of a new and deeper appreciation of what each man accomplishes on the shoulder of speeding roads. Nathan learns to accept the truth of the relationship between the young student in the Lonoff household and Lonoff; he accepts the relationship between the Lonoffs themselves – Lonoff is seen with sympathy as a writer who selfishly denies his wife the companionship of his hours because he saves his valuable time for his work, and the wife who is bereft of everything but her chores for the great writer, and yet not bereft, because the tasks she performs are valued by Lonoff in a mysteriously ultimate and fulfilling manner. Yet Roth has Nathan write this of his writer-hero: 'In his seven volumes of stories I could not think of a single hero who was not a bachelor, a widower, an orphan, a foundling, or a reluctant fiancé' (p. 71).

Ironically, it is Lonoff (alias Malamud) who transcends the singleness of his heroes by his vision of their participation in a universe that has a meaning, even if they cannot formulate or state the meaning. Malamud's heroes continue their good acts not because they are sure of their verity or their consequences, but because it is in their nature to do so. If they are fools they do not know it. Roth's heroes are more aware of their foolishness; they know even their best acts are absurd, but slowly *pace* Malamud (or Lonoff) they commit them and themselves to acts of absurdity that at least have some point of meaning and decency in a world they would like to believe in again. Perhaps they have never lost their belief in a benevolent world, for if all things are absurd, then it is not more crazy to believe in goodness than venality.

Yet Roth is no innocent like Candide. He presents his vision of a world gone separate from his talented heroes in a tone of mocking pain and revelatory yearning. The early works reveal the ache and the void when the fictions are searched for their textured signs: Roth's brilliant, at times savage, mockery is a cloak which can be lifted to show his need for reassurance. After all, like a good boy he became a writer to give tribute back to his parents. The later works

show the pain has grown, and the understanding with it. The ache
has not gone away, but like old age, every new day, and every new
achievement, brings further awareness of mortal frailty.

Consider, for example, the ending of *My Life as a Man*. (Roth's
endings are familiar litanies, beautifully rewritten each time to
round off individuating explorations into the psyche of loneliness
and human exile.) In *My Life as a Man*, the hero Peter Tarnopol has
been told of his ex-wife's death. She had taunted him, no less so
since their separation, with her jibes about his sense of caution, his
unwillingness to risk all to be a man. Her memory has proved lethal
in that it shapes the unrevised record of a failure for Peter. Her going
would seem then to end the cycle, and give Peter the opportunity to
move on to manhood. (The title is ironic in that Peter's life as a
married man and then as separate from his ex-wife shows him as
less than his own image of manhood.) His father urges Peter to go to
Maureen's funeral; Peter refuses. His father pleads with Peter not to
forsake this responsibility. For Peter, the plea from his father seems
one of regard for society, what others will think. Peter does not
realise his father may be speaking of Peter's responsibility to Peter.

His father tries to reach Peter with these words:

> You go to the funeral, Peter. That way nobody can ever call you
> pisher. . . . Listen to me, Peter, please – I've lived a life. Stop
> being out there on your own, *please*. You haven't listened to
> anybody since you were four-and-a-half years old and went off to
> kindergarten to conquer the world. You were four-and-a-half
> years old and you thought you were the president of General
> Motors. What about the day there was that terrible thunderstorm?
> Four-and-a-half years old – .

Like many Rothian heroes, Peter is clever enough to withhold
satisfaction from his parents as a compensation for the way he
believes they withheld satisfaction from him. But his father
continues:

> – it was a terrible thunderstorm. . . . there was thunder and
> everything, and you were in school, Peter, in Kindergarten.
> Four-and-a-half years old and you wouldn't let anybody even
> take you, after the first week. . . . No, *you* had to do it alone. You
> don't remember this, huh? . . . Well, it was raining, I'll tell you.
> And so your mother got your little raincoat, and your rainhat and

your rubbers, and she ran to the school at the end of the day so you shouldn't have to get soaked coming home. And you don't remember what you did? . . . You *balked*. You gave her a look that could have killed. . . . And told her off. 'Go home!' you told her. Four-and-a-half years old! And would not even so much as put on the *hat*! Walked out, right past her, and home in the storm, with her chasing you. Everything you had to do by yourself, to show what a big shot you were – and look, Peppy, look what has come of it! At least now listen to your family *once*.

This time Peter has listened. He says, 'Okay, I will' before hanging up.

Immediately Peter turns to the woman Susan who has become his lover and who has rushed to his apartment to be with him once she has heard the news. (That all his family and friends should be so concerned about the effect on Peter of his ex-wife's death is in itself revealing, for it shows Peter has not dismissed that part of his life; his ex-wife has in this sense never left him.) Indeed, Peter's father's advice was for this purpose precisely – that by burying the dead, we put a finish to them. Peter, in refusing to attend his ex-wife's funeral, is continuing to hold on to her, to use her for convenience sake, to salvage her for *ex post facto* rectifications of the past.

These are Roth's final words in the novel:

Then, eyes leaking, teeth chattering, not at all the picture of a man whose nemesis has ceased to exist and who once again is his own lord and master, I turned to Susan, still sitting there huddled up in her coat, looking, to my abashment, as helpless as the day I had found her. Sitting there *waiting*. Oh, my God, I thought – now you. And *me*! This me who is me being me and none other! (pp. 332–4)

The reader is left with the possibility that Peter may become a man and move on beyond the mistakes of the past. Peter may recognise that immaturity may be a transient, passing thing if one wishes it. But the exclamation points and the apostrophe to a force beyond his own vows suggest the conclusion is tenuous. Peter may be changing, he may be growing into himself and 'none other'.
May be.

The ending of *The Professor of Desire* is another case in point. This novel was written and published after *The Breast*, but its action takes place before the hero, David Kepesh, turns into a breast. In *The Professor of Desire*, Roth forces his hero to come to terms with the fact of the possibility of his father's death. The hero's lover, Claire, consoles him; she ameliorates his plight by saying the father is alive and well *today*. For the moment, today is enough; tomorrow may bring more news. Kepesh turns to Claire in bed, sucks her breast ('in a desperate frenzy at the choicest morsel of her flesh'), but all the while waits to hear 'the most dreadful sound' from the next room where his father lies sleeping (p. 263).

The allusiveness of the scene suggests Dylan Thomas's worm of death at the moment of coition, come and gone, the cycle of order and growth, but the scene is uniquely Rothian, for immediately preceding it has been presented Kepesh's fear of losing his passion for Claire, the woman he loves. Roth's heroes, in his later work, fear impotence more than the loss of love; for them, passion for a loved one is succeeded by impotence, and the consequence of impotence is the flight of the partner. Roth does not have his heroes consider that a lover may stay on even if the other partner becomes impotent; such a sacrifice seems awesome to Roth's heroes, and so impotence is the prelude to isolation and exile. The fear of impotence, as well as the fact of it, is then a punishment visited on Rothian men for some never-stated reasons or cause. But always the sense is given that the punishment is just, that a crime has been committed somewhere earlier that deserves such a fitting punishment. The novelistic situation is Kafkaesque in the most characteristic way of the Czech writer, and fittingly the spirit (or ghost?) of Kafka makes its presence known throughout this novel.

Kepesh is a professor of English. He is a professor of desire for many things. He seeks fulfilment of self, some communion with a force larger than mere self-satisfaction. He seeks understanding of those writers whom he has studied as a youth and who have greatly influenced him. Chief among these are Kafka and Gogol, but he is also moved by Mishima, Gombrowicz, and Genet, novelists he is preparing to teach in his next year's comparative literature class. Now in Prague to visit Kafka shrines, he thinks about his next year's reading assignments. He has decided to organise the semester around the subject of erotic desire, 'beginning with those disquieting contemporary novels dealing with prurient and iniquitous sexuality . . . disquieting to students because they are . . . the novels in which the author is himself pointedly implicated in what is morally most alarming' (p. 179). He is going to end the course with three masterworks 'concerned with illicit and ungovernable passions, whose assault is made by other means: *Madame Bovary, Anna Karenina,* and "Death in Venice"'.

It is fitting that erotic desire should be fingered as the centrum around which the professor's course revolves, for the professor runs his life around unfulfilled desire. Though he is in love with Claire, he cannot forget his ex-wife Helen. Like Peter Tarnopol, the past is not over for Kepesh, and he relives it constantly. Like Kafka, David Kepesh springs his life out of the ways he deals with his problems rather than in the solutions he finds to these problems. Like Kafka, Kepesh thrives on his own problems; he has learned to accept them as his guides and crutches; they in turn are not ungenerous in giving to him provisions for getting through the day.

Kepesh also seeks out his Jewish heritage in Prague. Thus he describes his visit to the Old Town Square in this manner after he has visited Kafka's grave:

I . . . am off to the Old Town Square, where Kafka and Brod used to take their evening stroll. When I get there it is after nine and the spacious melancholy plaza is empty of everything except the shadows of the aged façades enclosing it. Where the tourist buses had been parked earlier in the day there is now only the smooth, worn, cobblestone basin. The place is empty – of all, that is, except mystery and enigma. I sit alone on a bench beneath a street lamp and, through the film of mist, look past the looming figure of Jan Hus to the church whose most sequestered proceedings the Jewish author could observe by peering through his secret aperture.

It is here that I begin to compose in my head what at first strikes me as no more than a bit of whimsy, the first lines of an introductory lecture to my comparative literature class inspired by Kafka's 'Report to an Academy', the story in which an ape addresses a scientific gathering. It is only a little story of a few thousand words, but one that I love, particularly its opening, which seems to me one of the most startling in literature: 'Honored Members of the Academy! You have done me the honor of inviting me to give your Academy an account of the life I formerly led as an ape.'

'Honored Members of Literature 341,' I begin . . . but by the time I am back at the hotel and have seated myself, with pen in hand, at an empty table in a corner of the café, I have penetrated

the veneer of donnish satire with which I began, and on hotel
stationery am writing out in longhand a formal introductory
lecture (not uninfluenced by the ape's impeccable, professorial
prose) that I want with all my heart to deliver – and to deliver not
in September but at this very moment.   (pp. 180–1)

Roth includes the text of the professor's lecture notes. Without
irony Kepesh writes: 'I love teaching literature. I am rarely ever so
contented as when I am here with my pages of notes, and my
marked-up texts, and with people like yourselves. To my mind
there is nothing quite like the classroom in all of life' (p. 184).

It is a brilliant joining of the parts of exilic dilemma, displacement
and separation. Kepesh finds the whole of himself in the classroom:
he has found something which he can wholly move into, without
any lingering desire to keep a part in reserve, an alternative in a
secret closet to which he can repair when his dream castle or
supportive imagery falls down.

Paradoxically, as the professor is wholly himself in the classroom,
he is inspired by a literature of parts. What are his profoundest
reading experiences? Kepesh tells the reader they are Kafka and
Gogol and Chekhov, writers for whom the loss of part of the body or
spirit provided the base for their speculative literary journeys.
Kepesh describes his fascination with Gogol's 'Nose' – the story of
something lost which takes on the discovery of mythic proportions.
(For Gogol the nose became all the warts that had grown over
Russia; for Roth the mouth – isolated and apart – becomes his
symbol of rapacity and sucking-cess.) The choices of images from
parts of the body and the spirit represent Kepesh's fear of falling
apart, of losing hold on the orders he shouts at reality.

The most profound alliance for Kepesh – and I suspect for Roth –
is with Kafka's beetle, or roach. In *The Metamorphosis* the hero is
unmasked. He is all that everybody has suspected him of being –
spineless, crawling, infested, universally despicable with no
apparent redeeming qualities. If in Roth his heroes can escape
detection through their clever flights of imagination and their
whirlwind oral talents to move words around for the masking of
them, in Kafka the scheme stops and the procession is over. The
clever, even the solid bourgeois, are unmasked to reveal their naked
pathology.

Recently I gave an examination to a sophomore literature class I
teach at C.W. Post of Long Island University. In the examination

was a question about *The Metamorphosis*. I had asked the students to 'discuss the ways in which at least four writers deal with the issues of awareness and knowledge in the growth of human character. Comment on how these writers portray the growth of their characters from innocent and/or naïve young people into more knowing adults. Or you may wish to include discussion on how some characters do *not* grow, how these characters hold illusions as ways of coping with their stubborn immaturity and the persistence of their desires. Franz Kafka must be one of these writers.'

Here are three of the answers:

1. In *The Metamorphosis*, Kafka shows all of his characters to grow and mature. The roach showed, by turning from a human being into a roach, much consideration for his family. Although he had always helped to support his family, when his change took place he tried as much as possible not to be a burden to his family. He was very aware and sensitive to their feelings. An example of this is when he hid under the sofa when his sister came in to clean his room, so that she would not have to look at him. He also stayed in his room all the time, so he wouldn't scare them by his looks. By this horrible experience, he was able to grow and become a more caring roach. While before this change took place he was so wrapped up in his work he didn't have the time to.

   Also, his sister and his parents changed from this experience. His father, who had not worked in years and had become old and hunched, had gotten a job and was now strong and healthier looking. His sister also grew from the experience, as she continued to care for him even though she hated it. For example, she tried to move his dresser out so that he could climb the walls and be more comfortable, but it was too heavy for her to lift. At the end of the story, after the roach died, they had new hopes and dreams (like their daughter's getting married) which they never even thought about before the experience. They now felt they had a new beginning.

2. An example of growth in character or maybe in this case the not growing of a character is in Kafka's *Metamorphosis*. In this work a physical change does take place very obviously. A man turns into a cockroach. Though the character's body is transformed into another shape his mind remains mostly the same. The largest change in human characters occurs in the family. The sister and

parents lived off this man because they didn't work. The parents weren't strong enough and the sister had her music, which came first. As the family realised that their boy is still a cockroach they made changes in their lifestyles. Boarders are taken in and the family gets jobs. Their son begins to get angry at this treatment by the family and also angry that he is not needed. He never really accepts his life as it has become and he stops eating and dies from this along with the injury he received from his father. Physically he changes but there is no change on other levels. The family have become strong working people who realise that it is time to get rid of their son. Time to get rid of him because he will stay like a cockroach and also because they no longer need him.

3. Franz Kafka, in his book *The Metamorphosis*, presents a very clear picture of growth, even in the title alone. This story of a family which begins with a man Gregor Samsa, who is the sole supporter of his parents and his sister Grete which do absolutely nothing. His life has much meaning but he has no meaning inside. When Gregor is transformed to a cockroach, he becomes a person who has some enjoyment in his life which he has never had before. He plays in his room and can finally relax. His family, in the meantime, must do something to cope. They cannot just let life pass them by. The father must work, the sister must take care of him, and the three must face a crisis. They are growing differently than Gregor, but growing unknowingly. When it is time where Gregor dies, he is thrown out as if he never existed. His life, however, was not purposeless. His family are living. It is sad in that Gregor receives no appreciation, yet Kafka shows that Gregor put this family together. It is unknowing growth and it occurs all the time.

I think Philip Roth, perhaps even Kafka, would be amused by the misguided responses of these students. Yet the answers are not without their claim to value. Roth, and Kafka, are writing about the caring (and/or uncaring) being; they are exploring the priorities of characters in their ordered (and disordered) lives. Their vision may be horrendous to some readers, and normative for others. The vision is one of human exile, of the individual thrown out of the community (family or beyond), either through his own sense of unworthiness or his choice of superior flight into art.

Roth is more irreverent about the subject of literary calling in

Zuckerman Bound. He is, however, just as serious in his concern for the sense of exile and apartness in his characters as a consequence of the pursuit of art and personal testaments of morality. In one scene he writes:

> You see, not everybody was delighted by this book that was making Zuckerman a fortune. Plenty of people had already written to tell him off. 'For depicting Jews in a peep-show atmosphere of total perversion, for depicting Jews in acts of adultery, exhibitionism, masturbation, sodomy, fetishism, and whoremongery,' somebody with letterhead stationery as impressive as the President's even suggested that he 'ought to be shot'. And in the spring of 1969 this was no longer just an expression. . . . It didn't strike Zuckerman at all unlikely that in a seedy room somewhere the *Life* cover featuring his face (unmustached) had been tacked up within dart-throwing distance of the bed of some 'loner'. Those cover stories were enough of a trial for a writer's writer friends, let alone for a semi-literate psychopath who might not know about all the good deeds he did at the PEN Club. Oh, Madam, if only you knew the real me! Don't shoot! I am a serious writer as well as one of the boys! (*Zuckerman Unbound*, in trilogy volume, p. 188).

In his latest work, *The Prague Orgy*, Roth specifically treats literal exile. The hero Zuckerman, in a visit to Prague, has undertaken to obtain a manuscript by a famous and dead Czech Yiddish writer; the manuscript is in the hands of the Yiddish writer's former daughter-in-law. This woman, an ageing alcoholic actress whose husband (the dead Yiddish writer's son) has run off with another woman to the West, refuses to surrender the stories, which cannot be published in Czechoslovakia because the state has decreed that they promote alien parochial values. Before Zuckerman left for Prague he was beseeched by the Yiddish writer's son and his mistress to retrieve the manuscript. When Zuckerman asked why the task was so important to them – the dead writer's work was widely available in the West – the son could reply only in general terms. He has lost his belief in any permanent values, and any single ones too. He is beginning to doubt his sense of doubt, or, as he puts it, 'I don't believe in my doubt, frankly. I don't think I have any doubt at all. But I think I should' (p. 705).

Zuckerman, like the son Sisovsky, has plenty of doubt, and doubt about the value of his doubts. Like Sisovsky he thinks he *should* hold on to his doubt, perhaps because it is the most familiar of all his possessions. Nevertheless, if only because doubt allows for the possibility of belief, he goes about the business of luring, enticing, sequestering the manuscript away. Amazingly, the alcoholic actress, a boozy woman who tempts him with her ageing body and is as suffering a being as any sensitive drunk, gives him the manuscript of the stories. They have been hidden in a candy box; once someone (her husband?) gave her a box of chocolates, but no one has given her sweets for years.

As Rothian irony goes, the manuscript is seized almost as soon as Zuckerman returns with it to his hotel. It is taken away by the state police; Zuckerman is driven in a long black limousine to the airport and hustled out of the country. Nothing has been accomplished, except that the stories are definitively lost for publication, and perhaps all trace of their script and meaning as well, for the bureaucracy of state socialism will rationalise the situation into whatever purpose it decides.

Yet Zuckerman has learned something – not a glib lesson in freedom to write but something of the meaning of the creative urge to expression and the human need to share experience. All stories are fictions into which we pour ourselves; all fictions are stories out of which we find ourselves, Zuckerman the writer realises.

Or, as Zuckerman puts it, in describing literature and the craft of writing in Czechoslovakia:

> Here where the literary culture is held hostage, the art of narration flourishes by mouth. In Prague, stories aren't simply stories; it's what they have instead of life. Here they have become their stories, in lieu of being permitted to be anything else. Storytelling is the form their resistance has taken against the coercion of the powers-that-be. (p. 762)

If all terms are relative then words bring us back to the family of man we are inevitably cast out of and spend a lifetime trying to understand our ouster from. Yet our next step cannot be taken – profoundly – until we have walked away from the present station of our most intimate surroundings. And if we are still trying to understand, we walk slowly, hesitantly, holding on to the closing and never-closed door. Roth, who has been teaching literature classes for a long time and has said he would go crazy without the practice and enrichment of the experience, knows what an unending term is. His work is rooted in phases of the exile of the spirit, but it is also riddled with the undying and unconquerable pursuit of dreams of the return home.

NOTE

Quotations from various works by Philip Roth appear in the text, with the relevant page number given in parenthesis. The editions cited are as follows:

The Breast (New York: Holt, Rinehart & Winston, 1972).
Goodbye, Columbus (Boston, Mass.: Houghton Mifflin, 1959).
My Life as a Man (New York: Holt, Rinehart & Winston, 1974).
Portnoy's Complaint (New York: Farrar, Straus & Giroux, 1977).
Zuckerman Bound: A Trilogy & Epilogue (New York: Farrar, Straus & Giroux, 1985).

5

Strangers in a Strange Land: The Homelessness of Roth's Protagonists

ESTELLE GERSHGOREN NOVAK

Gershom Scholem quotes Charles Péguy as having said about the Jew that 'Being elsewhere, the great vice of this race' was also 'the great secret virtue, the great vocation of this people'. Scholem interprets this statement as having in it the contrary element of 'the desperate wish to "be at home" in a manner at once intense, fruitful and destructive'.[1] Certainly Philip Roth's characters suffer from both the vice and the virtue Péguy mentions, and Roth continually tells us that his characters bring with them that 'desperate wish to be at home' which both defines their neurosis and their essential being. Any discussion of this could easily turn into a discussion of alienation. But, in fact, a distinction has to be made between what we ordinarily call alienation and marginality and what is the condition of the Jewish character in Roth. The more assimilated the Roth character becomes, the more intense his desire to be at home in his environment, the more homeless he feels. It is his sense of himself as separate that is a continual reminder of his spiritual homelessness. This, and not any external force, creates his peculiar estrangement.

The paradox implicit in the creation of Roth's characters is that defined by Péguy and further explained by Scholem. Zuckerman, Tarnopol, Portnoy, Neil Klugman, and Eli Peck share the experience of the spiritual diaspora. The prototype for the character who feels elsewhere is Eli Peck in Roth's brilliant story 'Eli, the Fanatic'. The story opens with Eli brooding on what the townsmen of Woodenton, the Jewish townsmen, want him to do: 'Tell this Tzuref where we stand, Eli. This is a modern community, Eli, we have our families, we pay taxes. . . .'[2] The Jewish citizens of Woodenton are assimilated Jews who leave Brownsville for the suburbs. In the

50

suburbs they think they can be like anyone else, like their Protestant neighbours. So, if this is true, why are they so worried about the appearance of a Yeshiva on the hill, Leo Tzuref, its director, and the man in the black caftan, fringed undergarment, talmudic hat and earlocks? What it is that Ted Heller is afraid of in Tzuref is best expressed in his description of the Bible stories told to his child in Scarsdale, particularly the story of Abraham and Issac that frightens his daughter. Despite Irving Howe's notion that Heller is simply being stupid, what frightens the child, and what Ted would like to ignore, is the recognition of human evil, sin, and suffering. It is the image of suffering that the Woodenton Jews want to turn off, and it is the living with suffering that Eli Peck puts on when he puts on the black suit at the end of the story. They believe in the goodness of American life, in equality, and in the fulness of their assimilation. This is, after all, what defines the intensity of the desire to be at home. Eli's wife, Miriam, uses psychoanalysis to keep her normal. (The one book Eli says she brings to the marriage is *An Introduction to Psychoanalysis*.) She insists on peace and normality. It is the abnormality of Leo Tzuref, his difference in dress and language, that points up the local Jew's difference from his Protestant neighbours. It is that difference, that sense of the alien nature of their inner selves that frightens them.

Early in the story Eli Peck sees himself as one of them. 'He spoke for the Jews of Woodenton, not just himself and his wife' (p. 251), but later he finds the self which has always been elsewhere through his contact with Tzuref. Tzuref tells him that 'What you call law, I call shame. The heart, Mr. Peck, the heart is the law! God!' (p. 266). But it is not only Tzuref who speaks of the law's limitations to Eli. Eli speaks of them himself: 'The trouble was that law didn't seem to have anything to do with what was aggravating everybody' (p. 254). Here he is not speaking of personal aggravation of the heart, but of the community's aggravation. Tzuref and his children come into their midst from the displaced persons camps and remind them of the other world, the world that causes Eli Peck's neurosis, the world of the heart, the world of the diaspora, the alien identity of the Jew. Eli defines himself as not very strong, susceptible to what his neighbours 'forgivingly referred to as "a nervous breakdown"'. He is pained by Miriam's desire to make him normal. The law is normal, psychology encourages normality, and everyone in Woodenton desires nothing more than that normality.

Eli, in the title of the story, is called, 'the fanatic'. Eli's friend Ted tells him that the reason there is 'a good healthy relationship in this town' between the Jews and the Protestants is that there are no fanatics, fanatics like Tzuref, 'crazy people' (p. 277). Eli himself is identified with crazy people because he has nervous breakdowns, but his craziness is his simple failure to be normal, to believe that 'he deserves to be happy' as Miriam tells him. Fanaticism is defined as difference from others, being outside the normal. It's all right to have a few nervous breakdowns. See Dr Eckman and he'll take care of it, Miriam advises. As Ted Heller says, 'It's going to be all right, pal . . .' (p. 293). But Eli knows that his final choice to wear the black suit is different: 'But if you chose to be crazy, then you weren't crazy' (p. 295). He had chosen to wear the black caftan, the undergarment, and the talmudic hat and to go to see his child in the hospital.

If Eli suffers from nervous breakdowns, the man in the black caftan who frightens the community is in a state of nervous exhaustion. His experience with the Nazis has destroyed his normality. He is the diaspora Jew who has lost everything, everything except his suit, his religion. When Tzuref says, 'The suit the gentleman wears is all he's got' (p. 263), he means something more than the Jews in Woodenton can entirely comprehend. He has lost everything.

> 'A mother and a father?' Tzuref said: 'No. A wife? No. A baby? A little ten-month-old baby? No! A village full of friends? A synagogue where you knew the feel of every seat under your pants? Where with your eyes closed you could smell the cloth of the Torah?' . . . 'And a medical experiment they performed on him yet! That leaves nothing, Mr. Peck. Absolutely nothing!' (p. 264)

Eli responds by saying that he had misunderstood. He merely thought that the man was poor and couldn't afford another suit. Tzuref's response is: 'No news reached Woodenton?' What Roth is asking through Tzuref is the obvious question, 'Did the Jews of Woodenton know about the Holocaust?' and the answer is, of course, yes, they did know, but they chose happiness and peace rather than confrontation because confrontation creates unhappiness. The desperate desire to be at home among the Protestants drives them to reject what they share with Tzuref and makes them nervous about his presence in the community. It is the Jewish community, and not the Protestant community, that is unnerved by Tzuref's Yeshiva. It reminds them of Brownsville, of the Holocaust, of the diaspora, of everything that they have chosen to ignore.

The whole issue of normality becomes absurd for Eli when he comes into contact with the blackness of the Jewish experience. He begins by saying that 'I am them, they are me, Mr. Tzuref', but Tzuref replies, 'Aach! You are us, we are you!' Eli feels trapped by Tzuref at this moment, in a darkness which pains him. 'Eli shook and shook his head. In the dark he suddenly felt that Tzuref might put him under a spell. "Mr. Tzuref, a little light?"' (p. 265). It is in this same scene that Eli tells Tzuref that all the community is asking for is to 'protect what they value, their property, their well-being, their happiness' (p. 266). Miriam tells Eli that 'We deserve to be happy', and the community believes in the rightness of their own quest for happiness. Eli is right to say so. It is what civilisation has been working toward. But the very nature of happiness and peace for the Jew is always violated. His assimilation is never complete because he can never be completely happy. To be happy means to be at home. The Jew is not at home. Jewish neurosis, if that's what Roth writes about, is Freud's idea of neurosis. The dissatisfaction with place, self, and accomplishment is particularly characteristic of the Jew. Anything that reminds him of that dissatisfaction plunges him out of happiness and security in the American community and back into isolation. The ability to adjust and be normal means for Roth to deny the self that is other. The self here is represented by Tzuref and the 'greenie' in the black caftan. 'Happiness? They hid their shame,' Tzuref responds to Eli's effort to embody the American pursuit. To be happy the community has to get rid of Tzuref because Tzuref reminds them, not only of the Holocaust, but of their condition as Jews and of the Jew's unhappiness in the world of the galut. This is emphasised for Tzuref by the disjuncture of calendar time. Eli says to Tzuref, 'This is the twentieth century.' Tzuref's response is, 'For the goyim maybe. For me the Fifty-eighth' (p. 266). The Jew not only lives in another world spiritually, but by another calendar.[3]

Although he does not come from elsewhere literally as Tzuref does, in becoming the fanatic of the story's title, Eli attempts to duplicate the reality of the diaspora in both a spiritual and concrete sense, realising that he cannot ignore that part of himself that responds to Tzuref. It is the very essence of Eli's character to respond, to be upset, not to be normal, that is emphasised in the beginning of the story. His mission to Tzuref from the community weighs heavily on him. His briefcase with all the bits of paper from Tzuref weighs 'a ton' in Tzuref's presence. The face of the man in the black caftan is 'no other than Eli's'. They could easily have been in the same circumstance. This duality is emphasised and given a place in Eli's mind. When he has on the black suit and the 'greenie', the green suit, he says: 'And then Eli had the strange notion that he was two people. Or that he was one person wearing two suits' (p. 289). He gives the man his suits and he adopts the suit of the other. They exchange places. He experiences the diaspora physically through the suit. Contradicting his earlier avowal of identity with the Jewish community of Woodenton, he responds to Tzuref saying, 'I am me. They are them. You are you' (p. 267). He has not so much identified with Tzuref as made clear his identity as separate from that of the community which sees him as its representative.

Discomfort is the dominating trait of the Jewish character in Roth, sometimes physical discomfort as in the constipation of Portnoy's father, in Portnoy's impotence, or in Zuckerman's pain, but more often than not a spiritual discomfort. Eli feels the strangeness of the black clothes he puts on, but 'though he felt every inch of its strangeness. He felt those black clothes as if they were the skin of his skin . . .' (p. 293). He has costumed himself in a way that is more real than the green suit and all that it represents. Insane by the standards of Miriam and Dr Eckman, he knows that he is not mad. The tranquillising injection he is given 'calmed his soul, but did not touch it down where the blackness had reached' (p. 298). They cannot make normal and 'all right' the pain and suffering that the blackness has revealed to him.

Being elsewhere is the identity of Roth's protagonist. His very nature is based on his estrangement from his environment in the diaspora and even when he seems most at home, the intensity, the desperation with which he tries to assimilate reveals the undercurrent of discomfort with his environment. Roth deals with this alienation in psychological as well as social terms. The physical place, the suburb, is often the place where Roth's American Jews enact their spiritual diaspora, but the drive toward assimilation can take place in any environment.

In his voyage to Short Hills, New Jersey, from Newark, Neil Klugman of *Goodbye, Columbus* depicts himself as a tiny Gulliver in the land of the giant Brobdingnags. Sitting at dinner with Brenda Patimkin's family in Short Hills, he imagines himself reduced in size:

> It was a pleasure, except that eating among those Brobdingnags, I felt for quite a while as though four inches had been clipped from my shoulders, three inches from my height, and for good

measure someone had removed my ribs and my chest had settled meekly toward my back.[4]

But Neil, though he tries like Gulliver to accommodate himself to the world of Brobdingnags, is never wholly successful in merging himself with these strangers from another world, but always feels uncomfortable and outside. In order to maintain the absurd notion that he is as tall as the Brobdingnags Gulliver takes himself to the edge of madness. Neil Klugman never goes so far. He approaches the world of the Patimkins in Short Hills with a satiric sense of his relation to that world. Even his name suggests his role in the novel. As many critics have already pointed out, Klugman means 'clever' in Yiddish, but it also means 'cursed'.[5] Because of his position as ironic first-person narrator we get a clear sense of the way he perceives his situation with Aunt Gladys, with Short Hills and later with the Patimkins themselves. As he drives to Short Hills he imagines the world of the suburbs:

> It was, in fact, as though the hundred and eighty feet that the suburbs rose in altitude above Newark brought one closer to heaven, for the sun itself became bigger, lower, and rounder, and soon I was driving past long lawns which seemed to be twirling water on themselves, and past houses where no one sat on stoops, where lights were on but no windows open, for those inside, refusing to share the very texture of life with those of us outside.   (p. 8)

It is not that the Patimkins refuse to share the texture of their lives with Neil. Neil rejects them. The world of the suburbs is larger than life and closer to heaven. It is attractive to Neil, just as Brenda is sexually attractive, but it also has a characteristic lack of charity which will turn him away at the end.

While Roth allows Neil Klugman to enter a girl from Short Hills and to enter the world of the Patimkins, he shows us a Neil who is always uncomfortable. In his first meeting with Brenda Patimkin at the tennis courts, he learns that she has had her nose 'bobbed' or 'fixed' and is worried about its fragility. Neil asks, 'What is the matter with it?' Why did it have to be fixed? he wants to know. He goes on to ask if Ron, Brenda's bruiser of a brother, wants his nose to be fixed so that he might also be prettier. Though he says he doesn't 'mean to be facetious', he finds it difficult to be anything else (p. 13). He finds it difficult to repress his obvious sense of his satiric relation with the suburbs even when he has fallen in love. Neil's relationship with the world of the Patimkins is as fragile as Brenda's relationship with her Gentile nose. They both feel uncomfortable, but Neil has a clearer sense of his discomfort.

We sense Neil's discomfort through the metaphor of eating. His Aunt Gladys in Newark is constantly trying to empty her refrigerator, serving four different meals at four different times to four different people. Her whole relationship to food is based on charity, or giving away. 'Life was a throwing off for poor Aunt Gladys, her greatest joys were taking out the garbage, emptying her pantry, and making threadbare bundles for what she still referred to as the Poor Jews of Palestine' (p. 7). The Patimkins' relationship to food is wholly different. As Neil puts it, life is for Aunt Gladys, 'a throwing off' and for Brenda 'a gathering in'. The Patimkin refrigerator is described as overflowing with varieties of fruit. No one is worried about the fruit going bad because wealth can afford this luxury of what might go to waste and wealth doesn't give away easily either. Julie, angry at Neil for not letting her win at table tennis, accuses him of stealing fruit, 'You cheat! And you were stealing fruit!'

There is also the sense that the metaphor of the fruit is the traditional metaphor of stolen fruit and is connected to Neil's sexual relationship with Brenda. The imagery of the fruit in the refrigerator is the imagery of a man making love, the sheet of waxed paper clinging to the watermelon like 'a wet lip'. Of course, it is immediately after the scene with the fruit that Brenda and Neil do make love. He tells us that both he and Carlota, both strangers to the Patimkin family, were 'wooed and won on Patimkin fruit'. Neil Klugman enters the world of the Patimkins through food, through huge bowls of nectarines, plums, and cherries that he and Brenda share on summer nights.

When he first arrives at the Patimkin house, it is for dinner, and Neil watches the huge appetites of the Brobdingnags around him. The Patimkins tell him that he eats like a sparrow, and he imagines himself as a sparrow, a little animal like Gulliver in Brobdingnag. When visiting 'Patimkin Kitchen and Bathroom Sinks', he has a mental view of himself being asked by Mr Patimkin to oversee the unloading of a truck. In his reverie he hears Mr Patimkin: '"Klugman, what kind of worker are you? You work like you eat!" "That's right, that's right, I'm a sparrow, let me go." "Don't you even know how to load and unload?" "Mr. Patimkin, even breathing gives me trouble, sleep tires me out, let me go, let me go . . ."' (p. 92). His eating and his strength, an ability to deal with the material world, are closely related. He sees himself as having an ulcer within an hour of watching the men carry the sinks away toward the truck. The physical world tires him and gives his body pain. He can't seem to accommodate himself to the world of these giants without suffering in his relation to it.

Neil Klugman is never comfortable. From the very beginning of the novel we know that he is an outsider making his way into Short Hills, as a guest subject to the whims of his hosts and a lover subject to the whims of his mistress. But he is also not entirely at home even in Newark, where he stays with his Aunt Gladys while his parents take the cure for asthma in Arizona. He works at the public library temporarily because he hasn't made any plans yet. His contrast to the Patimkins is clear even in this. They make plans for everything. His colleagues at the library are almost as strange to him as the Patimkins, though less attractive. In his morning dream in Brenda's bed at the Patimkin house, he imagines himself adrift on a boat off one of Columbus's islands with the little Negro boy who comes to the library to look at Gauguin's pictures:

> and the Negresses moved slowly down to the shore and began to throw leis at us and say 'Goodbye Columbus . . . goodbye Columbus . . . goodbye . . .' and though we did not want to go, the little boy and I, the boat was moving and there was nothing we could do about it, and he shouted at me that it was my fault and I shouted it was his for not having a library card, but we were wasting our breath, for we were further and further from the island, and soon the natives were nothing at all. Space was all out of proportion in the dream, and things were sized and squared in no way I'd ever seen before.   (pp. 74–5).

Neil Klugman is like the Neil in the dream adrift on the ocean away from the paradise of one of Columbus's islands, unable to get back no matter how hard he tries. The American paradise is not for him any more than Gauguin's is for the little boy. It is the disproportion of the dream and its reference to Columbus, of course, that gives us the clearest relationship with Neil's real situation. He has just heard Ron's 'Goodbye Columbus' record, and he lives in the Patimkin house as a person all out of proportion to the people around him. His discomfort inside that world is reflected in the dreams by the disproportion of space. His sense of that disproportion in the dream wakes him into consciousness and gets him out of Brenda's bedroom just in time, but that consciousness of his disproportion to the Patimkins forces him to see them always from the outside, from the boat, even when trying desperately to remain on the inside.

When he is unceremoniously asked to babysit for Julie while the Patimkins drive to the airport for Harriet, he feels 'like Carlota, no not even as comfortable as that' and wants to go 'back to Newark, where I might even sit in the alley and break candy with my own' (p. 40). At the Patimkins he is not with his own. He is more at home, however, with Ben Patimkin than he is with Ben's children or with Mrs Patimkin. They both know what 'gonif' means; they are closer to their Jewish grandmothers who 'drank hot tea from an old jahrzeit glass'. Brenda and Ron don't know the Yiddish words, and Newark, where they once lived, is a distant memory. They have drifted onto the tennis courts, the basketball courts, over to Radcliffe, or to Ohio, into the suburban Hadassah, but mostly into the world of upper-middle-class American life. Brenda still wants to make love on the sofa from Newark in the storeroom at the Patimkin house, but the immigrant life of that city has no reality for her.

Though Ben Patimkin still has the 'diamond' in his nose which Brenda has had removed, he is the successful businessman of the suburbs who doesn't bear as close a relationship to Neil as does his poor brother Leo. Leo's memory of the pleasures in his life, oral sex with Hannah Schreiber before he was married, is a moment of happiness stolen from a life of bitterness, and when he, his wife, and his child leave Ron's wedding they look 'from the back . . . like people fleeing a captured city'. Though he seems to be on the inside, Neil, like Leo, feels outside the world of the wedding. Leo tells him that he's clever and will make it. But Neil's cleverness is cursed by the same thing that curses Leo, a sense of suffering and an uneasiness about the wealth of the Patimkins.

When he goes into a church in New York while Brenda is getting her diaphragm from the doctor, he meditates on what he wants from Brenda:

> 'Which prize do you think, schmuck? Gold dinnerware, sporting-goods trees, nectarines, garbage disposals, bumpless noses, Patimkin Sink, Bonwit Teller – '
> 'But damn it, God, that *is* You!'
> And God only laughed, that clown.   (p. 100)

If he gets Brenda, does he have to take along with it the whole Patimkin Kitchen Sink with the bumpless noses and their lack of charity, or, in its larger sense, Tzedakah? Unlike Gulliver who refuses to look at himself in a mirror after leaving Brobdingnag, Neil looks at his reflection in the glass front of the Lamont Library at Harvard. He questions his image, 'What was it inside me that had turned pursuit and clutching into love, and then turned it inside out again? . . . If she had only been slightly not Brenda . . . But then would I have loved her?' (pp. 135–6). It is only after losing Brenda to her mother that Neil recognises that the desire for Brenda could not be separated from a desire for the world she represented, the lust of the Jew for the American dream.

The undercurrent of Neil's vision of himself is dark. He sees himself not throwing off like Aunt Gladys or taking in like Brenda, but experiencing a 'numbness' in relation to life. Like the Negro boy in the library, he can't take his dream of paradise home with him because there it would be destroyed by reality, the reality of Aunt Gladys who says if there are Jews in Short Hills, 'They couldn't be real Jews, believe me' (p. 58). The reality is always Newark in the background and the fragility of the Gentile nose.

He must return to the self in the mirror or in dream to remind himself of who he is and where he belongs. All the time he is in Short Hills, he is really elsewhere. He wants desperately to be at home there, but it is both Brenda and Short Hills that ultimately make him feel homeless. In his relation to Brenda he feels a certain distance, but in his desire to feel comfortable in her environment, to make the American suburbs his and therefore to make Brenda his, it is his intensity that destroys him. This perfection of the sexual pleasure through the diaphragm at the end of the summer is what destroys paradise for him. Neil, in trying to acquire the very thing that would make his sexual relationship with Brenda perfect, 'turns winning into losing'. Brenda will always belong to the other world closer to heaven, where the air is cooler and people do not give of themselves to those on the outside.

The Philip Roth character can't win because he turns it into losing. Though not always the metaphor of baseball as in *The Great American Novel* or the sporting-goods tree in *Goodbye, Columbus*, this is the central metaphor for Roth's characters. Of course they are never losers in the ordinary sense of the word. While spilling his guts to Spielvogel, Alexander Portnoy is a functioning member of the American establishment, fighting the good fight for human rights. He is Commissioner for Human Opportunity in New York. Philip Roth's male protagonists are all good boys who have worked hard and wouldn't dream of being unsuccessful. But their relationship to success is always difficult, and it is this difficulty that defines their neurotic relation with the world in which they live, with their culture and civilisation.

Brooding about Bubbles and his fears of going blind from the sperm he has shot into his eye, Portnoy remarks, 'Oy, civilization and its discontents.'[6] Freud is never far from his mind when he is talking to Spielvogel and never far from his bed when he is masturbating. His need to use Freud is part of his neurosis. He must convince Spielvogel of his genuine intelligence and goodness. He needs to please, but, for all his reading of Freud, his self-analysis is probably as wrong as Spielvogel's diagnosis. But even in the absurdity of Portnoy's exposure of his illness on the couch there is some truth. In *Civilization and its Discontents* Freud tells us:

> So, also, the two urges, the one toward personal happiness and the other towards union with other human beings must struggle with each other in every individual; and so, also, the two processes of individual and of cultural development must stand in hostile opposition to each other and mutually dispute the ground.[7]

Portnoy's urge toward physical pleasure and therefore personal happiness comes into conflict with his desire to please other human beings, namely his mother and father and those in positions of authority. But this very conflict between the personal and the public that Freud hoped eventually psychoanalysis would normalise will never be normalised for the Roth character. The disease which is Portnoy's is the disease of homelessness that neither Eli Peck's Dr Eckman nor Portnoy's and Tarnopol's Spielvogel can cure. The central paradox of Alexander Portnoy is that this intellectualising – his attempt to 'normalise' his condition through Freud's views – only gives him the illusion that he truly understands his condition.

If Freud has argued that civilisation has achieved its highest aims through the very neurosis that he describes in *Civilization and its Discontents*, then the Jew is the prime example and Portnoy an archetype. Alex Portnoy, the 'A' student, the star of his 3rd grade play, acting Columbus discovering America and the Assistant Commissioner for New York's Commission on Human Opportunity, is the man successful in public life. But Portnoy has a divided nature; it is the division between the body and the spirit, between the world of American success and the world of the Jew that seems both to encourage that success and to destroy it.

In Spielvogel's diagnosis of Portnoy's problem it is the 'mother–child relationship' that is emphasised, but, as central as Sophie

Portnoy may be to the self-analysis of Portnoy, it is probably his father who is central to his crisis, his father whose 'intestinal tract is in the hands of the firm of Worry, Fear and Frustration'. Where is Portnoy's 'putz' but in his own hands most of the time surrounded by worry, fear, and frustration? His father's constipation is the predecessor of Alex's impotence. They are parallel problems. Neither can release what needs to be released. The father is unsuccessful in the world of America, particularly at 'Boston and Northeastern Life'. He is 'Doomed to be obstructed by this Holy Protestant Empire!' (p. 43) where the blond and the blue-eyed have the contacts and the success. Reliving his adolescent fantasies about his father and embarrassed by his father's 8th grade education, Portnoy tried to educate him by sending him the 'Partisan Review'. He is ashamed of his father's inability to hold the baseball bat properly, but has a tremendous admiration for his father's masculinity:

> between his legs (God bless my father!) he was constructed like a man of consequence, two big healthy balls such as a king would be proud to put on display, and *shlong* of magisterial length and girth. And they were *his*; yes, of this I am absolutely certain, they hung down off of, they were connected on to, they could not be taken away from him! (pp. 45–6)

These genitals belong to the same father who will never make it in the insurance business, will never be promoted as a Jew in a goyish company with a picture of the Mayflower on its stationery. Portnoy's view is split. The pleasure of having a father who has such testicles can never really take away the pain he feels when he sees his Jewish father a failure in Protestant America. Portnoy needs to please these parents who expect so much of him. But he does this only to find that rather than constipated and a failure like his father, he is a success and impotent. After discovering his impotence, Portnoy does what every intellectual would do. He buys the *Collected Works* of Sigmund Freud, begins his self-analysis and then goes to Spielvogel to present the invention of his self through Freud. He says that he is living a Jewish joke, Freud's Jewish joke, a sickness Freud suggests the Jews have from suffering. But from what does Portnoy's suffering derive?

That his father suffers in the reality of America and that social forces and prejudices prevent him from achieving success is clear enough. But how is this brilliant Portnoy, who imagines himself to be the centre of his parents' love, who has just been appointed by the Mayor, has solved a TV quiz scandal, and is busy helping out the downtrodden, how is he oppressed? The answer from Portnoy is that he has been oppressed and repressed by his parents. The real answer that Roth gives us is that he oppresses himself. He still lives in Newark in his past. And why does he do this? Why can't he be at home in his position of authority?

Alex Portnoy's fixation on his past is an escape from the uneasiness he feels with his present, and the past does explain the present in ways that the reader can piece together from Portnoy's account. His discomfort with his public position is surrounded by the guilt he feels for his physical pleasures – physical pleasures sought in places that will expose him as no more worthy than Gregor Samsa crawling on the floor of his room. Like Kafka's protagonists he is trapped in double binds. Masochism gives him pleasure because he feels guilty. He is guilty partly because he has been successful, and his success is partly the result of his guilt. If not for the revenge he feels he needs to exercise against those who oppress, those who in particular oppressed his father, he would not be able to do his job as Assistant Commissioner for Human Opportunity. He condemns those who oppress on the last page of the novel, 'The lying, the scheming, the bribing, the thieving – the larceny, Doctor, conducted without batting an eye. The indifference! The total moral indifference!' This is the Portnoy who sees himself as morally superior to the world around him, the righter of wrongs, but he is also the one who feels he will get caught because he cared to 'steal a slightly unusual kind of hump . . .' and can't get it up because of his 'crime'. Why, he asks, do they get away with it, and he can't? In Portnoy's view of the world, there is a definite connection between his sexual satisfaction and the world that oppressed his father.

Portnoy chooses his women, all the way from the imaginary shikses skating on the ice who are 'so gorgeous, so healthy, so blond', to Kay who 'never raised her voice in an argument', to Mary Jane Reed whose illiteracy turns him on. He thinks that he will discover America through Kay, educate it through the Monkey, or take revenge on it through Sarah. His relations with women approximate those with society. He thinks that, as Freud would say, his sexual instincts are connected to the death wish. But, in fact, he chooses those sexual objects which will either make him fall down on the ice like a schlemiel or will turn him away. Even with Mary Jane Reed he has difficulty using her name because it is 'too redolent of Christian symbolism' and so he reduces her to an animal, a monkey, below the level of civilisation (or the Marx Brothers' *Monkey Business*). Portnoy's need to drive himself into guilt is part of his discomfort with the reality of himself in society. He tells Spielvogel of his admonition to Monkey against saying anything about her cunt in the company of the Mayor. It is Portnoy, not Monkey, who feels uncomfortable. The nature of his rise to prominence can only make him feel miserable. He worries that he will be exposed for the orgy he engages in with Monkey and with Lina. He is continually imagining how the world will see him. When he visits Kay Campbell, the Pumpkin, on Thanksgiving he sees himself apologising, thanking them for inviting him, his being Jewish and all, and marvels at the 'good mornings', Elm Street, the American family. But he sees himself as the Yid from Newark, the insurance man's son, the rootless wanderer.

For all Portnoy's feelings of homelessness in America as the repressed Jew who needs to have the id put back in Yid, he wants to reform America, to go inside it and put the Oy back in Goy. But his exile comes, in the full circle of the comedy, in Israel when he is no longer in the diaspora making it with shikses. It is then he becomes impotent. Naomi, the Israeli Zionist, is the real socialist, the liberal. She takes him to task for his failure to establish any measure of equality in his job, criticising the whole of what he thinks of as his success. And she looks like his mother. 'Interesting. I associate her instantly with my lost Pumpkin, when in physical type she is, of course, my mother. Coloring, size, even temperament, it turned out – a real fault finder, a professional critic of me' (p. 292). In fact, he doesn't need Naomi as his critic because he has himself, but she serves as the model in his analysis for the mother-substitute who makes him impotent. She accuses him of being 'self-depreciating' and 'the most unhappy person I have ever known – like a baby'. When Portnoy responds by saying that 'self-depreciation is, after all, a classic form of Jewish humor', she replies, 'Not Jewish humor! No Ghetto humor.' We have a real sense that the exit from the diaspora to Israel will not cure Portnoy's neurosis. Ghetto humour is exactly what sustains Portnoy when he is most miserable. Naomi tells him that he 'was the epitome of what was most shameful in the culture of the Diaspora. Those centuries and centuries of homelessness had produced just such disagreeable men as myself – frightened, defensive, self-deprecating, unmanned and corrupted by life in the gentile world' (p. 299). As George Steiner tells us in his perceptive essay, 'Our Homeland, the Text':

> The State of Israel is an endeavor wholly understandable, in
> many aspects admirable, perhaps historically inescapable to
> normalize the condition, the meaning of Judaism. It would make
> the Jew level with the common denominator of modern
> 'belonging.' It is, at the same time, an attempt to eradicate the
> deeper truth of unhousedness, of an at-homeness in the word
> which are the legacy of the Prophets and of the keepers of the
> text.[8]

Roth's character is no more at home with the patriotism of the
Zionist's vision of a homeland in Israel than he is in Kay Campbell's
All American home. He is critical of the world around him, but also
feels an intense need to be loved by the world around him. He
couldn't camp out in the mountains with Naomi and the Zionists in
the short khaki pants. The Naomis of Israel, no matter how much
Alex may think they resemble his mother, are not what Portnoy
needs. In fact, they produce the exactly opposite effect.

If Roth's protagonists choose to suffer, they do not do so for the
Jews as Portnoy's and Zuckerman's parents or Milton Appel would
want them to. (And as the Jewish community would want Roth to
do.) They suffer for their own suffering. The paradox of the Roth
character as he emerges does not lie in externals, however vividly
Roth may draw them. It has more to do with an alienation from the
self, the split between civilisation and its demands and the demands
of the body. Portnoy's sense of estrangement, his difficulty, is nicely
explained by Steiner's rephrasing of Hegel, 'According to Hegel,
this "foreignness' becomes ontological. The sensibility of the Jew is
par excellence the medium of the bitter struggle between life and
thought, between spontaneous immediacy and analytic reflection,
between man's unison with his body and environment and man's
estrangement from them.'[9] Portnoy's struggle is just this. He
struggles throughout the novel between the Freudian text and his
feelings, between his body and his desire to strip the body and
analyse it. The problem for men like Portnoy and Zuckerman is that
their physical desires are inextricably tied to their emotions and their
emotions to their intellect, the intellect to guilt, and, of course, the
guilt to obligation. Psychoanalysis cannot explain the relationship of
civilisation to the self. The writer has to try to do this and in the
process be caught like Roth or Zuckerman with a public that refuses
to understand.

If you are Zuckerman and have published *Carnovsky* or Roth and
have published *Portnoy's Complaint*, you will be a literary success
and be criticised for wallowing in sexuality or making the Jews look

bad. But you will also suffer from, not constipation, not impotence, but a terrible pain that ties you down like Prometheus while your liver is being eaten away by vultures. As Clive Sinclair points out in his recent review of *The Prague Orgy*: 'In the final analysis the stories are just as important as the lives, perhaps more so, for it is in such stories that our most acute moral dilemmas are most finely articulated.'[10] And he quotes Zuckerman:

> No, one's story isn't a skin to be shed – it's inescapable, one's body and blood. You go on pumping it out till you die, the story veined with the themes of your life, the ever-recurring story that's at once your invention and the invention of you.[11]

This is Zuckerman, the suffering character whose art is his life and whose life is his art, not just a cheap imitation, but 'the body and blood'. For Portnoy the story he tells Spielvogel is the story he tells himself, as R. D. Laing would say, and it is indeed as true if not truer than Spielvogel's story printed up as analysis in the epigraph to the novel. And Tarnopol's story is multiple, with Zuckerman, Moonie, and Lydia as well as with Maureen. They are all true because they are all about the self.

It will be the text, the story, that will be the means for explaining the difficulties of Roth's characters. The solution is not in Israel nor in psychoanalysis. As George Steiner argues that the centre of Jewish existence is the text and its emendations the examination of the truth, so we can argue that the centre of existence for Roth's characters is textual. It is surely this centre of existence with which Nathan Zuckerman has to come to terms. He is part of a text that has already been written, the author of a text that is being misread and searching for the subject that has been lost in someone else's text of reality. Like Kafka he suffers in writing, and as Zuckerman he suffers both in not being able to write and having written. In his trilogy, *Zuckerman Bound*, Philip Roth has his protagonist, Nathan Zuckerman, brood over the problem of having lost his subject:

> Zuckerman had lost his subject. His health, his hair, and his subject. Just as well he couldn't find a posture for writing. What he'd made his fiction from was gone – his birthplace, the burnt-out landscape of a racial war and the people who'd been giants to him dead. The great Jewish struggle was with the Arab States; here it was over, the Jersey side of the Hudson, his West Bank, occupied now by an alien tribe. No new Newark was going to spring up again for Zuckerman, not like the first one: no fathers

like those pioneering Jewish fathers bursting with taboos, no sons like their sons boiling with temptations, no loyalties, no ambitions, no rebellions, no capitulations, no clashes quite so conclusive again. Never again to feel such tender emotion and such desire to escape. Without a father and a mother and a homeland, he was no longer a novelist. No longer a son, no longer a writer. Everything that galvanized him had been extinguished, leaving nothing unmistakably his and nobody else's to claim, exploit, enlarge and reconstruct.   (p. 446)

Appearing in the section 'Gone', this passage is echoed further on as Zuckerman brings in the fictional critic, Milton Appel, to show that with everything else gone, one critic, at least, believes that his talent has disappeared as well. 'Gone. Mother, father, brother, birthplace, subject, health, hair – according to the critic Milton Appel, his talent too' (p. 474).

Roth's Zuckerman feels homeless now, without the reality of the Newark he knew, without the father, the mother, and the brother that informed that reality, but with a desire to be at home in that world that is so intense as to be in itself destructive as Gershom Scholem has told us is the condition of the Jew. This estrangement is, however, the very subject he has for his writing, for his text, and his identity is informed by that self-destructiveness. The paradox of Zuckerman's remarks is that in Roth's ingenious parody of Greek tragedy with its three comic sections followed by a tragic picture of life in modern Czechoslovakia, instead of the three tragedies followed by the satyr play, he still has his theme. Out of the constipation of Zuckerman's artistic talents, Roth weaves a brilliant picture of the Jewish artist in modern America. Caught up in the fiction created by the regime of a totalitarian state, it is no accident that he is deported as a Zionist agent. And what was he doing in Czechoslovakia anyway? He was there to rescue the Jewish past in the form of an unpublished manuscript by a writer who was slain by the Nazis or maybe not slain by the Nazis. And this happens to Zuckerman, a writer vilified by the Jewish critics as a traitor to his people much as Roth was attacked in the Jewish press from *Goodbye, Columbus* to *Portnoy's Complaint*.

Zuckerman suffers from the pain that he thinks comes from his lack of a subject, a subject he looks for in Amy Bellette, the Anne Frank look-alike hiding at Lonoff's, and in Caesara, the actress who plays Anne Frank on the Irish stage, in Eva, the actress who plays Anne Frank on the Czech stage, and ultimately he looks for the manuscripts of the Yiddish writer. He looks into the past because he is estranged from the present. His parents are dead, and the Newark which he knew so well has disappeared. In returning to the city he knew and once wrote of so effectively, he finds it vanished. 'The African Methodist church . . .' which has moved into the synagogue where he once took Hebrew lessons symbolises the lost 'tribe' which he cannot recover. This return into the past is at least partly a flight from the present in which he cannot resolve the complex conflict between art and life. In the texts of the past such a complication does not seem to exist.

The conflict between art and life is a product both of the imposition of experience upon aesthetic principle and his personal conflict between the desire to replicate the real in art and his knowledge that such a willed creation is impossible. He tries to tell himself that what he learned of Aristotle's theory of art at the University of Chicago is right – that art, while an 'imitation' of reality is a structure entirely separate from life itself. But his dying father, Alvin Pepler, and his wife Laura's girl friend, Rosemary, will not believe him, nor will his public that reads the character of Carnovsky as Zuckerman and his life. Vulgar reality tells him that Aristotle is wrong even though he knows better.

His flight into the past is an attempt to escape the confusion between artistic reality and the painful world of his family, his admirers, and his critics. In order to approach reality in his art, ultimately he looks for reality in art itself. For Amy Bellette to respond to what happened to Anne Frank, to take revenge, she must do it with the diary. 'No, what she had been given to wield was *Her Achterhuis*, *va Anne Frank*. And to draw blood with it she would have to vanish again into another achterhuis, this time fatherless and all on her own' (p. 147). This is what Zuckerman must do. He must vanish into his book, fatherless, brotherless, motherless. Those who follow Zuckerman around 'had mistaken impersonation for confession and were calling out to a character who lived in a book' (p. 190). Zuckerman has lost what he thinks of as his real existence, but the reality that we discover at the end of the epilogue to the trilogy is that the Jewish character in Roth lives in the text, in the fiction, created either by him or by others. Zuckerman, who wants desperately to be virtuous, must continue, nevertheless, to tell the truth, and the truth is the text of *Carnovsky*, the truth of his story about Essie and the family in 'Higher Education', but his father will call him an enemy of the Jews, the judge will ask him why he must portray Jewish life as 'warped human behavior', and attackers will say that 'It is hardly possible to write of the Jews with more bile and contempt and hatred' (p. 239).

Despite his early belief in the high-minded Aristotelean ideas about art, he realises that Aristotle 'didn't mention anything about the theatre of the ridiculous in which I am now a leading character because of literature', nor does Aristotle realise the degree to which the artist desires to capture the real. Zuckerman wants desperately in art to 'approach the originality and excitement of what actually goes on! But if I ever did, what then would they think of me, my father and the judge' (p. 121). Caesara, the Irish actress, tells him that he only feels this way because he's 'intensity afflicted'. All of Roth's characters are afflicted with intensity because that is the nature of their existence that cannot be comfortable. And that intense desire to be inside of reality while feeling outside of it leads to the homelessness that they feel. Zuckerman jots down everything the kidnapper says on the telephone in his composition book and entitles it 'Dans le Vrai' from Flaubert's remark, 'Ils sont dans le vrai'. He tries to enter reality through art. Pepler will tell him that history, facts themselves, make the writer authentic, his agent that an artist should be a celebrity, and his father that he shouldn't write about the reality of their family because he put too much in. If Zuckerman's identity is his invention, his art, then he is pained by it almost as much as his audience.

Roth's Zuckerman is modelled after a figure from myth and literature, not after Prometheus bound down on his rock for having been heroic enough to steal fire for mankind, but after his scatterbrained brother, Epimetheus. Describing the shift from nineteenth-century to twentieth-century concerns, Carl Schorske remarked, 'Among the shifts from Promethean to Epimethean culture heroes, none was more striking than the turn from Marx to Freud.'[12] Roth's Zuckerman represents the figure of Epimetheus suffering his pain in the neck and down the back so that he cannot find a comfortable position in which to write. But his pain is even worse than that if we remember that Epimetheus, as opposed to his more famous brother who brought fire and knowledge to mankind and was punished for his deed, was the Titan who married Pandora, the woman fashioned by the gods to open a box that contained all the ills mankind has suffered from since. Only the little gift of hope that remained in the box made life bearable. Zuckerman suffers in *The Anatomy Lesson* and he searches everywhere for the clues to truth and healing, worrying over his self-indulgence in art. Like Kafka whom Zuckerman reminds himself of, he suffers the pain of self-analysis and makes that pain and self-analysis the object of an odd kind of laughter.

Zuckerman cannot find a comfortable position in which to write. The intense undiagnosed pain in 'his neck, arms and shoulders' leads him to wear a collar on the advice of one of his many doctors, but Zuckerman, dressed in the collar, looks for the cure in literature: 'That was commonly believed to be a function of great literature: antidote to suffering through depiction of our common fate' (p. 411). He reads George Herbert's poem, 'The Collar', 'hoping to find something there to help him wear his own', but he ends up throwing the book across the room because 'he refused to make of his collar, or of the affliction it was designed to assuage, a metaphor for anything grandiose' (p. 412). His discomfort is constant, but like Portnoy's father who is constipated ('bound') and like Portnoy himself in his impotence, Zuckerman looks for a cure. Zuckerman cannot be comfortable because Zuckerman's discomfort is not only his pain, but his feeling of homelessness in the world he inhabits. He insulates himself with 'double glazed windows' but he still can't write. He is torn apart by the self, both physical and mental. As he says, 'Every thought and feeling, ensnared by the selfness of pain' (p. 416). Zuckerman is bound by mental suffering and to cure the physical Jenny reads *The Magic Mountain* and draws pictures of American samplers with such adages as 'The only antidote to mental suffering is physical pain' from Karl Marx. Zuckerman, comparing himself to Hans Castorp, thinks the literary character is better at pain and suffering than he is. He walks out on his sessions with the analyst when the analyst tells Zuckerman that he is atoning for guilt through suffering.

What is Zuckerman's guilt? He is guilty of having placed truth, or art, the compulsion to write, above patriotism, above family. His brother accuses him of having killed his father. Yet, ambiguously, Zuckerman suggests that despite his father's reaction to his work and his brother's accusation, 'he had half begun to believe that if it hadn't been for his father's frazzled nerves and rigid principles and narrow understanding he'd never have been a writer at all. A first-generation American father possessed by the Jewish demons, a second-generation American son possessed by their exorcism: that was his whole story' (p. 446). It is, of course, the demons that Roth's Zuckerman needs to exorcise that are the very stuff of his art, the 'story', but not 'the whole story'. Milton Appel, in reconsidering 'what he called Zuckerman's "case" . . . ' decides that 'Though probably not himself an outright anti-Semite, Zuckerman was certainly no friend of the Jews: *Carnovsky's* ugly animus proved that' (p. 475). Appel cannot forgive Zuckerman's 'ghetto humor'. He doesn't find him funny. He argues in his attack against Zuckerman that he really is Carnovsky at fourteen delivering his 'declaration of independence' to his sister. Zuckerman is horrified, 'Appel had attributed to the author the rebellious outcry of a claustrophobic fourteen year old boy. This was a licensed literary critic? No, no – an overwrought polemicist for endangered Jewry' (p. 492). And everyone around him, and especially Milton Appel, sees the author of *Carnovsky* as not good for the Jews. The judge thought he should go and see the production of Anne Frank's diary, and Appel thinks he ought to write a defence of Israel. They all want him to affirm his Jewish patriotism. His father calls him a 'bastard', disowning his son the writer on his deathbed, and his mother's last written word, the only word she is capable of writing after a stroke and with a brain tumour, is 'Holocaust'. As Zuckerman writes to Appel, 'In your view, it really isn't deranged Islam or debilitated Christianity that's going to deal us the death blow anyway, but Jewish shits who write books like mine, carrying the hereditary curse of self-hate' (p. 501).

Zuckerman, bereft of his father, his hair, health, subject, and now his mother isn't sure about the six million either. He keeps running into versions of Anne Frank, her diary, because people respond to the book, not the girl. He says that he doesn't pretend to be Elie Wiesel. And about Israel? 'But I am not an authority on Israel. I'm an authority on Newark. Not even on Newark. On the Weequahic section of Newark. If the truth be known, not even on the whole of the Weequahic section' (p. 505).[13] What Zuckerman the artist is trying to do is to go into hiding in his art and what people like Appel do is accuse him of lacking in Jewish patriotism. But, in fact, Zuckerman may be the truest of Jews because he, the secular artist, has inherited the compulsion to produce the text that tells the truth about Jewish reality even if the text is unpatriotic.

Zuckerman's compulsion to tell the true story, the story that is central to the self, is also Roth's compulsion. His feelings of homelessness and loss are shared with all of Roth's characters. This is what finally gives Zuckerman his surreality; he is neither at home in his art, nor in the world where his art and his actions are misunderstood. The discomfort that Roth's characters feel makes them comic because comedy is based on discomfort. This lack of a comfortable position, be it a comfortable physical position in which to write, a comfortable position in politics, in sex, or in American Gentile society is always in part a mechanism that is both self-destructive and the only means toward self-discovery. It is this paradox that makes Roth's characters controversial for those who wish to find in them their own identity. The character's story is Zuckerman's invention and Zuckerman is the invention of the story Roth is telling. He will never be more than the homeless self, struggling to establish his identity in two worlds, in the world of fiction and in the world of reality, which is the world of the critics and the Czech authorities who want to make him into their author, into themselves.

NOTES

1. Gershom Scholem, *On Jews and Judaism in Crisis* (New York: Schocken Books, 1976) p. 82. 'Etre ailleurs, le grand vice de cette race, la grand vertue secrète, la grande vocation de ce peuple.'
2. Philip Roth, *Goodbye, Columbus and Five Short Stories* (New York: Meridian Fiction, 1962) p. 249. All subsequent quotations from *Goodbye, Columbus* and 'Éli, the Fanatic' are taken from this edition, and the relevant page number is given in the text immediately after the quotation.
3. Just as Tzuref lives in another time period so do all Jews. Edward Alexander, in an article entitled 'The Incredibility of the Holocaust', talks about time in relation to the characters in two stories, Kafka's story 'The Great Wall of China' and Sholem Aleichem's story 'Dreyfus in Kasrilevke'. Alexander says, 'The Kasrilevkites, like Kafka's south Chinese, lay claim to a supernatural knowledge which makes them superior to all merely political considerations. Hence they too seek refuge from the historical present by declaring it (and its newspaper reflection) incredible.' For these characters, as Alexander says, the historical present does not exist, but a far more significant time period, the eternity of olden times. See Edward Alexander, 'The Incredibility of the Holocaust', *Midstream*, 15, no. 3 (March 1979). George Steiner also remarks on this characteristic of the Jew as living in the eternity of a different calendar. 'It is because he lives, enacts privately and historically, a written writ, a promissory note served on him when God sought out Abraham and Moses, it is because the "Book of Life" is, in Judaism, literally textual, that the Jew has dwelt apart.' See Steiner, 'Our Homeland, the Text', *Salmagundi*, Winter–Spring 1985, p. 12.
4. Roth, *Goodbye, Columbus and Five Short Stories*.
5. Sanford Pinsker remarks on the meaning of *klug* in Yiddish: 'A number of critics have pointed out that the Yiddish word *klug* means "clever" . . . and one is reminded of the Yiddish curse, "A klug af Columbus" (A curse on Columbus!) which was a commonplace of the Lower East Side non golden streets' (see Sanford Pinsker, *The Comedy that 'Hoits'* (Columbia, Mo.: University of Missouri Press, 1975) pp. 10–11).

6. Philip Roth, *Portnoy's Complaint* (New York: Bantam, 1970) p. 206. All subsequent quotations from *Portnoy's Complaint* are taken from this edition.

7. Sigmund Freud, *Civilization and its Discontents* (New York: W. W. Norton, 1961) p. 88.

8. Steiner, 'Our Homeland, the Text', p. 24. In reading *Portnoy's Complaint* critics not only confuse Portnoy with Roth, but tend to see Portnoy as opposed to the Jewish tradition. Robert Forrey in his essay 'Oedipal Politics in *Portnoy's Complaint*' (in *Critical Essays on Philip Roth*, ed. Sanford Pinsker (Boston, Mass.: G. K. Hall, 1982) p. 272) argues that 'Portnoy's ultimate complaint is not only against the mother; it is also against language, against the word, the traditional repository of Jewish faith'. Portnoy, it seems to me, quite to the contrary, is locked in language and uses texts like Freud's to explain his life. He is not, as Forrey suggests, trying to escape language, but using language to explain what he finds to be unexplainable in his life. As Steiner points out, the real home of the Jew is the text. For Roth's characters the text becomes a place to look for home.

9. Steiner, 'Our Homeland, the Text', p. 6.

10. Clive Sinclair, 'The Son in the Father', review of *The Prague Orgy*, *The Times Literary Supplement*, 18 October 1985, p. 1167.

11. Philip Roth, *Zuckerman Bound* (New York: Farrar, Straus & Giroux, 1985) p. 782. All subsequent quotations from *Zuckerman Bound* are taken from this edition.

12. Carl Schorske, *Fin-de-Siècle Vienna: Politics and Culture* (New York: Vintage, 1981) p. xxiv.

13. Roth is responding here to the numerous critics who see him as merely a realist, critics such as Leslie Fiedler who finds in Roth's work memories of Newark, Robert Alter who has called him a Newark realist, and Irving Howe who accuses Roth of being a limited satirist who is merely writing realistic description of Newark with little or no universal significance. In Howe's attempt to make Roth into a Tolstoy manqué, he misses the point and fails to see Roth for what he is. Roth is a satirist who 'shoots wild' as all satirists, including Swift, do. But Howe, like the fictional critic Milton Appel (who is, of course, a mixture of many critics), cannot see the satire and sees only 'a swelling nausea before the ordinariness of human existence'. To all of Roth's Swiftean satire, exposure, a magnifying of discomfort, Howe can only respond with a deep moral disgust. (See Irving Howe, 'Philip Roth Reconsidered', *Commentary*, December 1972.)

6

Half a Lemon, Half an Egg

MARTIN GREEN

One of the many things that fascinate me about Philip Roth's work is *his* fascination with asceticism – with the deliberate frustration of desire, the denial of appetite, the refusal of gratification. My title combines two strikingly ascetic images, one taken from the Zuckerman novels, the other from the Kepesh novels. In *The Ghost Writer*, E. I. Lonoff asks for half an egg for his breakfast – a humorous gesture but not trivial, because of his habit of self-denial and self-limitation (p. 158);[1] and in *The Professor of Desire* David Kepesh tells Claire how Kafka shuddered at the sight of an office-mate eating a sausage for lunch, and said, 'The only fit food for a man is half a lemon' (p. 168).

Such images are moreover counterpointed, in Roth's work, by images of consumption, which is made to seem distasteful if not gross. The refrigerator of the Patimkins, in *Goodbye, Columbus*, is always bulging with food, their crockery is veneered with gold, their trees drop sporting goods. Portnoy remembers that eating and loving were twin forms of oppression in his childhood – his mother forced him to eat her food by sitting beside him with a bread-knife. The decors that arouse enthusiasm in Roth's young heroes are austere. When Nathan Zuckerman looks around Lonoff's house, he says to himself, 'Purity. Severity. Simplicity. Seclusion. All one's concentration and flamboyance and originality reserved for the gruelling, exalted, transcendent calling. I looked around and I thought, "This is how I will live"' (p. 5). His own current apartment has been described as 'the home of an unchaste monk' (p. 7), and in *The Anatomy Lesson* his place is called 'the pad of a well-heeled monk' (p. 488).

In terms of colour, the Lonoff house is white (the snow outside) and black (Lonoff's clothes and marginalia) and half-tones. The opposite spectrum is represented by Caesara O'Shea in her flame-coloured veils and cockatoo feathers, and by Helen Baird in her belt of emeralds. It is clear how uneasy the Roth heroes feel with such

73

gaudiness. (It is also clear, on reflection, how uneasy Roth is with it, as a writer; but that is a point to come back to.)

Roth's taste is, then, austere; and the coarseness of his humour and the explicitness of his erotica constitute no objection to this proposition if we are asking what does he think good taste to be. (Perhaps the energy with which he revels in bad taste is positively a sign of how important taste is to him.) But of course this does not mean that Roth in any sense 'believes in' ascetic values.

All the signs are that he does not. Kepesh's remark to Claire about Kafka is met by her with a sigh and a 'Poor dope'; he seems 'plain silly' to a healthy girl from Schenectady, New York (p. 168). That response reminds us that Kepesh doesn't find Kafka's predicament so easy to dismiss; but there is nothing to show that he sees it as anything *but* a predicament.

In *Goodbye, Columbus*, Neil Klugman asks God for direction, saying, 'If we meet You at all, God, it's that we're carnal and acquisitive, and thereby partake of You. I am carnal, and I know that You approve, I just know it. But how carnal can you get? Where do we meet? Which prize is You?' (p. 100). Of course, the author is inviting some irony at his hero's expense, but he remains proud of his acumen. (Roth would not be half so interesting if his heroes were not nearly always making the very best that Roth can imagine of their situations.) Though Neil is upset by some results of his carnality and acquisitiveness, he knows no alternative to those principles, and wants none.

One proof is that the rest of Roth's stories demonstrate the same themes: the predicaments get grosser – and grander – but the commitment that in some sense provokes them is irrevocable. The Kepesh novels are about carnality – how carnal can you get? – and the Zuckerman novels are about acquisition – where do I turn now in my acquisitiveness?

This anti-ascetic commitment is quite doctrinal, though – because Roth limits himself to the role of man of letters – slanted towards the aesthetic. Thus in *The Ghost Writer* we are told that it is not our high purposes but our humble needs and cravings that make us moving creatures (p. 21). Lonoff tells Nathan that an unruly personal life will serve him best as a writer (p. 33). And the whole story tells him to be carnal and acquisitive; Lonoff's ascetic life has made everyone he loves miserable.

Indeed, Nathan has already altered Babel's formula for the Jewish writer – autumn in his heart and spectacles on his nose – by adding 'and blood in his penis'. This is to be his Daedalian formula to ignite *his* soul's smithy (p. 49). And Claire Ovington – repeatedly declared to be an angel, a saint – is quite unascetic; about food (as we saw à propos Kafka) and about sex (where she can enjoy almost anything Nathan proposes).

In this anti-asceticism Roth stands in the main line of modern novelists – of modern thought. From the time when Samuel Richardson translated Puritan religious values into the terms of erotic personal relations, and the novel was born, there has been a remarkable continuity (with variations) in the preaching of love. Jane Austen, Charlotte Brontë, George Eliot, Henry James, Chekhov, Hardy, Lawrence – different though they are, all locate the ultimate value in erotic love between a man and a woman. Conflicting kinds of ultimate value, for instance those of spiritual asceticism, usually figure in their work as a blind alley or a perversion. They teach us indignant pity for those trapped in unhappy obligations like marriage, and make us want to see them released and desire fulfilled.

So does Roth. In *The Professor of Desire*, Kepesh says he had always believed sex to be sacred ground. At the climax to *Zuckerman Unbound*, Nathan tells his brother Henry to break out of the marriage in which he is miserable. This is a foolish impulse, for which he pays severely, but it is not, Roth implies, wrong. Nathan quotes Henry Chekhov (a more or less infallible guide) who said he had had to squeeze the serf out of himself drop by drop (p. 393). In *The Anatomy Lesson*, Nathan himself is reproached for his inhibitions: 'Outside the books, you act like you ain't even here. Moderation itself' (p. 488). The reproacher says he had learned his own freedom in anger, his healthy ruthlessness with his enemies, by reading Zuckerman while he was still in high school. Zuckerman/Roth is then a teacher of assertiveness.

This moral doctrine of the duty of self-assertion and self-gratification goes hand in hand with the literary doctrine of formal and moral realism. No doubt the middle term that connects them is Roth's intense interest in middle-class Jewish domestic life in Newark in the 1930s, '40s, '50s, and his profound respect for its values. Of course much of his work offends against the decorum of that life – *Portnoy's Complaint* is only the largest of those offences – but he himself through most of his career so far remains finally respectful of it. We feel, I think, that he keeps his loyalty to that life-style even as he claims his freedoms from it; his parents' marriage remains an ideal and his heroes from time to time reproach themselves for failing to reproduce it. He even appropriates his literary and ideological heroes by domesticating them; Kafka becomes his Hebrew teacher, his Aunt Rhoda becomes a Chekhov actress, Anne Frank becomes his girl friend and wife.

When a writer wants to present bourgeois life, with its small scale and its remoteness from the sublime and the heroic, it makes sense for him to use the techniques of realism: both the moral realism that exposes pretentiousness and cuts things down to scale, and the formal realism that records behaviour minute by minute in all its ignominy and inconsistency. Moral realism is a form of nay-saying, a limited use of asceticism; and formal realism has an elective affinity with that moral attitude. As for self-assertion and self-gratification, they can be part of the normal and decent values of the home: bourgeois domestic life, at least in our day, is no friendlier to meekness and martyrdom than it is to heroic grandiloquence. Of course self-gratification can go too far and destroy normality and decency. But (for most of Roth's career so far) he has claimed that such conflicts were not fights to the death. Thus subject-matter, moral doctrine, and literary technique, were all in harmony.

However, this is only one side – though I think the major side – to Roth's talent. In the 1960s he felt realism to be constraining, and wrote *Our Gang*, *The Great American Novel*, and (in 1972) *The Breast*. The last of these is a wonderful fictional idea – the revenge of fate on an enthusiastic teacher of Kafka and Gogol, as Kepesh himself suggests (p. 72). It is also a revenge by fate on the American-male obsession with women's breasts – and on Kepesh's appetite for more and better sex. As the immediate preliminary to his metamorphosis, he experiences 'Sex, not in the head, not in the heart, but excruciatingly in the epidermis of the penis, sex skin deep and ecstatic. In bed I found myself writhing with pleasure' (p. 10). And the next step is that he turns into a breast. (The story also catches up current fears and fantasies about sex-change operations – like Vidal's *Myra Breckenridge*.)

There is, however, no way to be realistic, morally or formally, about Kepesh's 'situation'; and therefore nothing can happen in the story. There is nothing for him or anyone else to do. And by keeping the first person voice (the most powerful agent of Roth's realism), the author paralyses our imagination even in response to the central image. We cannot respond because the voice undermines the image, undermines the whole project. Kafka wrote his

Metamorphosis in a narrative prose quite disengaged from the complex self-consciousness of Roth's prose. In the company of Kafka's voice, anything can happen. In Kepesh's company, that is not true.

One might guess that *The Breast* is all that survives of some large fantasy project built around Kepesh. What Roth finally published five years later as *The Professor of Desire* is literary realism again. But he attempted to include 'real life fantasy' – these blatantly exotic elements of experience incompatible with realism – by a different method. The hero falls in love with a woman he cannot 'believe in'. Helen Baird is beyond David Kepesh's imagination – she seems to be beneath it, to be 'corny', but he knows that the criteria by which he so condemns her are mean-spirited and stupid. They are categories appropriate to *his* experience but applied to her they can only find fault. This is because of her striking beauty and her exotic adventures, as well as because of her *cult* of her glamour and her history, as exhibited achievements, as displays. They are, to his sense, inauthentic just because they are public facts: 'Oh my God, I think, so beautiful and so corny' (p. 57). He is of course palpably wrong; she *is* strikingly beautiful, and she *has* done these exotic things.

'Corny' means lacking the stamp of authenticity which is given by ironic self-scrutiny, and by the self-contraction that induces; and ironic self-scrutiny is, within the conscience, the function of moral realism. Kepesh, like all Roth's heroes, bristles with that irony about himself – it is the vertebrae of his sensibility, the pungency of his style. But when Helen asks him, 'Why the studied detachment . . . what have you got against passion?', he admits the charge. 'Is the unbelievable character Helen or . . . ?' (p. 56). Clearly it is himself.

But such clarity does not help him to subdue his *suspicions*, his feeling that she is not for real. Her jewels, her adventures, her dealings with 'the men who *run* the world', above all her 'well-known and important' lover, who offered to have his wife killed so he could marry her – Kepesh feels they must come out of a grade B movie. And when this lover has Helen – now Mrs Kepesh – thrown into gaol and accused of drug smuggling, that does not convince him either. Though he flies to Hong Kong and sees her in gaol, he still cannot 'believe in' what is happening. His sense of reality – his moral realism – cannot accommodate facts of Helen's kind. On his way home, with Helen drunk beside him, Kepesh weeps, not over her, but over his students' Chekhov papers.

This would be great, except that *we* can't believe in Helen either. In Roth's prose – in his realistic portrait of her – Helen *is* corny. (So is Caesara O'Shea in *Zuckerman Unbound*.) You need Mailer's prose to accommodate such public personalities – see *The American Dream*. (By the same token, you don't turn to Mailer for brilliantly realistic depictions of family life.) Moral and formal realism belong to the domestic novel. It was the adventure tale, from Scott to Kipling and Mailer, which dealt in public history; and the two forms are mutually hostile.

It is interesting to compare the case of one great novelist who married a Helen Baird: D. H. Lawrence. Frieda Lawrence, too, was a beautiful woman, older than Lawrence, and with much more erotic and exotic experience when she married him. She, too, upbraided him with being 'monkish' and 'a young fogy'; and she often seemed morally shallow, self-preoccupied, made up of wilful, outer-directed gestures, a rhetorician not a poet of life. Lawrence gave her *Anna Karenina* to read, as a mirror of herself, just as Kepesh gave Helen; and both women wanted to rewrite the story, to make it reflect their own experience.

When Lawrence depicted Frieda in thoroughly realistic terms, in the domestic comedy scenes of *Kangaroo*, she is largely deprived of her glamour. Even in *The Rainbow* and *Women in Love* he strips from her her most exotic elements; she is no longer a German baroness, she is unrelated to Otto Gross and Max Weber; but he does invent a form – we can call it the novel as dramatic poem – which gives her scope. Lawrence gave Frieda a large place in his mind and art – he learned from her how to write differently. Roth was perhaps more impatient, more proud, more sure of himself: if there was a real Helen Baird, she was soon evicted from the throne of power in his mind. (Perhaps she left saying, as Maureen says in *My Life as a Man*, 'I could have been his Muse if he had let me.')

So Helen Baird is brilliantly conceived, and though she is not 'realised', such conceptions do not go for nothing; in fact failure has its own authenticating power. I at least am *moved* by the way Helen fails to come to life – I feel the creative anguish behind the page, the violence with which Roth flings his pen across the room as he sees that he can't do her. Nothing could more poignantly convince me of his plight as a realistic writer, shut off from so much he wants to write about.

But of course I'm relieved when he invents the devices that *do* bring that outer world within the reach of his domestic art: the integrating of stories by Chekhov and James into his own, and above all the domestication of the figures of Anne Frank and Franz Kafka. I must not repeat here what I have said elsewhere, but I will point to the Prague episode in *The Professor of Desire* as brilliantly clever and deeply moving. Kepesh's devotion to Kafka – Soska's devotion to Melville – his vision of Ahab as a symbol of America – the way the Czechs are forced to use Kafka to explain and excuse their daily experience – above all Soska's and Kepesh's ambivalence about their heroes: what are bookish people to do with their books but sink their teeth into them, 'instead of into the hand that throttles them' (p. 164). Here Roth gives expression to his political life, too.

This mention of Kafka, the Hunger Artist, returns us to the theme of asceticism. From Prague Kepesh flies on to Bruges, where he gives a paper on 'Hunger Art', and it seems clear that that story above all represents Kafka to Roth, and that Kafka above all represents something important. Part of that something must be asceticism. Kafka once had his stomach pumped because he felt that bits of food were sticking to its walls. Amongst Roth's other heroes, Gogol starved himself to death. James and Chekhov are figures of renunciation; and so, of course, is Lonoff. What does all this mean? And how does it relate to his domestic realism? Primarily it shows us Roth's readiness for disgust, the acute or exacerbated taste that accompanies his carnality. It is notable how often his heroes are contrasted with some figure of coarser sensibility. In *Zuckerman Unbound*, it is Alvin Pepler: 'The bullying ego, the personal audacity, the natural coarseness, the taste for exhausting encounters – what gifts' (p. 339). In *The Anatomy Lesson* it is Ivan Felt, who is compared with a dockworker, a circus strongman, a peasant – he has a plain, ungraspable face, a thick back, and shock-absorber legs (p. 487). And in *The Professor of Desire* Kepesh feels 'pitifully banal' besides Louis Jelinek, because the latter is not interested in pleasing anyone. There is no opposite contrast, between the Roth-figure and someone more refined and delicate: the nearest equivalent is the figure of Claire or Laura, and she is narrower in her range rather than more refined. Besides, she is a woman, and so the difference from her does not *define* Kepesh/Zuckerman.

It is that refined taste that keeps Roth in tune with Kafka and his other heroes. And taste is born when the great negative principle impregnates the imagination. When it is lived out thoroughly, the negative principle becomes asceticism: when it lives in and with the imagination, it employs itself rejecting all but the best – allows us certain pleasures, and immensely intensifies them, by rejecting 99 per cent of the sources that offer them.

Within ordinary domestic life, also, it is taste – in a different sense – which reveals the secret workings of the negative principle. There are things one just does not do, even when one does not invoke any rational or familial values to explain that refusal. Within most traditional societies there are special groups, special callings, in which people do practise asceticism. These are set apart from ordinary life, and ordinary people feel no obligation to imitate their strenuousness, but their presence (even in absence) exerts a pressure which helps form the criteria of normality and decency. You only escape that pressure when you renounce both taste and the ordinary virtues – a renunciation which in literary terms we call modernism. That is the choice before which Roth stands.

By all the signs, Roth is not interested in the great nay-sayers of *life* – in Gandhi and the late Tolstoy. His heroes (Kafka, Gogol, Chekhov) are men who *were* interested in, but who confined *themselves* to, art. Roth stands at a further remove – a remove symbolised for him, one guesses, by the Atlantic Ocean, by the historical split between the Free World and Eastern Europe. He is a Jew who got away; those who did not felt, and perhaps feel, the fascination of life-denial; he does not.

Thus he stands further back than his heroes from life-asceticism and moves further forward towards pornographic freedoms in art. In *The Professor of Desire*, where Kepesh alternates between 'decency' and 'indecency', the balance finally inclines to the latter. He is going to leave Claire, his principle of order and calm and duty. He has accepted Ralph Baumgarten's teaching that even Chekhov is unsatisfactory, because he is never 'implicated in the shit' (p. 130). Baumgarten, who is Kepesh's secret sharer (p. 137), says 'Virtue isn't my bag. Too bo-ring' (p. 130). He refuses to write about or out of the virtuous and pathetic aspects of his life, presenting himself to the world as an aggressive and unscrupulous animal. That is the model Kepesh sets out to follow. His seminar on desire will study books by Gombrowicz, Genet, Mishima – 'disquieting contemporary novels' about 'prurient and iniquitous sexuality' which do implicate the author in what he describes (p. 169).

In the Zuckerman novels, we see a connection between this new departure and a seemingly final break between the Roth-figure and his parents. After his father's funeral, Zuckerman finds himself haunted by the image of the dead Mussolini, hanging upside down, and realises that his father had been a repressive tyrant, of whom he is now free. In *The Anatomy Lesson* he crazily attacks his friend's father – who is lovable but who is trying to strengthen family bonds binding his son and his grandson to him and to each other. And of course Zuckerman's own father has broken *their* bond by (perhaps) cursing him with his dying breath. It seems that Roth is renouncing, amongst other things, those seriatim celebrations of domestic happiness which made him the Dickens of our time.

Of course he has announced such a renunciation before, a quarter of a century ago. In 1960, in 'Writing in America' he told us one could no longer write realistically about such a crazy country. He tried other modes, but came back to realism. Partly, no doubt, because he is wonderful at it; also, I would guess, because Céline, Mishima, and Gombrowicz cannot replace Kafka and Chekhov in his heart and mind. And even if this time they do, if this time Roth joins the modernists, his career as a whole will still form a classic link in a classic tradition: reaching back with his left hand he has held on to the writers who loved the ascetics and respected the ordinary, while with his right hand he reached forward for lawlessness, abjection, and outrage.

NOTE

1. References in the essay are to the following editions of Philip Roth's works:

   Goodbye, Columbus (1959; repr. New York: Bantam, 1963).
   The Breast (New York: Holt, Rinehart & Winston, 1972).
   My Life as a Man (New York: Holt, Rinehart & Winston, 1974).
   The Professor of Desire (1977; repr. New York: Bantam, 1978).
   Zuckerman Bound (New York: Farrar, Straus & Giroux, 1985).

7

Fictions of Metamorphosis: From *Goodbye, Columbus* to *Portnoy's Complaint*

DONALD KARTIGANER

I

At the centre of virtually all Roth's fiction, from the stories of *Goodbye, Columbus* to the *Zuckerman Bound* trilogy, is an action of character transformation: a bizarre metamorphosis in which a new self emerges to stand in striking opposition to the old. The strangeness of the transformation lies not only in its improbability or the grotesqueness of the new self, but in the survival of the old as a grudging yet tenacious partner. Like the different phases of desire in Freud's theory of psychic development, former and present selves coexist as the distorting masks of each other, preserving rather than reconciling the tension between them. The transformations, in other words, are always incomplete – dramas of changing rather than change, of characters struggling between competing claims to their identity.

Whatever the irresolution of the conflict or its potential pathology, the fact remains that the largest freedom, and moral core, of these fictions resides in the power of the central characters to play out the full range of their own discord: to magnify that divisiveness which Roth sees as fundamental to personality into a crisis of internal warfare. These are the men and women, as Roth has put it, 'whose moorings have been cut, and who are swept away from their native shores and out to sea' (*Reading Myself and Others*, p. 65). The shift into strange waters is at least half-willed; but it is not so much an escape from a personal and cultural past as an oddly courageous discovery and enactment of the conflicts embedded in it – conflicts that other characters, avoiding what they implicitly recognise as a kind of madness, choose to conceal.

In Roth's most extravagant novel of transformation, *The Breast*, David Kepesh finds himself metamorphosed into a six-foot, 150-pound female breast, while yet retaining the identity and habits of mind of a son, lover, and associate professor of literature. The grotesqueness of the conception is supreme – more than enough to appal readers who have learned to live on easy terms with Kafka's Gregor Samsa and Gogol's Kovalyov. And yet the upshot of this latest, not yet canonised *Verwandlung* is only to elevate into the grandest proportions tensions that have long existed in Kepesh: between the scholar and the sensualist, the man of reason and the man of lust, the man of reality and the man of pleasure.

As a single enormous, and enormously sensitive, erogenous zone, Kepesh experiences an ecstasy 'even more extreme' than during the twenty-one days of wild passion with Claire Ovington which have preceded the change (p. 21). At the same time, he remains both a reasonable man who sets boundaries to pleasure (Claire must fondle him for only thirty minutes of their hour-long daily visits) and as a professional academic inspired by his altered shape to new hermeneutic heights, as he probes the text of his transformation for cause and meaning. Is it a dream? a mad delusion? And if madness, what psychic blow has determined it – and why *this form*, 'big brainless bag of dumb desirable tissue', for the flight into lunacy (p. 66)? Or is the change real, to be explained as a remarkable extension of literature – the metamorphoses of Gogol and Kafka – into life: the critic's sublime triumph of *becoming* what even the boldest fiction can only fantastically propose? But with all the heady speculation, Kepesh remains hopelessly wedded to the image of his desire: mind and passion as antithetical, self-mocking terms of a transformation that can neither resolve nor complete itself – nor return to that once endurable, even enviable time of ordinary confusion.

In several of the essays and interviews collected in *Reading Myself and Others*, Roth has commented on the attraction in his fiction to the most exaggerated divisions of self. At the outset of *The Anatomy Lesson*, for example, Zuckerman is already torn between his writing identity, a freedom from all emotional and intellectual constraints but that of his compulsion to write, and the new, physical constraint of a mysterious *ache* that has effectively compromised his freedom into a pure 'selfness of pain' and sensual pleasure – 'It was all he was good for' (pp. 10, 108). But Zuckerman continues to be divided even in the further transformations he plans in order to rid himself of the torment of his present one. Were he only fantasising a new career as a physician *or* impersonating a pornographer, Roth notes, 'he wouldn't have been my man':

> The thing about Zuckerman that interests me is that everybody's split, but few so openly as this. Everybody is full of cracks and fissures, but usually we see people trying very hard to hide the places where they're split. Most people desperately want to heal their lesions, and keep trying to. Hiding them is sometimes taken for healing them (or for not having them). But Zuckerman can't successfully do either.   (p. 143)

Zuckerman's failure is also his peculiar triumph, and his link to other crucial figures in Roth who will not hide their fissures. Characters such as Eli Peck, Gabe Wallach, Lucy Nelson, Alex Portnoy, Peter Tarnopol, Kepesh, and Zuckerman suffer mightily for the tensions that rend them, yet they still prefer the anguish of all that they are to the comparative comfort of self-deceptive and repressive reconciliations. Nothing, no dimension of self, is to be given up. As Roth has observed about his most notorious invention, 'In Portnoy the disapproving moralist who says "I am horrified" will not disappear when the libidinous slob shows up screaming, "I want!"' (p. 299).

The action of division that Roth focuses on in his characters echoes significantly in his comments on the backgrounds and process of his own writing. In recounting the personal, social, and intellectual sources of his work, Roth emphasises the element of conflict animating each of them – as if they have become part of his consciousness, part of his usable past, primarily on the strength of that conflict. The most memorable aspect of his Jewish background as a youth, for example, seems to have been his sense of the disparity between his own experience as a Jew, growing up in a lower-middle-class, largely Jewish section of Newark, and the experience of European Jewry. Comfortable and secure, unintimidated, 'part of the majority composed of the competing minorities' and feeling inferior to none, Roth was nevertheless 'surrounded from birth with a *definition* of the Jew . . . as sufferer, the Jew as an object of ridicule, disgust, scorn, contempt, derision, of every heinous form of persecution and brutality, including murder'. The Jewishness of Roth's actual life and the Jewishness that 'surrounded' it were at once related and remote, unfathomably joined across the gap of a 'vast discrepancy' (p. 126).

Acknowledging his literary mentors, he recalls a comparable tension. In one version Roth presents himself as the disciple of Jake the Snake H., Arnold G., and Henny Youngman on one side, and Henry James on the other: 'the low-minded and their vulgarity' and 'the high-minded'; the masters of invective, obscenity, and the 'shlemieldom' that shines through cultural aspirations, and the Master of 'linguistic tact and moral scrupulosity', the heroic Worshipper of Art (pp. 81–2).

Applying Philip Rahv's classic bifurcation of American writers into Paleface and Redskin – the culturally refined and the unabashedly vulgar – to his own complex lineage, Roth insists on a dual identity: he is not to be categorised in either camp. He is a 'redface' – and by this he does not mean to suggest a reconciliation of the two types but to make what he regards as the more interesting claim that he straddles the fence that divides them. He employs in his fiction opposing energies, both of which arouse his affection and scepticism: 'The redface *sympathizes* equally with both parties in their *disdain* for the other, and, as it were, re-enacts that argument within the body of his own work' (pp. 82–3; my emphasis). The goal of his writing is 'to be true to these seemingly inimical realms of experience', to give voice to them – like the selves that divide his characters – as the combatants of a continuing warfare.

Even the act of writing is, for Roth, an act of confrontation. Beginning a novel is a matter of 'looking for trouble' (p. 140), looking for something against which to test oneself and one's last book. 'Fluency can be a sign that nothing is happening', whereas difficulty may indicate that new tensions are becoming available for fiction. The writer is chiefly an impersonator, for whom creation is a matter of performing a metamorphic drama of self and other, 'pass[ing] oneself off as what one is not' (p. 144). The 'real' writing self is not quite the one or the other; like the ventriloquist, 'he's most himself by simultaneously being someone else, neither of whom he "is" once the curtain is down'. Concocting a half-imaginary existence out of the so-called 'actual drama' is merely one of the terms of a larger, unresolved reality which exists only in the very act of impersonation. Thus the background of fiction, the influences, the impulses that inspire, the action of making novels – they all come to reflect, and finally culminate in, the dynamic character Roth needs at the centre of his work: 'My hero has to be in a state of vivid transformation or radical displacement. "I am not what I am – I am, if anything, what I am not!"' (p. 164).

II

All the stories of *Goodbye, Columbus* contain characters who find themselves doubling into complexity. Lou Epstein, for example, the fifty-nine-year-old founder of Epstein Paper Bag and doggedly responsible husband and father, becomes the disease-carrying adulterer: 'The change, the change . . . I don't even know when it began. Me, Lou Epstein, with a rash' (p. 156).[1] The change is as incredible to him as becoming a breast is to Kepesh. His solution, unlike that of Kepesh, is to bring on the heart attack that will allow him to succumb to his proper, single identity – to 'live normal', as Goldie frantically urges (p. 165). Ozzie Freedman, a precocious thirteen-year-old asking impertinent questions about the divinity of Jesus at Hebrew School, is suddenly the boy on the roof, wondering 'Is it me? Is it me?' (p. 106). Having scrambled in fright from the classroom, Ozzie now discovers a new feeling of 'Peace and . . . Power' (p. 107), from the edge of his new 'celestial' world presiding over 'the whole little upside down heaven' below him (p. 110). His transformation climaxes as the image of a Second Coming, sent in order to verify the possibility of the First – magically, after two millenia, converting the Jews.

But it is 'Eli, the Fanatic' that explores the theme of transformation, most deeply and disturbingly, and in ways that anticipate the more mature versions to come. The metamorphosis of Eli Peck is a process that begins as confrontation and ends as bizarre meeting. Eli is the young lawyer chosen by the Jews of Woodenton to persuade a recently arrived group of Hassidic refugees – the headmaster, assistant, and children of a Yeshiva – either to leave the community or minimise the sharp contrast of their presence. At issue are the values of moderation, common sense, the 'peace and safety' (p. 202) achieved by relinquishing the peculiar identity that *separates*, and the value of devotion to just that identity – and to the elaborate system of observance that is the key to its survival. Modern and tribal communities clash, with Eli as the bridge between them. Although he is the representative of the local Jews, Eli in fact defends the causes of each community to the other: 'the townsmen had a case', he is convinced, 'But not *exactly* . . .' (p. 183).

Roth presents this conflict with seriousness and even-handedness, whatever his simplifications of both suburban and Hassidic Jewry. Tzuref, the headmaster of the Yeshiva, gets most of the memorable lines:

'And a medical experiment they performed on him yet! That leaves nothing, Mr. Peck. Absolutely nothing!'
'I misunderstood.'
'No news reached Woodenton?' (p. 191)

But the Woodenton case – precisely because of the Holocaust, from which the Hassidic group is a last remnant – has its own resonance and force: 'What peace, Eli thinks, What incredible peace. Have children ever been so safe in their beds? . . . what civilization had been working toward for centuries. For all his jerkiness, that was all Ted Heller was asking for, peace and safety' (p. 202).

The conflict, however, is largely a matter of 'positions', forcefully argued but static, except as it reaches downward into the inner confusions of Eli Peck. Eli has been a lawyer who would often imagine himself pleading his opponent's case, as he has been a loving husband who finds inadequate his wife's devotion to the 'normal' in him and their life together (p. 183). Like the Woodenton Jews, Miriam wants 'calm circumstances . . . order and love' (p. 188) – while Eli, who has already fled normality on two occasions in the form of nervous breakdowns, has what might be called a neurotic passion for his own divisions. It is these divisions, displaced into the imagery of the current dispute, that finally explodes to the surface as the dramatic transformation of Eli into the Hassidic 'greenhorn', whose traditional black suit has so disturbed the community.

Having presented some clothes of his own to the Hassid, Eli is astonished to receive in return the man's outfit – 'the glassy black of lining, the coarse black of trousers, the dead black of fraying threads, and in the center the mountain of black: the hat' (p. 206). Eli's half-deliberate donning of the clothes, enveloping himself in the former guise of his own 'apparition' (p. 204), is the first great metamorphosis in Roth's fiction. It is a transformation whose power lies in the fact that these merging worlds are sustained, almost brutally, in their contradiction.

Throughout the entire episode, Eli remains himself as well as his imposture. He is the Jew at his own door, the stricken survivor and the young attorney whose name and identity he methodically pounds into the pavement as he zig-zags his way through the gaping crowd: 'E–li–Peck–E–li–Peck–E–li–Peck. . . . He knew who he was down to his marrow – they were telling him' (p. 212). Eli is madness insisting on its sanity, a determination to wear the suit he already knows his analyst will convince him to put away. Above all, he is the husband and the father impersonating the man who has lost both wife and child. This last doubling achieves its highest intensity as Eli, making his final utterance as a Hassid, just before the jacket is torn from his back, screams, *'I'm the father!'*: as if he were both restoring potency to the man who has 'nothing' and identifying the gap – the 'vast discrepancy' – that is the ground of their meeting.

'Eli, the Fanatic' makes no plea for orthodoxy or assimilation, and it is beside the point to accuse Eli Peck of either the conviction, or the preposterousness, of a true conversion. The power and moral thrust of the story lie in Eli's willingness, activated by the conflict in Woodenton, to confront once more his inner divisions, to release himself to the psychic upheaval of metamorphosis: the *changing* – for which there can be no denouement, no conclusive *change*.

Eli has, in other words, opened himself to a classic redemptive pattern – *Teshuvah*: to return, to repent – complicated by his inability to complete it. The 'state of vivid transformation' that Roth seeks in his characters, and in which Eli is caught, becomes the measure of his moral and creative life, his struggle 'to be more than he once imagined himself to be.'[2] But this is a struggle that can only turn, and turn again, within the tension of its utterly opposed possibilities. The extent of Eli's moral growth becomes the extent of his willingness to remain on the stretch, playing out the grotesque meeting of himself and his mask, before being led back to the normality of healed, or hidden, divisions.

III

Letting Go and *When She Was Good* are the novels Roth would later call his 'two indisputably earnest books', payments on a pledge he had made at the outset of his career to devote his fiction to the themes of 'conscience, responsibility, and rectitude' (*Reading Myself and Others*, pp. 77, 121). They are also his most conventionally realistic novels, faithful to the detail of locale and social context, the pressures of environment bearing down on character – above all, to the notion of credibility as a criterion for fiction.

Both books do, in other words, what novels are supposed to do, and in the way they are supposed to do it. The primary concern is the exploration of moral conduct, the novel being that 'genre that constituted the most thorough-going investigation of conscience that I knew of' (p. 78) – and the prevailing technique is the plausible representation of actual human affairs. Powerfully present is the sense of *containment* common to the novel, standards of credibility and a moral norm operating as boundaries within which writer and character must perform their various acts.

And yet *Letting Go* and *When She Was Good* both enact what I take to be Roth's characteristic drama of transformation, as Gabe Wallach and Lucy Nelson emerge as versions of doubled identity – unreconciled, and unwilling to conceal their divisions. Like Eli Peck, they bear the burden of metamorphosis – inherently implausible within the realistic mode and morally dubious, even perverse, within the normative value systems controlling the world of the text. And like Eli Peck, Gabe and Lucy are considered mad during the crisis of their transformations; they are the 'monsters' that neither society nor realistic fiction can normally accommodate. Thus both characters are a way of testing and in some measure breaking through the traditional novelistic form that has brought them to life.

In an important essay addressing the problems of being a realistic writer in America, Roth offers at least a partial explanation of why these testings must take place: '[T]he American writer in the middle of the twentieth century has his hands full in trying to understand, describe, and then make *credible* much of American reality.' Reality has simply become too wildly improbable; the writer who would uphold the realist creed of accurate observation is forced into the appearance of fantasy by the truth! Reality 'stupifies, it sickens, it infuriates. . . . [it] is continually outdoing our talents. . . . Who, for example, could have invented Charles Van Doren? Roy Cohn and David Schine . . . ?' (p. 176).

The characters of transformation provide Roth with a strategy for competing with the incredible characters of contemporary life. The people and circumstances, for example, embodying the codes of suburban and Hassidic Jewry are plausible enough; it is their uncanny meeting in Eli Peck that realises a madness. And this meeting becomes the passageway, as Roth writes in a later essay, 'from the imaginary that comes to seem real to the real that comes to seem imaginary, a continuum between the credible incredible and the incredible credible' (p. 91).

The difficulty Roth describes, however – that of the writer *matching* contemporary reality – may be the mask of a quite different difficulty beneath, which is the novelist's discontent with the containments of the realistic mode. The thread of this discontent runs through the traditional novel – *Madame Bovary*, for example, being the prototypical novel about a woman trying to get out of a novel (and into a romance).[3] By the middle of the twentieth century, of course, the constraints of the novel have been pretty well trampled down, with writers and their characters escaping them, as far as Roth is concerned, all too easily. Roth's dual task, then, becomes that of remaining faithful to the tradition while avoiding complete subservience to it. His solution is the creation of the character in transformation: the being who is *of* this contemporary world, composed of conflicts true to our time and place, but who challenges this world, confronts us with a behaviour we credit but refuse to understand except as a *mésalliance*, an unbalancing of forces that we, and the novel, insist must be brought to order. From such tensions come forth not only the professor-breast Kepesh and the ethical pervert Portnoy, but Gabe Wallach and Lucy Nelson: grimmer, less playful, more realistic versions of the struggles of Realism with itself.

Gabe Wallach is the character in *Letting Go* whose division is most openly expressed and least resolved by the end of the novel. He derives this division, as so many Roth characters do, from what he takes to be the essential qualities of his parents' personalities. Gabe's mother has been a woman of reason and self-control, of power over life – particularly over the various whims and fanciful designs of her husband: 'She had disapproved of his Yoga . . . his Reichian analysis, his health foods, and his allegiance in 1948 to Henry Wallace. . . . She checked cockeyed enthusiasm left and right' (pp. 42–4). Gabe's father is a man of feeling, who has not taken hold of life, trying to shape it to his desire, but 'who preferred the strange forces to grip him' (p. 45). He is the prey of his own passion, and he stands in need of his wife's reason and order even as he resents both the reason and his need of it.

Their relationship, although lasting, is like the other major relationships in the novel, Paul and Libby's, Gabe's and Martha's, in that it is marked by a sequence of need followed by resentment at the very fulfilment of need. Gabe, for example, though falling in love with Martha, 'was not falling in love with Martha's predicament' of two young children (p. 227); yet she justly accuses Gabe later of 'detesting' her for letting the children go to their father: 'I think you liked me noble better' (p. 466). Each partner eventually despises what he has made the other become, as if the response to need only makes more vivid its existence, and what is often felt as its shame. In a sense these relationships – and most of those throughout Roth's fiction – are as driven by principles of opposition as are the individual characters, and with as little chance for a reconciliation that is not merely a concealment of the tension.

Out of the influence of his parents, 'these two somewhat terrorized people' (p. 45), Gabe evolves a personal dynamic that reflects their conflict of feeling and reason: a dynamic of attachment and remoteness, engagement and separation, commitment and aloofness. In one of these modes he is a man of passion, who finds himself attracted to virtually every woman he meets and unable to restrain his advances. In the other he is the man persistently trying to disentangle himself from the relationships that ensue, all of which threaten his self-control. Running from the grasp of his widowed father or the array of women he finds himself wooing, he is also constantly intruding himself into other people's lives. Gabe is everyone's intermediary – visiting Paul's parents, Martha's children, delegating to himself the task of arranging Paul's and Libby's adoption of a baby, and then rising to what he considers the threat of Harry Bigoness to take the baby away. Gabe flees his involvements only to bind himself in the involvements of others.

The two modes constitute the gaping fissure of his character, neither one of which he is prepared to subdue. The climax of his condition is the section called 'The Mad Crusader', when Gabe carries his transformation to its most extreme point, becoming the grotesque coexistence of his opposing needs. In the episode of trying to persuade Harry Bigoness and his wife Theresa (the mother of Rachel) to sign the necessary papers allowing Paul and Libby to complete the adoption, Gabe indulges the side of his passion to the fullest, determined for once not to fail a commitment: '*Something was to be completed!* Finish! Go all the way!' (p. 598). But this commitment is being fulfilled in the interest of a family *not* his own, a married couple and child whose experience he can only vicariously know. Unmarried – incapable of being married – without child, Gabe becomes a crusader to save a marriage and a child. Remoteness and involvement become the dual masks whose tension draws Gabe into the madness of transformation: the *'decisive moment . . . my time of strength . . . followed so quickly and humiliatingly by the dissolution of character, of everything'* (p. 627).

Surrounding Gabe are characters comparably divided but who, by the end of the novel, have moved in the direction of some compromise of those divisions. Libby Hertz is the woman who *wants*: love, money, things, a child. She is a woman, Gabe believes, 'with desires *nobody* could satisfy . . . perhaps . . . fated . . . to a life of agonized yearning' (p. 239). Yet she has atttached herself to a man who desires only to explore his power of denial, who can scarcely comprehend, let alone respond to her yearning. Libby's resolution is to begin the approach to an acceptance of her situation: 'not to expect everything' (p. 620). She still fantasises, of course, that she can discover in Paul what is clearly not there, that she will free him from the past, *'will convince him of happiness'* (p. 619). But she seems prepared to cling to the structure of a marriage erected on frustration – to value the form despite the contradictions of its content: much as she performs the Chanukah ritual, which 'doesn't even require that you believe in God' (p. 539). Compromise is the final decision of Martha Reganhart as well. She wants a lover, she tells Gabe, not a husband, but in the chaos of Gabe's own contradictory needs she settles for the stable and supportive Sid Jaffe: 'I've got a right to hang on now' (p. 576).

More complex is the figure of Paul, for whom desire is not an inner pressure, contained by reality, but the gradually fading illusion of his life. His peculiar tragedy is in fact the very *absence* of the divisions others contend with, between the need for love and stability, for passion and order. Paul is not the man driven by the force of feeling, not the artist and lover he has imagined himself to be, but rather the man of responsibility, the man who *is* nothing other than the obligations he has inherited or chosen: 'he *was* Libby, *was* his job, *was* his mother and father' (p. 436). The 'glorious possibility' that he might be more – that at least there might be dreams he could poise against the pull of his constraints – succumbs to the single truth of his pursuit of the severest discipline.

Despite his self-image of writer-lover-independent soul, Paul has never actually desired more than to 'place a constant demand upon his spirit' (p. 85). He denies his obligations to his parents by making a marriage of even more stringent obligations: it is not desire but an opposing *duty* he confronts his parents with. Ultimately he links marriage and parents in his mind, wishing to break free of both, but finding himself drawn back – 'because *in* was the direction of his life. In and in and in' (p. 451) – to the grave of his father, to Libby and the adopted child.

Unlike Gabe, Paul does not truly test his past, does not revolve between opposing masks. He is far closer than he would like to think to his old friend Maury, whose adult life is simply the continuation of his childhood. Absent of desire, Paul can know the struggle he considers necessary to any genuine vitality only by choosing the obligations most difficult for him: by making a duty of the passion he cannot feel, by committing himself to forms whose spirit remains a mystery to him. He consoles himself for the frustration of lacking, rather than suppressing, passion by the determination that 'If I can't feel what I have to, I *do* what I have to' (p. 614).

The great cry of Roth's fiction, the source of its energy as well as its deep sadness, is the importance of change, coupled with the realisation of its ultimate impossibility. In *Letting Go*, Paul, Libby, and Martha experience change, but only as the move toward a partial though nevertheless substantial acceptance of, not what they *are*, but what they have been *given*. Change for them is the progress from testing to a degree of accommodation. This form of change is the law of the novelistic tradition itself, consistent with much of the tenor of *Letting Go* and possessing an unquestionable appeal for us. Musing over this book, after all, is that epitome of expectation and acceptance, Isabel Archer – and it is to her, and to Henry James, that *Letting Go* seems to look for its prevailing ethic.

Rebelling against this ethic, however, is the figure for whom change is not a bending to constraint but a full engagement of the opposing sides of self. Gabe Wallach survives the novel's acceptances. Having again fled his entanglements, this time to London, regarded by Libby (he believes) as a violator who must be forgiven – and by us as the 'monster' who has not learned the novel's characteristic pattern – Gabe yet remains at the centre of the novel's transformational power: the disturbing force who reflects Roth's need to revitalise the tradition by creating the 'credible incredible'. Gabe demonstrates the larger realism of unreconciled division rather than acommodation. He refuses the forgiveness that will allow him *'off the hook'*, preferring the continuing strain of his metamorphosis – still trying to *'make sense of the larger hook I'm on'* (p. 628).

Of all Roth's novels, *When She Was Good* is the most severely contained, locked in an unbroken banality that reaches into every corner of character, episode, and language. Willard Carroll's name for that banality is 'civilisation', and he regards Liberty Center as its most complete embodiment. His first glimpse of the town, its 'quiet beauty . . . serene order . . . [and] gentle summery calm' (p. 6), persuades Willard that here he will be free of the savagery of his father, 'a fierce and ignorant man' (p. 3), and the brute natural force his father had learned to deal with – perhaps by matching it with a brutishness and cruelty of his own. The largest commitment of Liberty Center is to the sublimity of its established routine: to cling to what is commonly done, commonly spoken and thought, and to protect it against the invasions of difference and emotional intensity – as if these were relics of that ancestral savagery that must be kept at bay.

The subtle strength of this civilisation is especially evident in its almost unlimited capacity for forgiveness. The more usual violations of convention – the crude language or philandering of Julian Sowerby, the period of idleness of Roy Bassart, following his discharge from the army, his briefly held illusion of himself as an artist, or even his conceiving a child out of wedlock with Lucy Nelson – these can be ignored or tolerated by society because they reflect no serious challenge to the legitimacy of routine itself. This is the case even with Whitey Nelson, the utterly irresponsible husband and father. Whitey fails as a provider, is a drunkard and petty thief, strikes his wife Myra (Willard's daughter), yet none of these things can overcome Willard's stubborn forgiveness, which is actually the other side of his fear that to throw Whitey out of the house would be a return to the old savagery – a defence of civilisation that would only signify its collapse. Whitey is driven from the family, and Liberty Center, not by Willard but by his own daughter Lucy, whose enduring anger at her father's inadequacy is the sign of her fatal confusion as to what civilisation is, and what it requires of its members.

Julian and Roy (and Whitey in spirit) remain part of the social unit because, while they occasionally transgress the forms of social behaviour, neither they nor the citizens of Liberty Center (with the exception of Lucy) recognise in these transgressions any significant clash with the content of the forms. In fact, the content can barely be said to exist, since it is the function of civilisation, of banality, not so much to span the distance between routine and underlying value as to conceal that value, subsuming it within the routine. Only Lucy is truly aware of the values and of their possible variance from actual behaviour – an awareness which ultimately results in her isolation from the community.

The triumph of banality in *When She Was Good* is the communal creation of a language wholly opaque, indifferent to separable meaning and comfortable in the supreme clarity of its surface. Language becomes a structure of pure form, dependent for its power not on its accuracy, and certainly not on any inherent beauty, but rather on the much firmer support of social consensus. In a society more civilised this gap between form and meaning would be called decadence; in a society less civilised, hypocrisy. But the genius of Liberty Center is that it lacks the self-consciousness of the one, the sophistication of *knowing* the irrelevance of forms, and the doubleness of mind, the deviousness of maintaining contradictory claims, of the other. The citizens of Liberty Center genuinely adhere to the forms *as forms* – having passed beyond the pragmatic or moral function of routine to an unconscious belief in its ritualised, sacred power.

To raise the question of the meaning of those forms, as Lucy Nelson dares to do, is to reintroduce savagery into the world. It is to threaten form with its possible frailty, to return language to its dangerous origins: when sign was no more than a human structure poised against a dark referent not to be named or controlled. It would be a regression to Willard's childhood and the 'terrifying inkling that there were in the universe forces . . . immune to his charm . . . remote from his desires . . . estranged from his desires . . . estranged from human need and feeling' (p. 5).

The language of Roy Bassart is so pure that it exonerates itself of any meaning distinct from its words. It means precisely and only what it says: a language neither of irony nor truth but of devout repetition of what has been said before. Drawing a firm line between being an 'individualist' and a 'loner' – 'there's a big difference' (p. 55); choosing the avenue of his rebellion against his parents – 'only with a car of his own would he ever be truly independent' (p. 61); or paying his dues to the long ordeal of getting Lucy Nelson to 'go all the way': '"Just trust me," he pleaded, "trust me, trust me . . ."' (p. 110) – Roy is a (necessarily) unconscious master of civilised language. When Lucy accuses him of using the word 'love' without meaning it, he can respond without qualm or alibi: 'I get carried away, Lucy. That's not a lie. I get carried away, by the mood.

I like music, so it affects me. So that's not a "lie"' (p. 110). As for Lucy, burdened by what she alone regards as a disparity between words and meaning – she is utterly mystified: 'What had he just said? She couldn't even understand . . .' (p. 110).

Later, in the climactic scene with Roy and the Sowerbys when she informs Roy that she is pregnant again, this time with the little girl he has always 'dreamed of' – 'Boy, wouldn't it be something if someday they had a little girl of their own' (p. 230) – he responds with the dismay of trying to address someone who no longer understands the basic rules of utterance or social behaviour:

'But, Lucy; oh my God – we were just talking.'
'*Talking!*'
He sank onto a step at the top of the landing, his head cradled in his hands. 'Yes,' he moaned. (p. 282).

'Just talking'. Implicit is a theory of language – 'not a "lie"', Roy would insist – that Lucy Nelson never understands: the relation between signifier and signified has simply vanished as an issue. The 'madness' of Lucy and the metamorphic drama she enacts are rooted in her dual, ultimately contradictory commitments to the language of Liberty Center and the need to test it before a bar of value outside language. The duality is a threat to the town, which can forgive everything except Lucy's fierce belief that the conventions truly mean *only* as they are fulfilled, that they possess no ritual power in themselves. Lucy is thus the character in the novel most devoted to the speech of the community and the one who violates it most seriously, the most convention-ridden and the least banal.[4]

Like everyone else in the town, Lucy speaks and thinks out of the context of an inviolable conformity. She quits her school band, for example, despite the rare sense it provides her of belonging somewhere, when she suddenly notices that the only other girls in the group are 'freaks' – 'and she wasn't!' (p. 88). Later, she is anxious to marry Roy without his family knowing that she is pregnant. Even her statement of educational goals to Mr Bassart betrays no indication of thought: 'Develop a logical mind . . . self-discipline . . . increase her general fund of knowledge . . . learn more about the world we live in . . . learn more about herself' (p. 119). Her later acquiescence to regular Sunday visits with Roy's parents is based on her determination that her son Edward will have an absolutely standard childhood: 'Why should he be denied anything that came as a matter of course to other children in other families? Visiting grandparents was a part of childhood: and whatever was a part of childhood he was going to have' (p. 216).

What intensifies yet subverts Lucy's attachment to the conventions is her unfailing habit of brandishing against them the values she believes they are intended to uphold. As a result, she becomes in Liberty Center the figure of radical division – torn between convention and the insistence on separable values that undermines convention, between the necessity of civilisation to screen its discrepancies and the savagery that exposes all. She becomes, in other words, another of Philip Roth's monsters of division such as Eli Peck, Gabe Wallach, and David Kepesh, all of whom defy the need of the surrounding social group to heal, or conceal, its tensions. Lucy's rage for an *authentic* conformity splits into the antithetical masks of one of Roth's oddest and most moving transformations.

Lucy is the woman who desires to make the banal *real*. The inherently irresolvable conflict of that desire – comparable to the meetings in other fictions of assimilated and orthodox Jews, of commitment and escape, sensuality and ethical restraint – becomes the identity she will not give up. 'Liv[ing] too much in the here and now' (p. 289), she will not defer that meeting of language and meaning whose shocking appearance convinces the community that she is insane.

The source of Lucy's simultaneous faith in, and questioning of, convention is of course the great disparity in her life between what convention has taught her is a father's proper role and her own father's actual behaviour. *When She Was Good*, Roth has written, 'deals with Lucy's struggle to free herself from the terrible disappointment engendered in a daughter by an irresponsible father. It deals with her hatred of the father he was and her yearning for the father he couldn't be' (*Reading Myself and Others*, pp. 151–2). That disparity traumatises Lucy primarily because it is not truly acknowledged. Grandfather Will insists that Whitey cannot finally be held accountable for his actions, cannot simply be ordered from the house, even as the conventions themselves cannot be held accountable to their alleged values.

Lucy's goal, however, is just such a standard of accountability, a dream of language and convention restored to a prelapsarian fullness of expression and action. She does not want Roy to pretend

to manhood and maturity, to use words to say 'what he thought she
wanted him to say' (p. 216), but to 'express . . . a real feeling, a real
desire. . . . [to] turn . . . into a man' (p. 231).

The terrible irony is that the fullness she seeks, like her yearning
for her father, derives its power from an experience with language, a
childhood, she did not have – and whose possibility is her profound
misreading of what convention is all about. Lucy's convention is at
once impossibly literal and ideal, linked to a communal code of
behaviour but stripped of the banality through which codes free
themselves of responsibility to the real world. Lucy reimagines the
conventional into an immaculate standard of behaviour – no
forgiveness here – that validates itself by the failures it requires. The
effect of Lucy's radical innocence of language is to preserve the
father Whitey failed to be, to wield that image like a weapon against
the partial fulfilments of a community no longer even aware of its
unwillingness to encounter the world. Discovering, to her horror,
that Julian's 'whoremongering' is no secret to his family, Lucy cries
out:

> 'You know? . . . You *know* what he is – ' She was incredulous.
> 'All of you in this room *know* what he is and what he has done and
> still you were going to allow . . . I don't believe it,' she said at last.
> 'That you can be so utterly unscrupulous and deceitful, so
> thoroughly corrupt and – '
> 'Oh Roy,' said Ellie, turning to her cousin. 'She's
> crazy.' (p. 280)

Despite her determination to live according to truthful speech,
Lucy's quest is utter fantasy: to reproduce in the present the
imaginary past, correcting what actually occurred: 'her child would
never know what life was like in a fatherless house. She would not
repeat her mother's life, nor would her offspring repeat her own'
(pp. 197–8). Yet the past survives, as a darker repetition than Lucy
fears – as if the failures of convention were nothing compared to the
failures of the dream of truth. For it is not her mother's life Lucy
grimly repeats but her *father's*. Lucy is the bully of her marriage, not
her husband Roy, Lucy who finally strikes Roy as Whitey has struck
Myra. As for the child, Edward, the evidence is that he has learned
to fear and hate Lucy: 'Because of your screaming, hateful, bossy,
hateful, heartless guts! Because he never wants to see your ugly,

heartless face again, and neither do I! Never!' (pp. 265–6). For the time, at least, Edward will grow up in a *motherless* house.

In the pursuit of a miracle of language – making real the past that should have been – Lucy only repeats a more bitter version of the past that was: her rectitude is the mocking mask of her father's irresponsibility. The ironies identify her special grandeur – as well, of course, as what the world concludes is her madness.

IV

In several interviews Roth marked *When She Was Good* as a watershed in his career, following which he turned to a comic emphasis missing in the first two novels: 'I was aching to write something free-wheeling and funny. It had been a long time between laughs' (*Reading Myself and Others*, p. 22). Behind this need Roth noted a number of causes. One was his rediscovery of 'a sit-down comic named Franz Kafka and a very funny bit he does called "The Metamorphosis"' (p. 21); another was the mood of the mid-1960s – incongruous with the 'unfiery prose . . . [and] puritanical heroine' (pp. 21–2) of the novel he had just published – a mood of 'infectious volatility . . . that was inspiring feats of self-transformation and self-experimentation in virtually everyone' (p. 121). A third influence, not specifically mentioned by Roth in this context, but looming large in the fiction from *Portnoy's Complaint* on, is a lie-down comic named Sigmund Freud and a couple of funny bits called *The Ego and the Id* and 'The Most Prevalent Form of Degradation in Erotic Life'.

As I have tried to make clear in this essay, Roth needed neither Kafka nor the 1960s – nor Freud – to arrive at his metamorphic mode. Virtually all his writing, from the beginning, is of transformation, of characters whose doom and desire is to engage the 'inimical forces' of their inner selves. And yet it is clear that the confluence of Kafka, Freud, a moment of mass spontaneity in American social history, and Roth's own imaginative needs, contributed to his growing awareness of the comic dimensions of an already intact vision. The contradiction Roth felt as a child between the comfort of his Newark upbringing and stories he heard of the suffering of European Jewry is one he eventually understood as *comic*: 'Being a Jew in New Jersey was comical just because it was somehow bound up with these ghastly events' (p. 126). So too, Lou Epstein's act of adultery, resulting in bewilderment and humiliation, came to strike Roth as not only 'an unlikely solution to his problems, a pathetic, even doomed response . . . [but] a comic one too, since it does not even square with the man's own conception of himself and what he wants' (p. 209).

With *Portnoy's Complaint* Roth disclosed fully for the first time the comic possibilities of metamorphosis. The novel twists and turns in an absolutely irreconcilable tension of id and super-ego, fleshed into life as the lustful and ethical selves of Alexander Portnoy. The tension becomes comic in the extravagance of each force – unbridled desire coexisting with moral outrage; in the amazing rapidity with which one force can seize, then lose, the upper hand ('To make the kind of joke that book seems to inspire' – (*Reading Myself and Others*, p. 71); and in Portnoy's nearly complete consciousness of the psychic war taking place within him. This is a neurotic who scarcely requires an unconscious to lead him unawares to his forgotten hungers: 'Dreams? . . . I don't need dreams, Doctor . . . I have this life instead' (p. 290).

Each Portnovian urge to pleasure or guilt provokes and subverts, reflects and distorts, the other. He is the composite of two Roth conceptions, 'the "Jewboy" (with all that word signifies to Jew and Gentile alike about aggression, appetite, and marginality) and the "nice Jewish boy" (and what that epithet implies about repression, respectability, and social acceptance)' (*Reading Myself and Others*, p. 35) – brought together as a single voice that struggles in vain to silence one of its competing languages.

By the end of his novel-long, free-associating monologue to Doctor Spielvogel, Portnoy recognises, with regret, the utter transparency of his divided personality. Having confessed the story of his impotence with an Israeli woman who resembles, he realises later, his mother, Portnoy cries out in chagrin, 'This mother substitute! Look, can that be so? Oh please, it can't be as simplistic as that! Not *me*! Or with a case like mine, is it actually that you can't be simplistic *enough*! . . . This then is the culmination of the Oedipal drama, Doctor?' (pp. 300–1). What Portnoy regards as the climax of his perversion – the three-way sex with the Monkey and Lina, the Italian prostitute – has led to the climax (that is, the impotence) of his guilt, exposing him as little more than a case history out of Freud's 'The Most Prevalent Form of Degradation in Erotic Life'. Portnoy is split neatly between sensuality and affection: 'Where such men love they have no desire and where they desire they cannot love'.[5]

But Portnoy's monologue has been richer than his momentary reduction allows, having elaborated with uproarious variety the history of his indomitable doubleness. In the scene with the Monkey and Lina, for only one example:

> I can best describe that state I subsequently entered as one of unrelieved *busy-ness*. Boy, was I busy! I mean there was just so much to do. You go here and I'll go there – okay, now you go here and *I'll* go there – all right, now she goes down that way, while I head up this way, and you sort of half turn around on this . . . and so it went, Doctor, until I came my third and final time. The Monkey was by then the one with her back on the bed, and I the one with my ass to the chandelier (and the cameras, I fleetingly thought) – and in the middle, feeding her tits into my Monkey's mouth, was our whore. Into whose hole, into what *sort* of hole, I deposited my final load is entirely a matter for conjecture. It could be that in the end I wound up fucking some dank, odoriferous combination of sopping Italian pubic hair, greasy American buttock, and absolutely rank bedsheet. Then I got up, went into the bathroom, and, you'll be happy to know, regurgitated my dinner. My *kishkas*, Mother – threw them right up into the toilet bowl. Isn't that a good boy?   (pp. 154–5)

Even at a moment of the id's supremacy, the ever-alert super-ego not only films the whole from its concealed spot in the chandelier, but arouses disgust from within, appropriating that part of the body Sophie Portnoy has claimed primary jurisdiction over – the digestive tract – to punish those orifices that lead in and out of it, and which poor Alex has tried to claim as his own.[6]

Such is the war that rages perpetually within and between the body and soul of Portnoy. He can neither satiate the fires of his desire – 'time marches on and lust peters out' (p. 116) – nor placate the guilt that interprets that very condition as a crime against maturity and normality. His every utterance turns on itself, speaking its dual languages simultaneously. Elaborating on his extravagant desire – 'desire continually burning within for the new, the wild, the unthought-of and, if you can imagine such a thing, *the undreamt-of*' – Portnoy cannot help but question whether it is his shame or his glory he is defending: 'Do I exaggerate? Am I doing myself in only as a clever way of showing off? Or boasting perhaps? Do I really experience this restlessness, this horniness, as an affliction – or as an accomplishment? Both? Could be. Or is it only a means of evasion?' (pp. 113–14). And every relationship with a woman eventually condemns itself by virtue of the relationship that it is not. The Monkey, the momentary fulfilment of all Portnoy's sexual fantasies, also repels him as a 'coarse, tormented, self-loathing, bewildered, lost, identityless' creature (p. 241); while all her superior predecessors, the Pumpkin and Sarah Abbot Maulsby for instance, 'lively, intelligent, self-respecting, self-assured, and well-behaved young women' (p. 243), lack precisely the sexual freedom that Portnoy requires and cannot allow himself unreservedly to enjoy.

Portnoy is content with no one, incapable of permitting a single satisfaction to remain uncomplicated by the need that is denied by it. He is like a new, degraded and yet amazingly resourceful Faust who has succeeded in withstanding the temptation to permanence: there is no moment to which he would say 'linger a while'. And so, clinging to the dilemma of his opposed desires, Portnoy emerges as still one more version of Rothian transformation, defying to the end the authorities who will not tolerate such divisions. The police, he fantasises, are ready to come in shooting because he has removed the tag from his mattress; or because 'I dare to steal a slightly unusual kind of hump, and while away on my *vacation*' (pp. 308–9). But Portnoy, gross parody of the Eli Pecks, Gabe Wallachs, and Lucy Nelsons who have come before him, remains the neurotic hero, screaming his refusal to diminish the scope and significance of his contradictions: 'at least while I lived, *I lived big!*' (p. 309).

In the novels following *Portnoy's Complaint*, Roth has continued the metamorphic mode in a comedy at times vulgar and at times gently elegiac, contemplating almost nostalgically the moments of high tension, before and still to come. The Zuckerman trilogy, whose subject Roth has described as 'the comedy that an artistic vocation can turn out to be in the U.S.A.' (*Reading Myself and Others*, p. 162), explores the increasingly complex transformations of the writer for whom impersonation is at once a profession, the subject of fiction, and the same drama of opposed forces that it is for everyone else.

In *The Ghost Writer* the young novice Zuckerman marvels at and embellishes with his own metamorphic compulsions the life of his mentor Lonoff, with its 'noble calling' of art and the adulterous affair with Amy Bellette. In *Zuckerman Unbound* the author of *Carnovsky*, suddenly a millionaire and celebrity, is now tormented by the fact that no one realises he is at bottom, as his agent puts it, 'only a humble, self-effacing yeshiva *bucher* and not the obstreperous author of such an indecent book' (p. 156). Zuckerman is indeed outraged that no one can recognise the moral soul that abides in this most scandalous fiction. Finally, in *The Anatomy Lesson*, Zuckerman is transformed into the Man of Sorrow, enduring an unaccountable physical pain, yet seeking further impersonations: middle-aged medical student – 'No words, just stuff' (p. 103) – and Milton Appel, once a literary critic to be reckoned with, but now the editor of *Lickety-Split* – *'everything's* in it' (p. 181). En route to a life of confidence instead of doubt, plain assertion instead of contradiction, Zuckerman is still enacting the metamorphic desire that splits itself and the language of his new ambitions: 'what looked like a new obsession to exorcise the old obsessions was only the old obsessions merrily driving him as far as he could go' (p. 283).

Roth's fiction of a transformation that not only never completes itself but ultimately takes pride in its refusal to do so, may remind us in certain respects of the Derridean concept of *difference* and the deconstructive project that has followed from it. The meaning of a text, like a character who could achieve coherence without repressing conflict, becomes the dream that must always be deferred, compromised by irreconcilable possibilities into a condition of absurdity or undecidability. The alternative to deferral is either blindness or the wilful imposition of a partial interpretive order. In a similar way Roth's protagonists act out a dynamic of clashing identities that can reconcile only by concealing a part of the self – an option that they almost always reject. Behind that rejection is a resistance to all totalisation or closure, to any product that threatens to defuse the power of process.

But the similarity is limited, for Roth's fiction also moves well beyond this philosophical and critical mode, that too often has seemed little more than an exercise in play pretending to profundity – juggling words while texts in fact pursue more definitive, if still complex purposes. Behind the metamorphoses of Roth's fiction, deepening their pathos, is a clear and passionate appeal to a more traditional transformation – one that the fiction finds impossible to fulfil, yet evokes everywhere as the possibility that inspires our acts. Always there is the summons to change, to move from what one has been to what one might be, to complete the ancient commandment of repentance. This is the high calling in the context of which all of Roth's strange transformations take place, disclosing a powerful moral urgency. The great poem of Rilke, 'Archaic Torso of Apollo', with which Roth concludes *The Breast*, describes a truncated statue, shorn of head and sex, perversion of a divine wholeness we can only guess at. Like Roth's monsters, the 'maimed' statue suggests a torn self that cannot help but dream of its once perfect form. Finally it turns on *us*, viewer and reader, enjoining us to the supreme moral act: '*You must change your life.*'

NOTES

1. I have used the paperback edition of Philip Roth, *Goodbye, Columbus* (New York: Bantam, 1963) rather than the original edition published by Houghton Mifflin because of the differences in the story 'Eli, the Fanatic'. The Houghton Mifflin edition has a number of changes from the version which first appeared in *Commentary* (April 1959); the Bantam edition reprints this original version. All other references are to the original editions of the novels and *Reading Myself and Others*.
2. Philip Roth, 'Second Dialogue in Israel', quoted in John N. McDaniel, *The Fiction of Philip Roth* (Haddonfield, N.J.: Haddonfield House, 1974) p. 101.
3. Woody Allen offers new versions of the escape from a text in his story 'The Kugelmass Episode' and the film *The Purple Rose of Cairo*.
4. Jonathan Raban, in an excellent essay to which I am indebted ('The New Philip Roth', *Novel*, 2 (1969) pp. 153–63), asserts that Lucy 'accepts the language of her environment at its face value, believing that the words still mysteriously retain their lost connotations'; 'Just talking' is 'mere wordplay, dissociated from resolution or action' (p. 159). I would only add to this the notion that while the language of Liberty Center is indeed empty, it possesses a ritualistic power that allows it to deflect Lucy's devotion to meaning. Banality is permeated with an almost magic authority.
5. Sigmund Freud, *Collected Papers*, vol. IV (New York: Basic Books, 1959) p. 207.
6. See Mark Shechner, 'Philip Roth', *Partisan Review*, 41 (1974) pp. 410–27, for an interesting discussion of the whole function of eating in *Portnoy's Complaint*: 'the table is the battlefield on which Alex's bid for manhood is fought and lost' (p. 417).

8

Fiction, Show Business, and the Land of Opportunity: Roth in the Early Seventies

DONALD G. WATSON

'But what if the world is some kind of – of *show*! Don't you understand me? What *if*, is all I'm saying!'[1] This proposition, voiced – as much in hope as in fear – by the pathetic talent agent Milton Lippman in 'On the Air' (1970), concerns almost every Roth protagonist from Neil Klugman to Nathan Zuckerman: are we – to borrow the title of Neil Postman's recent study of 'Public Discourse in the Age of Show Business' – amusing ourselves to death?[2] As long ago as 'Writing American Fiction' (1960), Roth had explicitly suggested an affirmative response in lamenting the journalistic sensationalism surrounding the deaths of two teenage girls on their way home from an Elvis Presley movie.[3] How unreal this tragedy had become, even to their mother, under the pressures of the popular media's transformation of reality into show business. Roth's fictions in the early 1970s struggle with the unrealities of mass culture, its commercialisation and trivialisation of America, its distortion of and antipathy to every American tradition of serious discourse.

From the debasement of national politics in *Our Gang* (1971) to the corruption of the mythical and heroic grandeur of baseball in *The Great American Novel* (1973), Roth experiments with ways of incorporating the show business of American culture into his fiction. Even in *The Breast* (1972) the media play a large role as spectators and potential consumers of David Kepesh's transformation, and in *My Life as a Man* (1974) the combination of baseball, sex, television, and show business produces one of the funniest scenes in Peter Tarnopol's first version of Nathan Zuckerman's adolescence.

Critical assessments of Roth's career, including those in this volume, seldom spend much time with Trick E. Dixon's machinations or Word Smith's history of the Patriot League and only glance at the first incarnation of Kepesh. *Our Gang, The Breast, The Great American Novel*, and to a lesser extent *My Life as a Man* do not fit the Philip Roth who writes primarily in a tradition of literary realism about the torments and adventures of men and women anchored in definite historical time and geographic place. Their outlandish fantasies surely outdo the grotesqueries of American reality, but we cannot simply identify the first as a literary response to the second.

Our Gang and *The Great American Novel* are the most fantastic. They are neither novels nor satires nor allegories, and calling them 'experiments' will not get us far. Roth himself has said that in *Portnoy's Complaint* (and in his next few fictions) he was clowning around, that in *Portnoy* he wanted to write something 'freewheeling and funny', that in *Our Gang* he wrote as the 'fantasist and *farceur*', that in *The Great American Novel* he wrote primarily for the sheer 'comic inventiveness' and 'the fun of it'.[4] If some found pornography, vitriol, and self-indulgence in these works, others set themselves the task of assimilating Roth's comic artistry into the traditions of American humour. In many instances the pursuit of critical sophistication can seem as wacky as the foibles of his more journalistic detractors.[5] The supermarket cashier drags across the laser beam half a dozen tabloids of *The National Enquirer* variety; bleep goes the machine and the green light flickers, as the bars in the Universal Product Code deliver their messages. Is the elderly man buying Fantasy for his arthritic, suffering wife, who lives with him in the mobile park down the highway? Do they need an escape from 'all the news that's fit to print'? The media and America being what they are, can anyone tell fiction from celebrity, fantasy from prophecy, fact from marketing? Yet these tabloids contain examples of Southwestern Humour, of the American Tall Tale, of Black Comedy, of Urban Folklore. Accommodating the inventions of tabloids within these Great American Traditions is no difficult feat; enfolding Roth within similar traditions of American Comedy similarly threatens to domesticate and trivialise the radical aggressiveness of his fantasies, to cook the rawness of his farce to the doneness of pot roast. Given these traditions of American

Literatoor, you see, Roth's fictions are, after all, quite Decorous. But, as Smitty and Hem know, critics can do anything.

If we want, we can take a less formal approach and reduce the highjinks of *Our Gang* and *The Great American Novel* to 'thematics': politics as sport, sport as politics, freedom versus convention, the debasement of the English language; with a bit of formal analysis, Roth becomes our Swift and Orwell, our premier parodist. Even his most sympathetic critics do him poor service when they assimilate his craziness to literary traditions their readers can readily recognise, and even Roth himself has contributed to his own domestication: an astute student of American Literatoor, he has himself contributed to his own misreading, offering his sympathisers such handles as 'Sheer Playfulness and Deadly Seriousness' as substitutes for critical thinking about his novels.[6] He can, no doubt, offer the most helpful assistance in reading Roth, but he can also over-intellectualise his own achievements. Similarly, explaining the experimentation with the erotic and the obscene as 'undoubtedly influenced by the mood of the times' offers the kind of truthful and innocent combination of biography and history likely to escape its context and simplify *Portnoy's Complaint*'s place in the Annals of Literary History.[7] Once again, though surely the formal, biographical, and historical tell some of the truth, Roth becomes Decorous, and reading through the serious analyses of Roth's novels, one will readily see that the most often quoted critical book about Roth is *Reading Myself and Others*.

The most crucial necessity, then, in writing about Roth's works (at least those of the early 1970s) may be establishing a balance between the fictions' anarchy and literary tradition. An experienced reader of the classics of western literature, Roth can be expected to draw upon and even feel cornered by the literary masterpieces of the past. In work after work, he includes the past masters as forces to be reckoned with, but, at least from *Portnoy* on, it is not the 'anxiety of influence' that Roth – or his fictional novelists, Tarnopol and Zuckerman – feels, but the anxiety that he and we may not be taking things seriously enough, or that he and we may be taking them far too seriously. This tension between François Rabelais and Matthew Arnold produces the fireworks of Roth's fictions.

Therefore, we would be badly off-key to mistake *Our Gang* and *The Great American Novel* for satires; rather they follow the ancient non-structure of the *satura*, whose original meaning was a 'plate of mixed fruit', a smorgasbord of genres, both written and oral, an inclusive anthology of all that can be thought about a subject given the freewheeling nature of associative logic and imaginative inventiveness. *Farce* originally meant 'stuffed', full of forcemeat and herbs, and these two fictions are farced: essentially both stuff a lot of comic inventiveness into a single premise.[8] If Roth's detractors complain about one-joke books, what would they say about *Lysistrata*, *Don Quixote*, *Felix Krull*, or even *Moby Dick*? Roth himself admits that *Portnoy* is an awfully long joke with a 'punchline' on the last page. But . . . what a joke!

Of course, one can over-emphasise such matters, make Roth into a *bricoleur*, and fancify and Frenchify his 'structures', or compare him with the Barth of *Giles Goat-Boy*. What is at the heart of this 'comic inventiveness'? Perhaps it is simply the spirit of farce, the nature of the Comic. To destroy gleefully the fixed and orthodox clichés of normality, to oppose the craziness of reality with the craziness of fantasy, to attempt to renew by burying the old. Clearly, both *Our Gang* and *The Great American Novel* attempt an assessment of American institutions and values: the presidency, the military, the Boy Scouts, the media, baseball, writing history, mythology, and so on: a 'duck soup' of Americana. Yet, at some higher (or lower) level of abstraction, we can say more. Roth places himself within the traditions of carnivalesque comedy, the kind of comedy which respects no boundaries and cares only to expose the folly of business-as-usual.

In a far-ranging examination of Rabelais, Mikhail Bakhtin wrote very wisely of this comic spirit as one which opposed the classical notion of man as complete and finished. Rabelais's 'grotesque images', he says, 'are ugly, monstrous, hideous from the point of view of "classic" aesthetics, that is, the ready-made and the completed'. Instead, the carnivalesque preserves 'copulation, pregnancy, birth, growth, old age, disintegration, dis-memberment. All these in their direct material aspect are the main element in the system of grotesque images. They are contrary to the classic images of the finished, completed man, cleansed, as it were, of all the scoriae of birth and development'.[9] The Decorous imagines man from the neck up, sweeps the porch, files the dirty socks in the hampers, and gets its house ready for the rabbi's visit. All has been defined, and all that remains is obedience to the definitions: Decorum. What Bakhtin calls 'the lower bodily stratum' becomes 'grotesque', a violation of man's nobility, society's order, and nature's sublimity. The Decorous substitutes social definition for self-definition, becoming a (fill in the blank) for Becoming. 'But as of now I am nothing so sharply delineated as a character in a book. I am still amorphous Roth', says Roth in denying his 'invented selves', Portnoy, Lonoff, Zuckerman;[10] the amorphousness of the human condition denies the centrality of the completed, finished man of western civilisation and frees the writer for satire, parody, fantasy, and every grotesque invention of the comic imagination. What the Decorous leaves out returns; Milan Kundera's praise of Roth's Maureen provides one example: her vulgarity shames the human condition, and we desperately flee from the nightmare of her incorrigible tastelessness. One defence of the Grotesque well applies to her indecorous horridness: if we summon the demons into our presence, perhaps we may then begin to deal with them; if we don't they remain in our sub-consciousness where they will maintain their control over us.[11] Any number of Kafka's fictions and parables illustrate the principle, as does the tradition of Freudian psychiatry, and so do the novels of Philip Roth. The inseparable, repressed or distanced by Decorum or Fear or Wishful Thinking, still remains with us and in us.

The writer's business, then, may be to summon the demons, to include the excluded, but not necessarily to exorcise the first or to socialise the second; it simply involves not leaving out anything and reminding us that we do live with them both. This artistic intention helps reconcile Roth's fantastic fictions and his realistic novels and seems so unassailable in an age of Joyce and Kafka, yet oddly enough around this inclusiveness has revolved the bitterest attacks on Roth's fiction. Listen to Irving Howe on Roth's 'vulgarity':

By vulgarity in a work of literature I am not here talking about the presence of certain kinds of words or the rendering of certain kinds of actions. I have in mind, rather, the impulse to submit the rich substance of human experience, sentiment, value, and aspiration to a radically reductive leveling or simplification; the urge to assault the validity of sustained gradings and discriminations of value, so that in some extreme instances the concept of vulgarity is dismissed as up-tight or a mere mask for repressiveness; the wish to pull down the reader in common with the characters of the work, so that he will not be tempted to suppose that any inclinations he has towards the good, the beautiful, or the ideal merit anything more than a Bronx cheer; and finally, a refusal of that disinterestedness of spirit in the depiction and judgment of other people which seems to me the writer's ultimate resource.[12]

Howe says more in defence of good taste and 'dispassionate objectivity', but his comments clearly presuppose a fixed notion of man cleansed of the scoriae of birth and becoming, a fixed morality which knows what 'the good, the beautiful, and the ideal' are, and a fixed tradition of decorous and 'dispassionate' scrutiny of whether or not those measures of human conduct and literary discourse are being achieved: more or less, Bakhtin's definition of 'classical aesthetics'. (Bad taste belongs at Grossinger's in the midnight performance of the stand-up comedian's relentlessly vulgar ethnic jokes.) But do we read fiction for its disinterested and 'pure-spirited' descriptions of 'reality' (whatever that is in an age of show business), to see if the author 'got it right' this time? 'From whom shall we receive the Commandments?' asks Roth in *Reading Myself and Others*: 'The Patimkins? Lucy Nelson? Tricky E. Dixon?'[13]

If vulgarity is the reductive levelling of experience, then it plays a large part in Roth's fictions, attracting and repelling his characters by its alluring and shallow promises of athleticism, sexual liberation, riches, fame, glamour, comfort, and other assorted simplicities. Klugman, Portnoy, Tarnopol, Kepesh, Zuckerman, all suffer and are ironically exposed for pursuing the simple and vulgar solutions to the problems posed by their desires; each pulls back from the discomfort of identities and relationships debased by frenetic single-mindedness of a Brenda, Naomi, Maureen, Helen, Caesara, even a Claire Ovington. In the public sphere, the Media and the People contribute to the vulgarisation of American politics as much as does Tricky E. Dixon. The title *Our Gang (Starring Tricky and His Friends)* stresses the show business emphasis, and television interposes itself as a major character in the fiction. Tricky shares with Roth's more 'realistic' protagonists the comic discomfort of living in a world with no fixed values and of having to cope with the radical discontinuities produced by the fragmentation of reality into credible performances before indifferent audiences.

Our Gang begins with a quotation from Richard Nixon's 1971 anti-abortion speech, a text which expresses his 'personal belief in the sanctity of human life'. What could be more inoffensive, less open to dispute than the sanctity of human life? Or, as Tricky later laments, more 'inane'?[14] Yet it triggers a sequence of relentlessly logical interpretations and counter-interpretations, as the incongruity between the good, the beautiful, and the ideal and the grotesque realities of American vulgarity is repeatedly revealed. The 'troubled citizen' is bothered by the hypocrisy involved in defending human life and defending Lieutenant Calley's murder of twenty-two Vietnamese civilians, at least one of whom may have been pregnant; the press questions Tricky's motives, suggesting that he is creating and catering to a new and vast segment of supporters for his re-election by raising the issue of foetal rights. Finally, in an ironic and Dantesque *contrapasso*, Tricky is turned into the abortion he has been all along:

> The cause of death was drowning. He was found at seven A.M., unclothed and bent into the fetal position, inside a large transparent baggie filled with a clear liquid presumed to be water, and tied shut at the top. The baggie containing the body of the President was found on the floor of the hospital delivery room.[15]

From today's vantage point, more than a decade after Richard Nixon's total disgrace, *Our Gang* seems more playful than vitriolic, its satire more directed at the inanities of the Media and the People who must bear the responsibility for the vulgarisation of our national life, for the blinding of our powers of perception, for the blandness and indifference with which we regard politics, for the effacement of continuity in our history, for the triumph of show business. Tricky always concerns himself with his performance – his operation to remove the sweat glands from his upper lip succinctly captures the theatrical priority of the visual rhetoric of machiavellian appearances – and his advisors measure the viability of political decisions by how they will play on television and what the media will make of them. Yet ultimately the people share the culpability for our having a Tricky as our President; as the Legal Coach says: 'Luckily, Mr. President, the people of this country are still by and large passive and indifferent enough not to get all stirred up by this kind of irresponsible sensationalism on the part of the media.'[16] What the people want, Tricky and his advisors decide, is a scapegoat; what the people want, television news decides, is comfort: the bland clichés and empty rhetoric of Erect Severhead, Peter Pious, and Brad Bathos. Certainly, they do not want their rights flagrantly violated, but even their freedoms may be subtly circumvented, as Tricky suggests in rejecting the Spiritual Coach's solution to the problem of the dissenting Boy Scouts: 'This is a free country, and certainly one of your fundamental freedoms here is choosing the place where you want your child to be killed.'[17]

What *Our Gang* most effectively exposes is the complete absence of value, ideology, and history from the nation's political life. The media operate within rigidly formulaic and discontinuous segments: the clichéd press conference, the rhetorical speech, the on-the-scene report, the saccharine commentary. It believes that the people want platitudes: 'A mood of cautious optimism surged forward just at dusk,' comments Severhead in 'a cogent news analysis' from the 'stunned capital'. 'For no one dares play politics with the momentousness of a tragedy of such scope, or the scope of a tragedy of such momentousness. If tragedy it be. Yet tragedies there had been, and the nation founded upon hope and trust in man and in the deity, has continued to survive.'[18] This inanity creates the possibility of a Tricky's being elected in the first place, and, as Roth wrote soon after the 1960 presidential debates, the electronic culture's displacement of the traditional values of political discussion has been truly astonishing.[19] Though a ridiculous and by no means sympathetic figure, Tricky by his acknowledgement of and determination to conform to the unwritten supremacy of show business resembles the Land Surveyor who endeavours to observe the decrees of the Castle; unlike the world of Kafka's fiction, however, the world of the electronic media does not allow a place for the world. Typographic man has disappeared, as has the initial text of Nixon's defence of the 'sanctity of human life'.

American history has also been tidied up in *The Great American Novel*. Eighty-seven-year-old sports writer Word Smith is determined to rectify the forgetfulness of the American people and restore the glorious Patriot League to its annals:

> I am speaking of what no one in this country dares even to mention any longer. I am speaking of a chapter of our past that has been torn from the record books without so much as a peep of protest, *except by me*. I am speaking of a rewriting of history as heinous as any ordered by a tyrant dictator abroad. Not thousand-year-old history either, but something that only came to an end *twenty-odd years ago*. Yes, I am speaking of the annihilation of the Patriot League. Not merely wiped out of business, *but willfully erased from the national memory*.[20]

Again, the unnamed 'powers-that-be' are responsible for

perpetrating this heinous crime against the truth. Smitty must contend with a conspiracy of 360 sports-writers whose silent and intentional forgetfulness keeps the great Luke Gofannon out of the Baseball Hall of Fame. If the Ruppert Mundys of the Patriot League do not play through the 1942 and 1943 seasons before network cameras, they nevertheless must struggle with a staggering number of extracurricular factors which threaten the Great American Game: apart from the war effort which necessitates their giving up their home park to the Marines for a training camp, the Patriot League suffers the trivialisations of the sport by greedy entrepreneurs who turn entertainment into circus, patriotic rhetoric into economic profit. Baseball is show business writ large: myth, comedy, and commerce. Its history is American history in the sense that we have invested so much of our emotional energies and mythical imaginations in its representations of the national life.

Roth gives us plenty of potential for allegorising his fable, as the Mundys play out their season against the backdrop of the war abroad against Hitler. A ragtag collection of cripples, misfits, under-aged and over-aged players wanders through America, homeless and unloved, denied even the possibility of returning home, finally written out of the record completely, while the physically fit heroes of the nation empty the Big Leagues of all its athletic talent and fight in Europe and the South Seas. The homeless Ruppert Mundys suggest the American-Jewish population united in an attempt to maintain its integrity and to contribute to the great American institutions at the same time, but this identification works only sporadically.[21] Rather, the Patriot League is the reverse side of the heroic mythologising of the national character. Roth places this novel within the context of the 'demythologising decade' of the 1960s, within the disorienting, shocking, and alienating fiasco of Lyndon Johnson's trying to extend the mythology of the wartime America of World War II to the era of Vietnam:

> It was not a matter of demythologizing baseball – there was nothing in that to get fired up about – but of discovering in baseball a means to dramatize the *struggle* between the benign national myth of itself that a great power prefers to perpetuate, and the relentlessly insidious, very nearly demonic reality (like the kind we had known in the sixties) that will not give an inch in behalf of that idealized mythology.[22]

As in *Our Gang*, it is the American ideology and the idea of America that is at stake, and it is often the media who are responsible for fabricating the comforting images of a bland and bourgeois 'perfection' for the people who want just that. Many incidents in this sprawling chronology of the Patriot League illustrate this play of journalistic mythmaking and the demythologising tendencies of 'reality', but I will single out only one: the story of Bob Yamm and O. K. Ockatur, of midgets in baseball, one of the most effective fantasies of the novel (as well as one of the funniest) in revealing the incompleteness of the 'benign national myth'.

For one brief shining moment in our history, America truly became the Land of Opportunity: the fourteen-year-old ninety-two pound second baseman, the one-legged catcher, the fifty-two-year-old third baseman, the one-armed outfielder, and others make the Mundys a 'haven for the handicapped' but enjoy the glory of playing in the majors, an opportunity which would otherwise be denied them. And so does Bob Yamm, a genuine forty-inch-high midget signed on by the fiercely competitive and unscrupulous owner of a sixth-place club to pinch hit. When the Patriot League president objects that the 'dignity of the game and the integrity of the league' is threatened by the midget's presence, Yamm argues his constitutional 'rights as an American and as a human being'. Not only does Yamm succeed as a pinch-hitter, he also attracts an admiring public: 'All at once . . . the entire nation took not only brave Bob Yamm to its heart, but all American midgets with him, a group previously unknown to the vast majority of their countrymen.'[23] The media publish a blitz of photo stories about midgets helping in the war effort, growing corn in Victory Gardens, having fun on New Year's Eve, working in various occupations. Yamm celebrates himself with the appropriate hyperboles of American mythology, God-and-country, love-and-family, and Mrs Yamm appears on radio and in the news as the wholesome, self-reliant designer of her own marvellous sunsuits. The world just below our waists is the edenic America, paradise writ small, but still proof of the viability and glory of our traditions, of the truth that we live in a Land of Opportunity. However, for every flag-waving, true-blooded American midget, there will be a bitter, demonic counterpart. Yamm opens the door to glory for midgets everywhere, raising the consciousness and liberating the oppressed, and through it comes O. K. Ockatur, a right-handed midget pitcher, clearsighted about the reality of being a midget and angry at the twist of fate that has confined him to the body of a dwarf. Their rivalry is ideological more than sporting, and Ockatur blinds Yamm with a high inside fastball which the valiant Yamm, taking the bat from his shoulder for the first time, swings at to avoid the disgrace of looking at a called third strike. Yamm represents the benign national myth which can accommodate midgets so long as they are just the same as the rest of America, only smaller, Ockatur the reverse: the suppressed reality which will always resist idealised mythology, never giving an inch.[24]

Smitty's history of the Patriot League provides other equally suggestive parables which demythologise the benignity of a comfortable ideology and expose the impoverishment of American culture by opportunistic journalists and capitalists who care little for baseball's integrity. *The Breast* is one long parable, another experiment in fictional discourse. Kepesh's transformation into a female breast seems in one way the ultimate simplification, a return to infancy, an abandonment of masculinity and its difficulties, an absolute pursuit of the Pleasure Principle, yet Kepesh's supreme unhappiness again evidences that attraction to and repulsion from the reductive levelling of experience. Unlike Gregor Samsa, he questions the reality of his metamorphosis: he denies it, preferring to think himself a quadraplegic, or a mental patient, or dreamer who cannot awake. Unlike Gregor, he seeks an explanation for its happening: he has enjoyed his sexual pleasures too much, is too comfortable, has taught too much Gogol and Kafka, placed too much value upon the extraordinary pleasures of extraordinary sex. Unlike Gregor, he is a man alone: he lives apart from his girl friend yet sleeps with her and finds that situation ideal, and he finds himself 'convalescing' within the confines of a hospital rather than within a family, a more radical solitude than Gregor's, however unsympathetic most of the Samsas are, his sister excluded. Without sight or mobility, his communication with the world is more radically altered than Gregor's, and he recurrently wonders if he is being televised. The transformation, therefore, prompts an ambivalent but intense reconsideration of his own performance as a human being, previously and under the present circumstances:

> And why do I even care if I am not alone when I think I am? If I am under a soundproof glass dome on a platform in the middle of Madison Square Garden, if I am on display in Macy's window –

what's the difference to me? Wherever they have put me, however many may be looking in at me, I am really quite as alone as anyone could ever wish to be. Best to stop thinking about my 'dignity,' regardless of all it meant to me when I was a professor of literature, a lover, a son, a friend, a neighbor, a customer, a client, and a citizen. If ever there was a time to forget about propriety, decorum, and personal pride, this is it. But as these are matters intimately connected to my idea of sanity and to my self-esteem, I am, in fact, troubled now as I wasn't in all my former life, where the style of social constraint practiced by the educated classes came quite easily to me, and provided real satisfaction. Now the thought that my morning sessions with Miss Clark are being carried live on intra-hospital TV, that my delirious writhings are being observed by hundreds of scientists assembled in the galleries overhead . . . well, that is sometimes almost as unbearable as the rest of it. Nonetheless, when Dr. Gordon assures me that my 'privacy' is being respected, I no longer contradict him. I say instead, 'Thank you for that,' and in this way I am able at least to pretend to them that I think I am alone even if I'm not.[25]

So convinced is Kepesh of the uniqueness of his own experience and of the inability of the media to resist the sensationalism of his 'experience' that he imagines that his case will be televised on the six o'clock news, publicised on the front page of the *Times*, disseminated by 'tomorrow's tabloids', and that his impersonations of Olivier's Shakespearean performances are being taped. Finally, despairing of his 'dignity', he imagines joining the pop culture, becoming rich, and being surrounded by groupies young and old who will service his sexual demands around the clock. 'But what if the world is some kind of – of *show*?' The combination of a feeling of absolute solitude, of aloneness, with the fear that the whole world is watching is terrifying – but intriguing, beckoning him into the vulgarity of the Land of Opportunity:

And I will be deliriously happy. *And I will be deliriously happy.* Remember Gulliver among the Brobdingnags? How the maid-servants had him strolling out on their nipples for the fun of it? He didn't think it was fun, poor lost little man. But then he was a humane English physician, a child of the Age of Reason, a faithful follower of the Sense of Proportion trapped on a continent of outlandish giants; but this, my friend and accomplice, is the Land of Opportunity, this is the Age of Self-Fulfillment, and I am the Breast, and will live by my own lights![26]

The contrast between Swift's age and Kepesh's, between the Age of Reason and the Age of Show Business, is recurrently invoked in Roth's fictions.

The transformation of man into breast can never be explained satisfactorily, but the change does prompt in Kepesh an examination of conscience which forms the fundamental interest of the story. Has he 'professed' what he has taught to his students? Has he sold out to the comforts of a secure but bland existence in the variety of roles he lists and in which he finds ease and a real satisfaction among the educated classes? Has he succeeded in fashioning his own mediocrity by refusing a commitment to Claire Ovington?

> And *there*, I thought, is my trauma! Success itself! There is what I couldn't take – a happy life! 'What is that?' asks Dr. Klinger, quizzically. 'What was it you couldn't take?' 'Rewards – instead of punishment! Wholeness! Comfort! Pleasure! A gratifying way of life, a life *without* – . . . I'm saying that my happy new life was too much for me! It's why I lost my desire for Claire – it was all too good to last! So much satisfaction seemed – seemed unjust!'[27]

Even Arthur Schonbrunn, parody of the successful, desiccated academic humanist, is committed to something, even if it is only an aesthetic of elegance, sartorial, literary, and cultural. Kepesh, the 'passionately well-meaning literature teacher', does not believe in his own profession: why should not he perform before crowds at Shea Stadium and make 'a pot of money'?

> To read more books? To write more critical essays? Further contemplation of the higher things? How about contemplation of the lower? I will have hundreds of thousands of dollars – and then I will have girls, twelve- and thirteen-year-old girls, three, four, and five at a time, naked and giggling, and all on my nipple at once.[28]

Reduced to the vulgar simplifications of sexual stimulation and intellectual contemplation – listening to Olivier perform *Othello* –

Kepesh cannot accept either. Pitied by the woman he loves, humoured by his father, humiliated by the laughter of his mentor, chairman, and friend, further discomforted by the platitudes of his psychoanalyst, separated even from the college edition of Shakespeare's works which lies so near at hand, severed from his biological masculinity, Kepesh is as alone as any character in Roth's or anyone else's Land of Opportunity.

Kepesh's psychiatrist, Dr Klinger, counsels him that he cannot escape the gaze of Mr Reality; Kepesh leaves us, quoting Rilke's certainty that we cannot escape the 'gaze' of Apollo. Someone is always looking. Nathan Zuckerman, adolescent hero of Peter Tarnopol's two 'Useful Fictions' in *My Life as a Man*, knows this well enough but decides to work within its framework, especially in the first story, 'Salad Days'. Young Zuckerman has found a willing sexual partner in Sharon Shatzky, ravishing, rebellious, but 'pampered middleclass daughter of Al "the Zipper King" Shatzky', wealthy and suburban manufacturer. Their adventurous sex is heightened by the presence of the four parents, and Sharon, uninhibited and 'anxious to please', takes the starring role:

> Best of all were 'the shows.' For Zuckerman's pleasure and at his instigation, Sharon would stand in the bathroom with the door open and the overhead light on, performing for him as though she were on a stage, while he would be seated in the dark living room at the other end of the corridor, seemingly looking in the direction of the television set. A 'show' consisted of Sharon unfastening her clothes (very slowly, deftly, very much the teasing pro) and then, with the little underthings at her feet, introducing various objects into herself. Transfixed (by the Phillies game, it would appear), Zuckerman would stare down the hallway at the nude girl writhing, just as he had directed her to, upon the plastic handle of her hairbrush, or her vaginal jelly applicator, or once, upon a zucchini purchased for that purpose earlier in the day. The sight of that long green gourd (uncooked, of course) entering into and emerging from her body, the sight of the Zipper King's daughter sitting on the edge of the bathtub with her legs flung apart, wantonly surrendering all five feet nine inches of herself to a vegetable, was as mysterious and compelling a vision as any Zuckerman had ever seen in his (admittedly) secular life.[29]

This scene surely would offend those readers sensitive to the violations of literary decorum, to the pornographic, obscene, and vulgar; for truly it is all of those. But the scene is framed in so many ways that it becomes rich with meaning and humour. In the narrative itself, the four parents – Zuckermans and Shatzkys – sit complacently on the Shatzky's terrace, thinking of how nice Sharon looks in her new winter coat, occasionally glancing through the door (a frame) to the reception room at Nathan who appears to be engrossed in the Phillies game on TV (another frame) but who is really looking at Sharon through the frame of the open bathroom door, as she performs with the zucchini as on a stage, with the overhead light on, 'writhing' according to his directions. Nathan has set up this scene, framed it the way an artist frames 'reality', albeit art fashioned by a rebellious adolescent. Nevertheless, his 'shows' are ways of ordering the chaos or of creating an alternate reality to that of the suburban disorder of values; the cleverness of remaining within their frame, of not disturbing the security of their complacency, of creating a frame-within-a-frame, is a comic triumph of fantasy. Nathan's ironic superiority, however, is further compounded and turned against him by other ironies. He finds he cannot enjoy such sexual freedom as totally and as singlemindedly as Sharon does; she is too 'coarse, childish, ignorant', too vulgar. The scene itself suggests as much in the way in which Nathan enjoys the voyeur's detachment in the surrogate vegetable which distinguishes phallus from penis and gives the starring role to the substitute part. Oh, what fun the Freudians and Lacanians would have with this displacement! Clearly, Nathan has sublimated his erotic fantasies somewhere into a sequence that includes parental solicitude and complacency, baseball and its attendant male heroics in Roth's mythos, and 'shows' on a stage, framed by the bathroom door. In this L-shaped dog-leg of a triangle, parents, Nathan, and Sharon form the points which can never connect in any normal way. If it all seems rather innocent enough (and surely it is), it nevertheless reveals the radical separation of sexual desire and compulsive need, body and mind, and the retrospective guilt which afflict every Roth lover.

Further, the ironies are compounded by the Chinese-box narrative structure of *My Life as a Man*. Peter Tarnopol has created the whole incident as part of a story which will assist him in exorcising the demons of his own adolescence, and the Tarnopol is in turn Roth's creation, a character who very much resembles his creator. More frames! Tarnopol himself admits at the end of this 'useful fiction' that he can go no further and must give over his invention of Nathan to some more *serious* author:

> To narrate with fidelity the misfortunes of Zuckerman's twenties would require deeper dredging, a darker sense of irony, a grave and pensive voice to replace the amused, Olympian point of view . . . or maybe what that story requires is neither gravity nor complexity, but just another author, someone who would see it too for the simple five-thousand-word comedy that it very well may have been. Unfortunately, the author of this story, having himself experienced a similar misfortune at about the same age, does not have it in him, even yet, midway through his thirties, to tell it briefly or to find it funny. 'Unfortunate' because he wonders if that isn't more the measure of the man than of the misfortune.[30]

Tarnopol has not really been exorcising his demons but displacing his aggressions and denying his committedness to the moral seriousness of fiction and life, castrating himself by producing a puerile fiction in which his passive and symbolically dismembered surrogate inflicts an outrageous but a private revenge against the uptight and materialistic middle-class older generation.

Young Zuckerman dramatises his own alienation from the object of his desire through the 'natural' medium of our age: the histrionics of televised 'shows'. Tarnopol, who aspires to continue his career as a novelist, once wanted to live somewhere in the literary stratosphere between *The Wings of a Dove* and *The Brothers Karamasov*, but instead finds himself a performer in a soap opera.[31] Partly the electronic culture has mastered our imaginations, and partly 'shows', television, and film serve as images for the super-egos which watch ourselves performing our own lives. Portnoy pauses long enough in acting out his fantasies with the Monkey and Lina in a hotel room in Rome to wonder how this orgy looks: 'I the one with my ass to the chandelier (and the cameras, I fleetingly thought) – .'[32] The Age of Show Business intensifies our self-conscious befuddlements; our super-egos feed our need for self-dramatisation. If this America is truly the Land of Opportunity, all these needs can be easily accommodated.

As Roth's interview in this volume asserts, we are indeed amusing ourselves to death. It takes a very, very radical crisis of identity to make us stop and ask ourselves questions about our self-entertainments. The intense glow of reason still gazes from the maimed torso of Apollo: 'Du musst dein Leben andern' – it sounds more dramatic in the original – 'You must change your life.'[33] Orwell was wrong about the inevitable ascendancy of Big Brother totalitarianism in the West, and Huxley was right about the inexorable process of self-destruction through which post-typographic man would turn himself into a passive recipient of pleasurable fulfilments of his wants.[34] The threats to our wholeness come from within not from without.

Since Blake, many have believed that the Road of Excess leads to the Palace of Wisdom. If it does, Roth's characters find it poorly signposted but nevertheless the only highway worthy of our journey, surely more interesting than the boring, mundane repetitiveness of the scenery along the Interstate. Even in the Age of Show Business, presided over by the Great Trivialiser, it remains their destiny to provide us with travellers' reports.

The heaviest baggage in their creator's and sometimes their own odyssey through this Land of Opportunity is the literary tradition, the past masters of the language; it slows down the thinking, the ethical, and the serious, but it also provides the surest security and stability on a journey with few reliable landmarks and signposts. *Our Gang* is fraught with the political morality of the English tradition, beginning with the epigraphs from Swift and Orwell and ending with the quotation from *The Book of Revelation* in a slightly revised version of the King James translation. In the first, Gulliver reports his Houyhnhnm master's difficulty in comprehending 'that Faculty of Lying, so perfectly well understood, and so universally practised among human Creatures'; the second captures the essence of Orwell's laments about the 'decay of language' in his great essay, 'Politics and the English Language'. The concluding passage, which receives its own page after Tricky's long 'come-back' speech and which strikes one as an odd addition, seals the apocalyptic urgency of the strain of 'tragic satire' appropriated from the tradition of Gulliver's Fourth Voyage and 'The Modest Proposal' and suggests that the redemption of the political world is not to be expected this side of The Last Days. In the acceptance of massacres as everyday occurrences, the formulaic character of the press conference, the self-serving logic of the presidential advisors, the demonising rhetoric of Tricky's machinations, the empty platitudes of the network reporters and commentators, the Faculty of Lying and False Representation gets a strenuous work-out. What keeps the forces of linguistic decay at bay is the authorial voice behind the parody. Dante's ordered world is evoked by the full circle of the ironic *contrapasso*, Tricky in the baggie, and the grandeur of Milton's heroic style can be heard through its distortions in Tricky's campaigning against Satan in the book's final section. *Our Gang* is too overwrought to be simply a vicious, vitriolic attack upon Richard Nixon; the literary past supports its relentless logic and strengthens its apparently flimsy narrative architecture. More than that, it provides a sense of continuity in a political world fragmented into discontinuous, forgettable segments and opposes the typographical culture of the written word to the easily manipulable and ever changing visual rhetoric of the electronic media.

Although Smitty and Hem agree that the Great American Novels of Hawthorne, Melville, and Twain have been overrated, and although their only defender is a superficial Vassar girl full of handbook generalisations from the College Outline Series, the literary past makes its presence felt in *The Great American Novel* as a stabilising element in the world of benign but bland ideology and rampant commercialisation and trivialisation of American mythology. Roth's attitude, essentially one of reverence despite the acuteness of the parody, places the destruction of the Mundys against the greater glory of American nineteenth-century mythopoetics: 'Smitty is to my mind correct in aligning himself with Melville and Hawthorne, whom he calls "my precursors, my kinsmen." They too were in search of some encapsulating fiction, or legend, that would, in its own oblique, charged, and cryptic way, constitute the "truth" about the national disease.'[35] The difference between Moses and General Oakhart, the distance between Mister Kurtz and Mister Fairsmith, and a huge collection of large and small discrepancies throughout the fiction generate a perspective which transcends the jokes, anecdotes, and bizarre fantasies which make up the fiction and which gives coherence to Roth's 'attempt to imagine a book about imagining that American myth'.[36]

The Breast, unthinkable without Gogol and Kafka, uses Shakespeare and Rilke as well to suggest an order beyond the surprises of Mr Reality and the irrational impulses of sexual desire. And through literature's imaginings, Kepesh with a burst of insight tells Klinger, we imagine ourselves:

'I loved the extreme in literature, idolized those who wrote it, was virtually hypnotized by the imagery and the power – . . . So I took the leap. Made the word flesh. Don't you see I have out-Kafkaed Kafka.' Klinger laughed, as though I meant to be only amusing. 'After all,' I said, 'who is the greater artist, he who imagines the marvelous transformation, or he who marvelously transforms himself? Why David Kepesh? Why me, of all people, endowed with such powers? Simple. Why Kafka? Why Gogol? Why Swift? Why anyone? Great art happens to people like anything else. And this is my great work of art!'[37]

Of course, it isn't Kepesh's doing exactly, as he tells us in the closing pages by quoting Rilke's sonnet, but the passage above – in this most fantastic of fantasies – succinctly paraphrases the Great Tradition's idea of the novel's provision of equipment for living the moral life, for fashioning the self, for transforming the word into the flesh-and-blood actuality that is greater than the artistic product. Self-transformation – 'You must change your life' – is the end, and literature is the means. This assertion, however wryly coloured by the incongruity of its being spoken by a six-foot, 155-pound mammary gland, more than technique or allusiveness or parody, ties Philip Roth's fictions to the order and continuity of our literary past.

Kepesh and Tarnopol present studies of abuses of the power of literature to transform the self. Tarnopol's fictions are 'useful' in their holding out the promise (false, as it turns out) that he can resolve his personal problems; instead, they help him sidestep them. As we learn more of David Alan Kepesh in *The Professor of Desire*, we see how thoroughly he – like Tarnopol – believes in literature's assistance in promoting life from the neck up. As Kepesh sits at an outdoor café in Prague, he drafts a first-day lecture for his next semester's university class on Novels of Passion; Desire 341 will give these students the lessons they need for dealing with the erotic life of late adolescence. Oblivious to the irony of writing down a heartfelt and spontaneous confession, Kepesh writes away, while a Prague prostitute plays nearby with her lapdog.[38] He, too, has mistaken control for order, teaching for show business; what he says becomes problematic in the process of writing it down: he is preparing a script for a performance. Yet the content of his remarks is the same as that of the Breast's boasting (or of Roth's interview in this volume): literature as a means of understanding the world and the self. As an alternative to the Official Version, as a carnivalesque inversion of business-as-usual, as a full length portrait of the whole man rather than a snapshot of man from the neck up, as the Excess that includes, rather than the Decorum that limits, Roth's fictions renew and regenerate, bury and revive.[39]

However encircled in irony, the novelist's language and his fictions may be the best means of finding our way in this Age of Show Business through this Land of Opportunity.

NOTES

1. Philip Roth, 'On the Air', *New American Review*, 10 (1970) p. 20. This piece has never been reprinted.
2. Neil Postman, *Amusing Ourselves to Death: Public Discourse in an Age of Show Business* (New York: Viking, 1985). The debate about the effects of television is now decades old, but Postman's contribution is an exceptionally clear examination of some of the broad cultural issues.
3. Philip Roth, *Reading Myself and Others*, expanded edn (New York: Penguin, 1985) pp. 173ff.
4. Ibid., pp. 22, 24, 76.
5. See the helpful and partly convincing but, I believe, overdone analyses of Walter Blair and Hamlin Hill's *American Humor* (New York: Oxford University Press, 1978) pp. 472–87, and Bernard F. Rogers, Jr, *Philip Roth* (New York: Twayne, 1978) pp. 75–9, 115–19. Rogers points out that Roth studied with Blair and with Napier Wilt at the University of Chicago.
6. Roth, *Reading Myself*, p. 111.
7. Ibid., p. 121.
8. On these points see Barbara Babcock-Abrahams, 'The Novel and the Carnival World', *Modern Language Notes*, 89 (1974) pp. 911–37, especially pp. 918–19. Her work is based upon Mikhail Bakhtin's *Rabelais and His World*, trs. Helene Iswolsky (Cambridge, Mass.: M. I. T. Press, 1968); and Julia Kristeva, 'Bakhtine, le mot, le dialogue et le roman', in her *Semiotike* (Paris: Editions du Seuil, 1969).
9. Bakhtin, *Rabelais and His World*, p. 25.
10. Roth, *Reading Myself*, p. 128.
11. This approach to the grotesque has been explored in Wolfgang Kayser, *The Grotesque in Art and Literature*, trs. Ulrich Weisstein (New York: McGraw-Hill, 1966 [1957]), especially pp. 179–89.
12. Irving Howe, 'Philip Roth Reconsidered', *Commentary*, 54 (December 1972) pp. 75–6. I had at first thought that silence was the better response to Howe's attack, but his remarks clearly delineate some of Roth's central interests.
13. Roth, *Reading Myself*, p. 84.
14. Philip Roth, *Our Gang* (New York: Random House, 1971) p. 32.
15. Ibid., p. 152.
16. Ibid., p. 51.

17. Ibid., p. 49.
18. Ibid., p. 150.
19. See 'Writing American Fiction' (1960), in Roth *Reading Myself*, pp. 173–91.
20. Philip Roth, *The Great American Novel* (New York: Bantam, 1974 [1973]) p. 18.
21. Roth circumvents our taking this allegory too seriously by ironising it; see ibid., pp. 95–102.
22. Roth, *Reading Myself*, pp. 89–90.
23. Roth, *The Great American Novel*, pp. 209, 210, 211.
24. An alternative response is to see Roth's fable of the midgets as a comment upon the admission of black athletes in the major leagues. I do think my suggestions are incompatible with such an interpretation; the fiction is rich in suggestiveness. Moreover, Roth's midgets have their basis in the real life shenanigans of Bill Veeck, as many other apparently crazy incidents in the novel also have a kernel of 'fact' in the annals of the Great Game.
25. Philip Roth, *The Breast*, revised ed. (New York: Penguin Books, 1985) pp. 22–3. Roth revised *The Breast* (1972) for *A Philip Roth Reader* (New York: Farrar, Straus & Giroux, 1980). Most of the revisions are stylistic rather than substantial.
26. Roth, *The Breast*, pp. 85–6.
27. Ibid., pp. 72–3.
28. Ibid., p. 84.
29. Philip Roth, *My Life as a Man* (New York: Penguin Books, 1985 [1974]) pp. 25–6.
30. Ibid., p. 31.
31. Ibid., p. 195.
32. Philip Roth, *Portnoy's Complaint* (New York: Bantam, 1970 [1969]) p. 154.
33. Roth, *The Breast*, p. 89.
34. See Postman, *Amusing Ourselves to Death*, pp. vii–viii, 155–6.
35. Roth, *Reading Myself*, p. 92.
36. Ibid.
37. Roth, *The Breast*, p. 82.
38. Philip Roth, *The Professor of Desire* (New York: Farrar, Straus & Giroux, 1977) pp. 124–7.
39. Again, see Bakhtin, *Rabelais and His World*, especially chs 1 and 3.

9

Portnoy's Prayer: Philip Roth and the American Unconscious

SAM B. GIRGUS

In his extraordinary essay on 'The Unconscious' (1915), Freud writes:

> An instinct can never become an object of consciousness – only the idea that represents the instinct can. Even in the unconscious, moreover, an instinct cannot be represented otherwise than by an idea. If the instinct did not attach itself to an idea or manifest itself as an effective state, we could know nothing about it. When we nevertheless speak of an unconscious instinctual impulse or of a repressed instinctual impulse, the looseness of phraseology is a harmless one. We can only mean an instinctual impulse the ideational representative of which is unconscious, for nothing else comes into consideration.[1]

Freud's simple description of the difference between the conscious and the unconscious in terms of the distinction between ideas, which relate to consciousness, and instincts, which are outside of this psychic realm, represents Freud's genius for theoretical construction. His concept of an 'ideational representative' of instinctual impulses constitutes the key, as Paul Ricoeur indicates, to understanding 'how the unconscious can be reintegrated into the realm of meaning by a new interrelation – "within" the unconscious itself – between instinct (*Trieb*) and idea (*Vorstellung*): an instinct can be represented (repräsentiert) in the unconscious only by an idea (*Vorstellung*).'[2]

In addition, this association of ideas and the unconscious also helps to explain how the unconscious partakes in the transmission of cultural ideas and values. Accordingly, for Juliet Mitchell, the unconscious comprises the centre of the process of the individual's integration into and adaptation to culture. For Mitchell one of the great contributions of Freudian psychoanalysis concerns its elucidation of the involvement of the unconscious in the interaction between the individual and culture. She writes, 'In each man's unconscious lies all mankind's "ideas" of his history; a history that cannot start afresh with each individual but must be acquired and contributed to over time. Understanding the laws of the unconscious thus amounts to a start in understanding how ideology functions, how we acquire and live the ideas and laws within which we must exist.'[3] The concept of 'ideational representatives' that enlightens the darkness of the unconscious also provides a format for incorporating and relating to the ideas that form culture. The unconscious relates to ideology and the ideas of culture in part because it knows itself through ideas. This drama of the unconscious in culture that Freud scripted and Mitchell discusses constitutes a crucial aspect of the significance of Philip Roth's *Portnoy's Complaint*. When poor Alexander Portnoy sent forth his extended whine in 1969 from the couch of his silent psychoanalyst, Dr Spielvogel, most readers and critics heard it as a grumbling and *kvetching* from the interior of the Jewish-American soul, a psychic ghetto of unconscious fears and insecurities. In retrospect, however, it can be argued that in writing *Portnoy*, Roth was mining more than a seemingly bottomless pit of Jewish *angst*. He was, in fact, dealing in a new way with questions of sexuality and the unconscious that have been central to American literature and culture. While his work maintains a long tradition of seeing love and ideology in the context of the making of American culture, Roth also adds a new chapter to the history of the American unconscious. He seeks to counter the forces of repression and guilt and to answer fears of dependence and weakness with an alternative ideology of understanding and enlightenment. Never proffering psychological placebos that dissimulate the guilt, fear, and anxiety of the human psyche, refusing to sentimentalise or minimise the inherent difficulty of achieving love and happiness, Roth, nevertheless, advances the contemporary battle for liberation by dramatising the conflict of hidden and manifest psychological forces.

Portnoy's Complaint constituted a breakthrough on many different levels and directions. Roth was propelled by *Portnoy* to a new plateau of international recognition and fame. Whether you liked the novel or not, its instant popularity established Roth as a literary celebrity. It gave him the success of a John Updike or William Styron. In addition, the novel also seemed to break new ground for the genre of the Jewish-American novel. Already under attack for his critical perspective of Jewish subjects and characters, Roth's treatment in *Portnoy* of the domineering mother and the self-effacing father and the galaxy of Jewish fears, prejudices, and insecurities pushes his penchant for social parody and black humour to a new extreme. What to Roth was the exposure of self-assimilation, appeared to others to be the blatant distortion and exaggeration of self-hating anti-Semitism and the vulgarisation of a deep tradition of authentic liberalism and social commitment. Also, the novel's uninhibited burlesque of such sexual subjects as masturbation and oral sex and its explicit descriptions of bathroom scenes and bodily functions certainly entailed a dramatic extension of the boundaries of acceptable taste.

At the same time, Roth's body of work, including *Portnoy's Complaint*, occupies an important place in a vital tradition of Jewish-American writers and thinkers who are deeply intrigued and concerned about the meaning of the American idea and experience. Ranging from Abraham Cahan and Louis Brandeis through Anzia Yezierska and Henry Roth to Saul Bellow, Johanna Kaplan, E. L. Doctorow, and Norman Mailer, this group of writers and intellectuals revivifies the rhetorical and narrative structures of the myth and ideology of America. Often considering the symbol and ideal of America in terms of redemption, renewal, and revolution, they write as New Jeremiahs to awaken individual and national conscience and to modernise the symbols and metaphors of the American idea. As writers of fiction and literature, they transformed the modern novel. *Portnoy's Complaint* exemplifies this new novelistic form. At its core in the figure of Portnoy is the new 'hero of thought' who embodies the consciousness of his times. Other aspects of the novel include the setting of the urban wilderness, the quest for upward mobility and success as well as moral affirmation, the psychological theme of anxiety, and the sociological motif of alienation.[4]

However, one other major element or theme in his new narrative structure is especially important in demonstrating how *Portnoy's Complaint* relates to the development of the American unconscious. This is the theme of the *shikse*, or Gentile love-goddess. In *Portnoy* the psychological and social role of the *shikse* establishes a vital thread from the unconscious desires of the hero to a crucial aspect of

American culture as perceiving America in sexual and feminine terms. From its beginnings America was seen, as Annette Kolodny says, as a feminine pastoral image. While the land was female, men were hunters or yeoman farmers. For Kolodny these universal symbols achieve a special significance in America because here such symbols actually entered history and personal experience. In *The Lay of the Land* she writes,

> If the initial impulse to experience the New World landscape, not merely as an object of domination and exploitation, but as a maternal 'garden' receiving and nurturing human children, was a reactivation of what we now recognize as universal mythic wishes, it had one radically different facet: *this* paradise really existed. . . . Only in America has the entire process remained within historical memory, giving Americans the unique ability to see themselves as the willful exploiters of the very land that had once promised an escape from necessities.

Following Henry Nash Smith's *The Virgin Land*, Kolodny argues that from our earliest history such figures as William Byrd of Virginia and Robert Beverley of North Carolina devised 'a uniquely American pastoral vocabulary' the heart of which dramatised 'a yearning to know and to respond to the landscape as feminine'.[5]

Kolodny provides many examples of early thinking of the New World, and of America in particular, as a woman to be possessed. William Byrd saw in the landscape 'a Single Mountain [in the Blue Ridge range], very much resembling a Woman's breast' and a 'Ledge that stretch't away to the N. E. . . . rising in the Shape of a Maiden's Breast'; Walter Raleigh portrayed Guiana as 'a country that hath yet her maydenhead, never sackt, burned, nor wrought'; for John Smith the New England coast aroused intimations of a New Eden because of 'her treasures having neuer beene opened, nor her originalls wasted, consumed, nor abused'; the rebellious and profligate Thomas Morton believed America to be a '*Paradise* with all her Virgin Beauties', while John Hammond expressed a more chivalrous attitude in his desire to protect the innocence of 'The Two Fruitful Sisters Virginia and Maryland'. Since one may consider these statements as sixteenth- and seventeenth-century rhetorical exaggerations that do not represent modern attitudes, it should be noted that expansion into the West was explained throughout our history in similar metaphors. Thus, those who went to the unsettled territory of Wisconsin were promised to see that 'the land foams with creamy milk, and the hollow trees trickle with wild honey'.[6]

Portnoy's treatment of the *shikses* in his life develops this motif in American literature and culture. The Gentile women in the novel are not merely Americans; they embody America. As such they become vessels for the expression of Portnoy's deepest desires and insecurities. He recalls that his first encounter with such girls occurs during the winter ice-skating on the lake in Irvington Park, a town that neighbours Portnoy's 'safe and friendly Jewish quarter'.[7] He writes,

> But *shikses*, ah, the *shikses* are something else again. Between the smell of damp sawdust and wet wool in the overheated boathouse, and the sight of their fresh cold blond hair spilling out of their kerchiefs and caps, I am ecstatic. . . . How do they get so gorgeous, so healthy, so *blond*? My contempt for what they believe in is more than neutralized by my adoration of the way they look, the way they move and laugh and speak – the lives they must lead behind those *goyische* curtains.   (pp. 144–5).

For Portnoy the beauty of these wonderful creatures is enhanced by their surface representation of a whole culture. He says,

> These people are the *Americans*, Doctor. . . . O America! America! It may have been gold in the streets to my grandparents, it may have been a chicken in every pot to my father and mother, but to me, a child whose earliest movie memories are of Ann Rutherford and Alice Faye, America is a *shikse* nestling under your arms whispering love love love love!   (pp. 145–6)

Portnoy's prayer for love from an American *shikse* is not so far removed from the mixture of love and belief that mystified the vision of earlier admirers and explorers of the wonder of America. Roth's blend of humour, exaggeration, parody, and pathos renders a Jewish version of this American phenomenon. Through the *shikse* motif, Roth relates sexuality to culture. He particularises the process of how the unconscious works in placing the individual within culture. The sexual basis of Portnoy's fascination for America demonstrates how the unconscious factors of guilt, ambivalence, and fear that are usually associated with sexuality also play an important part in the acquisition of culture itself. Thus, Portnoy combines his most extreme sexual fantasy with his desire to be a real

American by conjuring up the name of 'the real McCoy' (p. 127) for any imaginary *shikse* who unites pure lust with pure American features. She is the real thing in terms of both her sexual abandonment and her cultural identity. As he schemes to pick up *shikse* skaters, he also contrives new names for himself, thus seeking an identity that will reciprocate hers. He thinks to himself, '"Portnoy, yes, it's an old French name, a corruption of *porte noir*, meaning black door or gate. Apparently in the Middle Ages in France the door to our family manor house was painted . . ." et cetera and so forth. No, no, they will hear the *oy* at the end, and the jig will be up' (p. 149). When he finally manages the pick-up he thinks he will need 'to speak absolutely perfect English. Not a word of Jew in it' (p. 164). He introduces himself to the girl as Alton C. Peterson but is so obsessed with 'what I'll say when she asks about the middle of my face and what happened to it (old hockey injury? Fell off my horse while playing polo after church one Sunday morning – too many sausages for breakfast, ha ha ha!)' that he loses his footing and goes 'hurtling forward onto the frost bitten ground, chipping one front tooth and smashing the bony protrusion at the top of my tibia' (p. 164). The wounds, clearly, are psychic, guilt over the denial of his father, a form of death wish. Also his Gatsby-like fantasy indicates a fear that his love will not be strong enough to allow for his transformation by 'this perfect, perfect-stranger, who is as smooth and shiny and cool as custard, will kiss me – raising up one shapely calf behind her – and my nose and my name will have become as nothing' (p. 151).

Portnoy's pattern of relating sexuality, the unconscious, and America persists in his subsequent relationships with women. There is Kay Campbell, the All-American 'Pumpkin' – so named because of 'her pigmentation and the size of her can' (p. 216) – who brings Portnoy home from Antioch for a Thanksgiving dinner that anticipates the wonderful 'Grammy Hall' scene in Woody Allen's *Annie Hall*. Later, there is Sarah Abbot Maulsby, labelled 'The Pilgrim' because of her Yankee appearance, prestigious pedigree and élite social background. The inherent connection between the forces of the unconscious and sexuality and the incorporation of the ideas and forms of culture is especially clear in Portnoy's attitude toward Maulsby. Moreover, Portnoy's personality provides further demonstration of a Jewish version of the historic connection between sexuality and the making of American culture. Thus, for Portnoy sex with *shikses* constitutes a rediscovery of America. Through sex the metaphor of the penetration of the virgin land and the symbolism of the cultivation of the land become Portnoy's personal reality. Such penetration equates psychologically to possession and domination. 'What I'm saying, Doctor, is that I don't seem to stick my dick up these girls, as much as I stick it up their background – as though through fucking I will discover America. *Conquer* America – maybe that's more like it. Columbus, Captain Smith, Governor Winthrop, General Washington – now Portnoy. As though my manifest destiny is to seduce a girl from each of the forty-eight states' (p. 235). Ultimately, Portnoy's most important and emotionally significant relationship with a Gentile goddess involves Mary Jane Reed or 'The Monkey'.

The intensity of the sexuality between Mary Jane Reed and Portnoy compels him to confront the quagmire of unconscious forces that help make him so miserable. The relationship with Mary Jane suggests a crisis of love itself. Driven by inner doubts and fears into humiliating and abandoning her in Rome and into subsequent impotence with an Israeli woman, Portnoy must examine the psychic pain beneath his living joke about *shikses*. He realises that the desire for assimilation through sex indicates a deep association of sexuality, the unconscious, and cultural adaption. However, at the core of this psychosocial phenomenon are questions about the nature of love and growth that Portnoy obstinately avoids until crippling guilt demands confrontation. Roth's use of Freudian analysis to explain this psychological situation is not terribly subtle. As Steven David Lavine says, 'Roth's first step is to offer a psychological reading of Portnoy's behavior even more complete than Portnoy's self-analysis. . . . The application of Freud's ideas to *Portnoy's Complaint* is straightforward.'[8] In his excellent essay, Lavine expands upon Roth's own discussion of Freud to describe the sources for Portnoy's illness. The key to this discussion comes from Freud's 1912 essay on 'The Most Prevalent Form of Degradation in Erotic Life' which is part of his 'Contributions to the Psychology of Love'. Roth even titles one of the chapters in *Portnoy* after this essay. However, the brilliant insights of this essay actually originate in Freud's masterpiece of 1905: *Three Essays on the Theory of Sexuality*. In the latter, Freud structures human sexuality in terms of sexual impulse or aim and the love object of that aim. He argues that the connection between object and aim are far more tenuous than most people assume. In fact, the instability of the bridge between object and aim accounts for the pervasiveness of deviations in the form of perversions and homosexuality. Furthermore, the tendency in western culture to idealise or overvalue the sexual object greatly complicates the object-aim relationship. In a footnote added in 1910 Freud indicates the implications of such overvaluation.

> The most striking distinction between the erotic life of antiquity and our own no doubt lies in the fact that the ancients laid the stress upon the instinct itself, whereas we emphasize its object. The ancients glorified the instinct and were prepared on its account to honour even an inferior object; while we despise the instinctual activity in itself, and find excuses for it only in the merits of the object.[9]

This tendency to idealise the object at the expense of the power of the sexual impulse encourages, according to Freud, a separation of sexuality from love. Accordingly, in the 1912 essay that occupies so much of Portnoy's attention, we learn that this separation of love and sexuality results in such forms of degradation as impotence and frigidity. Of course, Portnoy's fixation with his knife-wielding mother, who still thinks of him as lover, demonstrates Freud's theory that in neurosis unresolved Oedipal drives provide the edifice for the idealised sexual object. The resounding silence of Dr Spielvogel, the object of Portnoy's monologue, indicates that this patient repeats Freud's own experience of self-analysis. However, such self-awareness and insight do not serve to mitigate the pain involved in his dilemma.

Mary Jane Reed, or 'The Monkey', creates the crisis that forces Portnoy to engage the ghosts of lust and guilt that haunt him. Epitomising Portnoy's penchant for degrading women by renaming them, Mary Jane's pleasure in sexuality satisfies his greatest fantasies and finally elicits a degree of feeling and affection that astounds him. 'What a night! I don't mean there was more than the usual body-thrashing and hair-tossing and empassioned vocalizing from The Monkey – no, the drama was at the same Wagnerian pitch I was beginning to become accustomed to: it was the flow of feeling that was new and terrific' (p. 190). The moment of love and excitement occurs during a car trip to New England and several factors help make it happen. Out of discretion for his position as Assistant Commissioner for the New York City Commission on Human Opportunity, he signs them into cosy inns and hotels as a married couple by using the name of an old friend from Newark, a delinquent of sorts who never faced the prohibitions of Portnoy's parents. Mary Jane enjoys the pretence of being a newlywed on the trip and calls him by his alias, Arnie. The new name encourages the illusion of a reckless identity. Also, the beauty of the New England scenery nourishes their mood.

> Saturday we drove up to Lake Champlain, stopping along the way for The Monkey to take pictures with her Minex; late in the day we cut across and down to Woodstock, gaping, exclaiming, sighing, The Monkey snuggling. Once in the morning (in an overgrown field near the lake shore) we had sexual congress, and then that afternoon, on a dirt road, somewhere in the mountains of central Vermont, she said, 'Oh, Alex, pull over, now – I want you to come in my mouth,' and so she blew me, and with the top down!' (p. 191)

Probably given public acceptance of previously taboo sexual practices, Roth today would be hard pressed to invent a sexual act or situation shocking enough to current audiences to dramatise Portnoy's conversion to a new way of thinking – perhaps celibacy or chastity would work. Nevertheless, to his amazement Portnoy finds himself undergoing a temporary metamorphosis into a man who both loves and feels. 'What am I trying to communicate? Just that we began to feel something. Feel *feeling*! And without any diminishing of sexual appetite!' (p. 191). The new harmony of sex and love, body and mind achieves a special degree of intimacy when Portnoy gambles on both her character and intelligence and teaches her about William Butler Yeats's 'Leda and the Swan'. She justifies his faith in her by having an orgasm. He touches her and says, 'Sweetheart! You understood the poem!' (p. 194). They celebrate with 'idyllic' love making 'under the red and yellow leaves' of New England and with 'glorious acrobatics' in their Woodstock room, all of which leads to a crucial discovery: 'What a deal! And yet it turns out that she is also a human being – yes, she gives every indication that this may be so! *A human being! Who can be loved!*' (p. 194).

Unfortunately, Portnoy's revelation of her humanity leads him to the horrible question of his own feelings and values. Yes, he realises, she can be loved, 'But by *me*?' (p. 194). Of course, through Portnoy's pornographic imagination and consciousness, Mary Jane Reed remains a joke. However, as usual, the joke is on Portnoy because she also is presented with enough credibility as to dramatise Portnoy's own sickness. Ironically, it turns out to be she who wishes to grow and change, while Portnoy seems incapable of escaping the confinement of his own ego and guilty conscience. Thus, she does not provide Portnoy with an answer to his sexuality and life but only a question about his ability to learn to love, while Naomi, the Jewish Pumpkin from Israel, punishes him by engendering impotence.

In the way he confronts the question of love, Portnoy, it is important to remember, is not alone as a character in either Jewish novels or in American literature. The themes of the overvaluation of the sex object, the transference of this form of idealisation on to the image and symbol of America and the related problems of love, sexuality, and moral development are all intrinsic to American literature and culture. In our century both Fitzgerald and Hemingway established basic patterns for discussing these themes that reflect the modern environment. It can be argued, therefore, that Roth's work actually maintains and modernises this tradition. What more compatible company could Portnoy request than Jay Gatsby who worships Daisy Buchanan by confusing her with the green light of American success and renewal. Both Gatsby and Tom Buchanan are archetypal American males who idealise their women as mother figures while also holding them in contempt for their carnality, thereby placing all women in the impossible position of being responsible for men's illusions and disappointments. For Gatsby the real woman is of no consequence in comparison with the dream and mission she represents for him. To survive in this situation the American woman must become a Jordan Baker of sexual ambiguity and hardness. Of course, Gatsby pays for his illusions with his life. Because of their mutual idealisation of the American woman, it is not too hard to imagine Gatsby and Portnoy engaged in conversation about The Real McCoy during a luncheon with their friend Meyer Wolfsheim. In the same vein, Portnoy certainly would understand the devastation desire demands in the world of Jake Barnes and Brett Ashley. Although he would be leery of the way she and her friends regard Jews, Portnoy would see Brett as the flip side to Daisy, a competing pagan goddess of insatiable sensuality who ultimately leaves men as lifeless and dead as Gatsby. The classic Hemingway response to this situation of lovelessness and death involves the creation of the famous Hemingway hero who adopts a style of indifference and toughness that Humphrey Bogart popularised into a new manner of speaking and acting. Thus Jake Barnes in *The Sun Also Rises* says, 'Then I thought of her walking up the street and stepping into the car, as I had last seen her, and of course in a little while I felt like hell again. It is awfully easy to be hard-boiled about everything in the daytime, but at night it is another thing.'[10] Supposedly Frederick Henry in *A Farewell to Arms* also will adopt a hard-boiled posture of existential detachment after his beloved Catherine Barkley dies. Catherine, we recall, also was an English goddess who devoted herself to creating a world safe from death and loneliness for the boyish Frederick. This results, of course, in his utter dependence upon her. Thus, from the perspective of the Hemingway hero, the failure of Frederick's and Catherine's 'separate peace' and of the wall they build around themselves suggests the need for an even greater constriction and withdrawal of self. The vulnerability love induces in these Hemingway novels teaches the need to protect the self against dependence on anyone or anything. The psychology of these heroes dramatises Freud's statement in 'Analysis Terminable and Interminable' (1937) about attitudes toward dependence:

> At no other point in analytic work does one suffer more from an oppressive feeling that all one's repeated efforts have been in vain, and from a suspicion that one has been 'preaching to the winds', than when one is trying to persuade a woman to abandon her wish for a penis on the ground of its being unrealizable or when one is seeking to convince a man that a passive attitude to men does not always signify castration and that it is indispensable in many relationships in life. The rebellious overcompensation of the male produces one of the strongest transferences-resistances.[11]

Of course, to simply state that Portnoy radically differs from the Hemingway hero constitutes a serious venture in understatement. Although facing similar sexual forces of overvaluation, dependence and impotence, Portnoy in contrast to the Hemingway hero comes from a culture where 'they wear the old unconscious on their *sleeves!*' (p. 97). While Hemingway assiduously strives to merely suggest the life of the unconscious, Roth obviously trumpets it forth. Moreover, Hemingway's famous style of omission, his dedication to writing so as to give greater potency to what remains hidden also relates to his treatment of the unconscious. For example, at the end of chapter 12 of *The Sun Also Rises*, Jake describes fishing and life at Burguete with a friend. Not until the very last line of the paragraph do we realise that the fine details actually dissemble Jake's inner thoughts of love and jealousy concerning Brett.

> We stayed five days at Burguete and had good fishing. The nights were cold and the days were hot, and there was always a breeze even in the heat of the day. It was not enough so that it felt good to wade in a cold stream, and the sun dried you when you came out and sat on the bank. We found a stream with a pool deep enough to swim in. In the evenings we played three-handed bridge with an Englishman named Harris, who had walked over from Saint Jean Pied de Port and was stopping at the inn for the fishing. He was very pleasant and went with us twice to the Irati River. There was no word from Robert Cohn nor from Brett and Mike.[12]

This is a style that seems to replicate the very processes of repression that it dramatises. It suggests an ideology of hardfaced aversion to emotional expression. It challenges the hint of dependence with detachment and counters feelings and emotions by concentrating on surface detail. As Saul Bellow so pointedly wrote years ago:

> For this is an era of hardboiled-dom. Today, the code of the athlete, of the tough boy – an American inheritance, I believe, from the English gentleman – that curious mixture of striving, asceticism, and rigor, the origins of which some trace back to Alexander the Great – is stronger than ever. Do you have feelings? There are correct and incorrect ways of indicating them. Do you have an inner life? It is nobody's business but your own. Do you have emotions? Strangle them. To a degree, everyone obeys this code.[13]

Roth, of course, proffers a serious alternative to this code that represents more than a mere difference of style between a Jewish voice and All-American stoicism. In spite of his neurosis and weakness, Portnoy works toward an ideology of love and growth as opposed to mere resistance and distance. That ideology could be described primarily in Freud's phrase from 'The Most Prevalent Form of Degradation in Erotic Life' that serves as something of a centerpiece for Roth's novel: 'To ensure a fully normal attitude in love, two currents of feeling have to unite – we may describe them as the tender, affectionate feelings and the sensual feelings.'[14]

Accordingly, Portnoy discovers that the source of his greatest weakness also constitutes his greatest strength. He realises that these beautiful *shikse* love objects are yearning for someone like him who can deal with emotion and think of love with something more than resigned independence.

> Only what I don't know yet in these feverish years is that for every Eddie yearning for a Debbie, there is a Debbie yearning for an Eddie – a Marilyn Monroe yearning for her Arthur Miller – even an Alice Faye yearning for her Phil Harris. Even Jayne Mansfield was about to marry one, remember, when she was suddenly killed in a car crash. Who knew, you see, who knew back when we were watching *National Velvet*, that this stupendous purple-eyed girl who had the supreme *goyische* gift of all, the courage and knowhow to get up and ride around on a horse (as opposed to having one pull your wagon, like the rag-seller for whom I am named) – who would have believed that this girl on the horse with the riding breeches and the perfect enunciation was lusting for our kind no less than we for hers?   (p. 152)

It occurs to Portnoy that the inner confluence of sensuality and tenderness that proves necessary for love and happiness applies to both men and women. Portnoy learns that because women also need to associate feelings with sexuality, they will be attracted to individuals who are not afraid of emotions and the so-called inner life. Thus, Portnoy's inner turmoil, which he perceives as signs of embarrassing weakness and immaturity, can appear to others as visible evidence of a vital emotional life.

> Who knew that the secret to a *shikse*'s heart (and box) was not to pretend to be some hook-nosed variety of *goy*, as boring and vacuous as her own brother, but to be what one's uncle was, to be what one's father was, to be whatever one was oneself, instead of doing some pathetic little Jewish imitation of one of those half-dead, ice-cold *shaygets* pricks, Jimmy or Johnny or Tod, who look, who think, who feel, to talk like fighter-bomber pilots!   (p. 152)

Ironically, Portnoy's new insight into the importance of being oneself and loving oneself is difficult to put into action. For Portnoy the most obvious objective of growth and maturity becomes the most elusive. Roth summarises this aspect of the book in the theme of becoming a man, of achieving a mature selfhood and identity. In effect the book opens and closes with Portnoy's pleas to become a man. Early in the novel he says, 'Bless me with manhood! Make me brave! Make me strong! Make me whole!' (p. 37). Similarly, the book closes with Portnoy flying into Israel but weeping over the memory of the men he used to watch play ball when he was a kid. 'And that's the phrase that does me in as we touch down upon *Eretz Yisroel*: to watch the men. Because I love these men! I want to grow up to *be* one of these men!' (p. 245). This hope of growing into manhood and the difficulties attendant upon that task persist in Roth's fiction. David Kepesh in *The Professor of Desire* confronts the same challenge and realises in Prague, Czechoslovakia, that Kafka suffered the same experience of fighting for his manhood. 'Of all things, marking Kafka's remains – and unlike anything else in sight – a stout, elongated, whitish rock, tapering upward to its painted glans, a tombstone phallus.' Upon further examination of the grave, Kepesh realises the Oedipal overtones of the fact that 'the family-haunted son is buried forever – still! – between the mother and the father who outlived him'.[15] Similarly, Peter Tarnopol in *My Life as a Man* is reduced to putting on his wife's clothes during a fight and proclaiming that he wears the 'panties in this family'. He later asks, 'How do I ever get to be what is described in the literature as *a man*? I had so wanted to be one, too – why then is it always beyond me?'[16]

In *Portnoy's Complaint* Roth places the subject of being a man in the context of what many consider to be Freud's most profound study, *Civilization and Its Discontents*. As Portnoy says, '*Oy*, civilization and its discontents!' (p. 183). Obviously, neither Freud in this masterpiece of psychoanalysis nor Roth in his dramatisation of some of its major ideas believes they have devised a final answer to mankind's unhappiness in society and culture. In fact, Freud's disavowal of an ultimate cure for unhappiness has inspired generations of psychologists into espousing programmes and practices that promise easier resolution of pervasive problems. Relatively early in his career, Freud countered such hopes for absolute answers with the statement that in the battle against mental sickness 'we succeed in transforming your hysterical misery into common unhappiness'.[17] Accordingly, in *Civilization and Its Discontents* Freud does not render a final solution but an analysis of man's continuing unhappiness and self-inflicted misery even in the face of enormous technological progress. He argues the immutability of primitivism in human nature. Unsatisfied love, desire, and violence are ineradicable, and the attempt to cleanse these forces from the human psyche only causes them to grow stronger under the repression of the unconscious. Freud maintains, therefore, that we need to accept this aspect of human character and psychology. We need to leave room for this inherent primitivism. As Portnoy says, 'Because to be *bad*, Mother, that is the real struggle: to be bad – and to enjoy it! That is what makes men of us boys, Mother' (p. 124). Out of appreciation for the power of instinctual energy, Portnoy cherishes Mary Jane's ability to put 'the id back in Yid' while he only puts the '*oy* back in *goy*' (p. 209). Portnoy accepts Freud's argument that the failure to account for this libidinal aspect of human nature not only results in inevitable depression and disillusionment over man's moral imperfection, as occurred during the First World War, but also can produce neurosis. Fuelled by instinctual energy that turns upon the self, the super-ego or moral conscience becomes another form of sickness. As Freud says, 'Since civilization obeys an internal erotic impulse which causes human beings to unite in a closely-knit group, it can only achieve this aim through an ever-increasing reinforcement of the sense of guilt.' He goes on to declare that 'the price we pay for our advance in civilization is a loss of happiness through the heightening of the sense of guilt'.[18] Portnoy, of course, demonstrates Freud's claim that such frustration results in individual and cultural neurosis. Thus, Portnoy complains about 'That tyrant, my super-ego, he should be strung up, that son of a bitch, hung by his fucking storm-trooper's boots till he's dead!' (pp. 160–1).

All of Roth's work, but especially *Portnoy's Complaint*, argues Freud's life long principle that the first step toward moral responsibility, freedom, and maturity demands an honest confrontation with the brutal and searing conflict between love and guilt. Driven on one side by boundless desire and haunted on the other by crippling guilt, existence still thrusts upon man the needs to love and to be moral. Portnoy cries,

> The things that other men do – and get away with! And with never a second thought! To inflict a wound upon a defenseless person makes them *smile*, for Christ's sake, gives a little *lift* to their day! The lying, the scheming, the bribing, the thieving – the larceny, Doctor, conducted without batting an eye. The indifference! The total moral indifference! They don't come down from the crimes

they commit with so much as a case of indigestion! But me, I dare to steal a slightly unusual kind of a hump, and while away on my *vacation* – and now I can't get it up!   (p. 273)

For Freud the proclivity to invent illusions of false freedom and happiness compounds the difficulty of this human condition. For Portnoy, however, the luxury and indulgence of such illusions seem long past. There is instead the idea of a new beginning, of a new life with the moral, emotional, and intellectual obligation to seek the dim light of analysis. Moreover, this vision of enlightenment through the painful process of analysis carries with it certain political and cultural assumptions about the psychological and philosophical basis of individual freedom. In Freud the potential for human freedom exists but only within the context of the individual and cultural structures to sustain it. As Lavine says,

> All the turning and twisting in search of an escape from the past, all the desperate energy of Portnoy's monologue, all the desire to leave nothing unsaid, indeed, even all the hate directed at his family, grew from Portnoy's desire for the dignity that comes with independent moral choice. For Roth, this very energy and persistence of the desire for freedom and dignity are the evidence – or, better, the sign – that man may indeed have some freedom and dignity.[19]

Regardless of what some critics feel about Roth's work, he certainly sees himself as a leader in the effort to gain both freedom and dignity. He imagines freeing those who imprison themselves in their own illusions, beliefs, and fears. Thinking of Kafka and *The Trial* he asks: 'If only one *could* quit one's pulpit, one might well obtain decisive and acceptable counsel. How to devise a mode of living completely outside the jurisdiction of the Court when the Court is of one's own devising?' He seriously considers *Portnoy's Complaint* to be an important weapon in the battle for such freedom.

> I sometimes think of my generation of men as the first wave of determined D-Day invaders, over whose bloody, wounded carcasses the flower children subsequently stepped ashore to advance triumphantly toward that libidinous Paris we had dreamed of liberating as we inched inland on our bellies, firing into the dark. 'Daddy,' the youngsters ask, 'what did you do in

the war?' I humbly submit they could do worse than read *Portnoy's Complaint* to find out.[20]

No doubt others, including Hemingway and Fitzgerald, preceded Roth on that beachhead of liberation that leads to Paris. However, he can claim leadership of a Special Forces brigade. In the extended war for liberation and freedom, Roth devised brilliant strategies in some significant battles. These battles are now part of a long war that has been fought in the American unconscious since our founding. He helped to sabotage and demolish for at least a while the foundation and edifice for the American goddess. He saw the dangers of dependence and admitted he was a victim. He looked into the hard-boiled American face of detached indifference. Instead of blinking, he complained. He served in the underground as a double agent working on behalf of both sexual instinct and the force of conscience to help unify them in the greater cause of bridging sexuality and feeling. Equally important, he saw that any gains in the battle could be lost in a peace based upon the illusions of the permanent pacification of the intractable forces of hatred and guilt. Thus, in spite of the controversy surrounding his career and work, Roth stands as a leader in the modern movement to make life more loving, more meaningful, more peaceful.

NOTES

1. Sigmund Freud, 'The Unconscious', in *The Standard Edition of the Complete Psychological Works* (London: Hogarth Press, 1957) vol. 14, p. 177.
2. Paul Ricoeur, *Freud and Philosophy: An Essay on Interpretation*, trs. Denis Savage (New York: Yale University Press, 1970) pp. 115–16.
3. Juliet Mitchell, *Psychoanalysis and Feminism* (New York: Vintage, 1975) p. 403.
4. For a more extensive study of this tradition as well as Philip Roth's place within it see Sam B. Girgus, *The New Covenant: Jewish Writers and the American Idea* (Chapel Hill, N. Carolina: University of North Carolina Press, 1984).
5. Annette Kolodny, *The Lay of the Land: Metaphor as Experience and History in American Life and Letters* (Chapel Hill, N. Carolina: University of North Carolina Press, 1975) pp. 5, 8.
6. Ibid., pp. 9, 11–12, 67.
7. Philip Roth, *Portnoy's Complaint* (New York: Random House, 1969)

p. 143. All subsequent references to this book will be to this edition and will be included parenthetically in the text.

8. Steven David Lavine, 'The Degradation of Erotic Life: *Portnoy's Complaint* Reconsidered', *Michigan Academician*, 11 (1979) pp. 358, 359. See also Judith Paterson Jones and Guinevera A. Nance, *Philip Roth* (New York: Frederick Ungar, 1981), and Maurice Charney, *Sexual Fiction* (London and New York: Methuen, 1981) pp. 113–31.

9. Sigmund Freud, *Three Essays on the Theory of Sexuality*, trs. James Strachey, introd. Steven Marcus (1905; rpt. New York: Harper Colophon Basic Books, 1975) p. 15, n. 1.

10. Ernest Hemingway, *The Sun Also Rises* (1926; rpt. New York: Scribner, 1954) p. 34.

11. Sigmund Freud, 'Analysis Terminable and Interminable', in *The Standard Edition of the Complete Psychological Works* (London: Hogarth Press, 1964) vol. 23, p. 252.

12. Hemingway, *The Sun Also Rises*, p. 125.

13. Saul Bellow, *Dangling Man* (1944; rpt. New York: Bard, 1975) p. 7.

14. Sigmund Freud, 'The Most Prevalent Form of Degradation in Erotic Life', in 'Contributions to the Psychology of Love', in *Freud: Sexuality and the Psychology of Love*, ed. Philip Rieff (New York: Collier, 1963) p. 59.

15. Philip Roth, *The Professor of Desire* (New York: Farrar, Straus & Giroux, 1977) p. 175.

16. Philip Roth, *My Life as a Man* (New York: Holt, Rinehart and Winston, 1974) pp. 246, 299.

17. Josef Breuer and Sigmund Freud, *Studies on Hysteria*, in *The Standard Edition of the Complete Psychological Works* (London: Hogarth Press, 1955) vol. 2, p. 305.

18. Sigmund Freud, *Civilization and Its Discontents*, trs. James Strachey (1930; rpt. New York: Norton, 1962) pp. 80, 81.

19. Lavine, 'The Degradation of Erotic Life', p. 363.

20. Philip Roth, *Reading Myself and Others* (New York: Farrar, Straus & Giroux, 1975) pp. 8, 108.

10

'None Other': The Subject of Roth's *My Life as a Man*

PATRICK O'DONNELL

Imagine a reader reading, for the first time, Philip Roth's *My Life as a Man*. She, let us say, dimly remembers reading the infamous and shocking *Portnoy's Complaint* as an undergraduate, but now recalls little of the novel with the exception of the hero's repulsive sexuality and a bizarre female character bearing the nickname of 'The Monkey'. More recently, she has read *The Ghost Writer* and, enjoying the seeming lightness and brevity of that novel, has started *Zuckerman Unbound*. But she soon tires of Zuckerman and his exploits, so she stops reading the second instalment of the 'Zuckerman Trilogy' somewhere in the novel's first third, and gives up reading Philip Roth for the moment. Then, in a bookstore, she sees that several of Roth's novels have been reissued in attractive paperbacks by Penguin Books; she sees one entitled *My Life as a Man* bearing on the cover the interesting illustration of a hand holding a knife. Ignoring the usual and (to her mind) meaningless panegyrics on the back cover, she makes the assumption, given the name and title on the front cover, that this is Roth's autobiography, a confession from (now she remembers *Portnoy* more fully) a parodist of confessions. She buys; she reads.

What this fictional reader first encounters upon opening the cover of *My Life as a Man* is a blurb about the author. 'Philip Roth,' she reads, 'was born in Newark, New Jersey, in 1933. He is the author of twelve books of fiction.'[1] Here follows a list of the author's works with dates of publication in parenthesis – this helps her 'place' the book she is presently reading and those she has read in a chronological order; now, whether she consciously knows it or not, she has in mind a history of her reading of Philip Roth. Turning the page she sees a title page which repeats information she already knows, the name of the book she is reading and the name of the author. Seeking further knowledge, she turns again, quickly skips

144

past the uninteresting small print of the publication data, then sees the dedication page: 'To Aaron Asher and Jason Epstein'. She does not know who these people are, though she notes by their names that they appear to be, like Roth himself, Jewish. Perhaps, she thinks, they are friends of Roth – teachers, mentors, editors – those to whom he would like to make reference as influences in his life.

Turning again, she finally comes to something meant for her: 'A Note to the Reader'. The note says that 'The two stories in Part I, "Useful Fictions", and Part II, the autobiographical narrative "My True Story", are drawn from the writings of Peter Tarnopol.' Immediately, confusion sets in. What she thought to be Roth's autobiography is now, she finds, a novel containing two short stories and an 'autobiographical narrative' by someone else of whom she has never heard. But recalling *The Ghost Writer*, she sees that Roth is up to his old tricks in, seemingly, writing a novel about an author who will probably have a haunting resemblance to the author described in the blurb she has just read. She leafs to the next page, and discovers an epigraph by one Maureen Johnson Tarnopol, a diary entry which reads 'I could be his Muse, if only he'd let me be.' She must infer that the diarist is Tarnopol's wife, and that what she is about to read will have something to do with husbands and wives, artists and muses. Again, *The Ghost Writer* enters her mind as she remembers the strange triangular relationship Nathan Zuckerman imagines between himself, the author he visits in the Maine woods, and the puzzling student who Zuckerman thinks might be his 'muse', Anne Frank. Turning the page, she sees repeated again the title of the book she is reading in 30-point type. On the next page, she sees the title 'Useful Fictions' designating the two short stories by Peter Tarnopol. She turns the page once more to see the title of the first useful fiction, 'Salad Days', and, at last, the beginning of the novel. She reads in disbelief what appears to be a biographical sketch describing the childhood of Nathan Zuckerman. Zuckerman again! What could Philip Roth be up to? A novel by Roth about a writer, Tarnopol, who is writing stories about himself and another writer, Zuckerman, Roth's *alter ego*? Confused, somewhat disgusted, and mildly insulted she closes the book before it has properly begun, vowing to save Philip Roth and authorial labyrinths for another day.

My depiction of this curious, moderately well-informed, but naïve (that is, 'first-time') reader is, to be sure, a caricature, but I think it renders a fairly accurate description of what one must go

through in 'beginning' *My Life as a Man*. In order to discover Nathan
Zuckerman, the subject of 'Salad Days' (who is in my reader's 'past'
what he will be in Philip Roth's 'future', or that of any present-day
reader who reads Roth's novels chronologically), the reader must
pierce through several textual veils: the cover, the autobiographical
sketch of Roth, three title-pages, a dedication page, a note to the
reader, and an epigraph from the diary of a character who will not
appear until Part II of *My Life as a Man*. This, as I have elsewhere
argued in a discussion of *The Ghost Writer*, overdetermines the
concepts of 'author', 'reader', and 'beginning' as questionable at the
outset of a fiction – they are what one must 'get through' before the
story can even begin.[2] A dedicated reader of Roth's fiction must get
through even more: one can not help but be disturbed in knowing
that, like Maureen Tarnopol, Roth's wife died in an automobile
accident after a six-year separation from the author. Even the
'chronological' reader I mentioned earlier – the reader of 'the
complete Roth' – may experience confusion and literary vertigo in
re-reading *My Life as a Man*, where a protagonist of Roth's uncreated
canonical future 'reappears' as the uncanny double of an earlier
protagonist, Tarnopol, himself uncannily close to 'Roth' in matters
of biographical detail.[3] An unsympathetic reader might claim that
the only responses to such textual inversions is to note that Roth
(not 'Roth'), like Tarnopol, is a narcissist. A reader who thinks like
Spielvogel might diagnose the problem as a case of simple,
obsessive self-interest on Roth's part: everything he writes (this
reader would say) must refer in some way to himself – his life as
an artist, his Jewish-Americanness, his childhood, his difficult
marriage and its tragic end, his battle with fame.[4] To this reader, all
of the textual veils which so frustrated my 'naïve' reader are
pasteboard masks thinly disguising the real subject of Roth's novel –
Roth himself, wrapped up in his marriage, his affairs, his
psychoanalysis, begging the reader's indulgence for this three-
hundred-page-plus display of self-indulgence.[5]

   I have created here several heuristic readers of *My Life as a Man*
because I think these constructed responses expose the central issue
of the novel, which is not a matter of simple self-love (either Roth's
for himself as autobiographical entity, or 'Roth's' for himself as
self-conscious author, or Tarnopol's for himself as authorial *alter ego*)
but of the subject and reference of fiction. Responding to
Spielvogel's charges of narcissism in what he perceives to be a
cosmetically altered version of his own case history, scandalously

reproduced in Spielvogel's article 'Creativity: The Narcissism of the Artist', Tarnopol defends himself in this way:

> And if I may, sir – his *self* is to many a novelist what his own physiognomy is to a painter of portraits: the closest subject at hand demanding scrutiny, a problem for his art to solve – given the enormous obstacles of truthfulness, *the* artistic problem. He is not simply looking into the mirror because he is transfixed by what he sees. Rather, the artist's success depends as much as anything else on his powers of detachment, on *de*-narcissizing himself. That's where the excitement comes in. That hard *conscious* work that makes it *art*! Freud, Dr. Spielvogel, studied his own dreams not because he was a 'narcissist', but because he was a student of dreams. And whose were at once the least and the most accessible of dreams if not his own.   (p. 240)

Ironically enough, this polemic on the aesthetics of the self arises out of Tarnopol's rage at Spielvogel's fictionalised version of his self-image. Here, it is as if the writer had forgotten the lesson of detachment propounded by his own art, though he might argue that, since the subject of Spielvogel's 'fiction' is not Spielvogel himself ('the closest subject at hand') it is based in ignorance. Nevertheless, what Tarnopol articulates as the 'problem' of art in this passage is, precisely, the problem of the 'subject' scrutinising himself in the hand-held mirror of (in Tarnopol's case) writing – holding the mirror, he would argue, at a distance, thus guaranteeing the detachment and authenticity of self-scrutiny. But how does 'the closest subject at hand' refer to itself? How, in the world of John Ashbery's magnificent meditation on Parmigianino's 'Self-Portrait in a Convex Mirror', is the self as subject anything but a prisoner of its own reflection (thus narcissistic), an 'inside' barred from what is without?

> The soul has to stay where it is,
> Even though restless, hearing raindrops at the pane,
> The sighing of autumn leaves thrashed by the wind,
> Longing to be free, outside, but it must stay
> Posing in this place. It must move
> As little as possible. That is what the portrait says.[6]

It would seem that Tarnopol's self-portrait in 'My True Story' also says that he must move as little as possible. In the end, he is isolated at a fictionalised Yaddo, where he reflects extensively on those obverse images of self-hatred and self-love embodied, respectively, in his dead wife, Maureen, and his abandoned mistress, Susan. It is here that Tarnopol writes, in some near and implicit future, his 'life as a man'. It is here that he faces up to himself as the 'subject' which, like all subjects, must escape the confines of book or mirror to a larger world of fact, reference, and others by which it might know itself, though only as a series of fictions rendered in a language of referrals to and deferrals from its questionable 'essence'.

Dr Spielvogel would agree that Tarnopol's 'self' is trapped, but he would reject the poignancy of Ashbery's lines in favour of his own diagnosis, which privileges the actuality and dynamism of the past over the static present of self-reflection's prison. Spielvogel locates the source of Tarnopol's problems not in the sole self, but in the other, or mother. According to Tarnopol's version of Spielvogel's analysis:

> It was hardly unusual . . . to have felt loved by the 'threatening mother'; what was distressing was that at this late date I should continue to depict her in this 'idealized' manner. That to him was a sign that I was still very much 'under her spell,' unwilling so much as to utter a peep of protest for fear *yet* of reprisal. As he saw it, it was my vulnerability as a sensitive little child to the pain such a mother might so easily inflict that account for 'the dominance of narcissism' as my 'primary defense.' To protect myself against the 'profound anxiety' engendered by my mother – by the possibilities of rejection and separation, as well as the helplessness that I experienced in her presence – I had cultivated a strong sense of superiority, with all the implications of 'guilt' and 'ambivalence' over being 'special'. (p. 217)

An old-fashioned Freudian, Spielvogel inflicts on Tarnopol a steady stream of psychoanalytical jargon which the patient, under the spell of the analyst's authority, grudgingly accepts as one explanation for his problems with women. Tarnopol argues at first that he has never thought of his mother as threatening in any sense, that she *'adored* me, worshipped me across the board', that 'it was her enormous belief in my perfection that had very likely helped to spawn and nourish whatever gifts I had' (p. 213). But Spielvogel's diagnosis partially convinces Tarnopol that it was this very role his mother played as nourisher/muse to his 'perfections', along with his censoring of her more threatening aspects, that has resulted in the complex labelled 'narcissism'.

Evidence that Tarnopol gives credence to the implicit tautology of the diagnosis can be noted in his frequent citation, whenever he talks about his 'case history', of Spielvogel's terminology: for Tarnopol, quotation is always a reference to some predecessor or figure of authority, be it Tolstoy, Flaubert, or Freud via Spielvogel. The obsessive quoting one finds in certain passages of the novel reflects Tarnopol's fear that his attempts to inscribe his 'original' in 'My True Story' may merely be a form of repetition: as Edward Said has noted, 'the more writing appears to be quotation, the more writing thinks of itself as, in some cases even proclaims itself, rewriting'.[7] Doubtless, Spielvogel derives his 'language' from Freud's comments on 'the ideal ego':

> To this ideal ego is now directed the self-love which the real ego enjoyed in childhood. The narcissism seems to be now displaced onto this new ideal ego which, like the infantile ego, deems itself the possessor of all perfections . . . here again man has shown himself incapable of giving up a gratification he has once enjoyed. He is not willing to forgo his narcissistic perfection in his childhood: and if, as he develops, he is disturbed by the admonitions of others and his own critical judgements . . . he seeks to recover the early perfection, thus wrested from him, in the new form of an ego-ideal.[8]

Both Freud's definition of narcissism and Spielvogel's depiction of its manifestations in Tarnopol are curiously circular in that they attempt to explain a present 'state' through a projection backwards to a fictional origin which the patient may have misread. Both implicitly or explicitly locate the source of 'the problem' in the mother, who over-gratifies the (male) child. The adult then seeks a return to this state of 'perfection' by projecting it on to a fictionalised 'ego-ideal', another who should be a (nurturing) mother. When reality intrudes – in Tarnopol's case, when women refuse to conform to this fictional model – then the narcissistic defence redoubles its efforts. Thus Tarnopol chooses women like Maureen and Susan who, different as they are, share the quality of demonstrating 'that sense of defenselessness and vulnerability that has come to be a mark of their sex and is often at the core of their relations with men' (p. 172). Such women/victims, when they are abject, fulfil a primary narcissistic need (so in love are they with Tarnopol that they will eventually try to kill themselves rather than live without him) while embodying an ambivalent counter-desire for punishment and the return of the threatening mother, particularly in the case of Maureen.

Whatever questions might be raised about the validity of narcissism and its dynamics to explain 'Tarnopol', it is a 'useful fiction' whose authority he accepts, whose explanatory power is great enough to allow for the formation of a certain version of the self-as-narcissist. For Spielvogel, Tarnopol is a literary text to be read, and this diagnosis a form of literary criticism. The 'truth' of this critique applied to the recollection of the self lies, for Tarnopol, in its manipulation of 'evidence'. When he complains to Susan about Spielvogel's article, he responds most vociferously to what he views as its flaws in composition:

> Just read on. Read the whole hollow pretentious meaningless thing, right on down to the footnotes from Goethe and Baudelaire to prove a connection between 'narcissism' and 'art'! So what else is new? Oh, Jesus, what this man thinks of as *evidence*! "As Sophocles has written," – and that constitutes *evidence*! Oh, you ought to go through this thing, line by line, and watch the ground shift beneath you! Between every paragraph there's a hundred-foot drop! (pp. 246–7).

This is to regard one's own self, fictionalised by Spielvogel, as a form of composition – in this case a bad one since Spielvogel has not observed the rules of logic and evidence which, managed properly, signify the truth and authority of the exposition. Later, as he reads Maureen's diary, Tarnopol expresses dismay at her inability to convert the diarist's private musings into public fictions: 'Oh, Maureen, you should never have spared my ego your writing career – better you should have written down everything in that head of yours and spared me all this reality! On the printed page, instead of on my hide!' (p. 322). Whether it is his 'hide' that is the text or his psyche, Tarnopol defines the self in 'My True Story' as a text which gains its 'reality' from other texts, compositions, or translations of 'life' into 'art'. Tarnopol graphs the self within a matrix of references which are judged for their qualities of authority, explanatory power, consistency and tautological 'intertextuality', or referability to other, sponsoring fictions. These combine to make up the linguistic prison of self-reference within which Tarnopol defines 'himself' as a literary subject. Narcissism, or self-love, may be the name he accepts for this form of self-composition, but it is only one of many authorised texts which he accepts as sources for the constitution of the subject. Thus, Tarnopol's 'problem', which is the problem of the novel, resides in the definition of the self as subject or, as I wish to show, in a critique of subjectivity portrayed as a form of textual criticism.

What is the subject of *My Life as a Man*? It would, indeed, seem to be Tarnopol, his life and his 'manhood' as they are represented through autobiography and those 'useful fictions' which can perform as stand-ins for autobiography. Yet, unlike the speaker of 'Self-Portrait in a Convex Mirror', who knows himself as that quiescent separateness from everything without, Tarnopol rarely speaks of himself save as he is being seen or interpreted by some other. 'My True Story' might be seen as a mock-autobiography in that it describes everything and everyone but 'who' Tarnopol is. It begins with what appears to be a biographical summary of the author's career, a repetition of that depicting Roth on the first page of the text, but it quickly falls into parody as Tarnopol's life as a man and artist is summarised by such quips as '*Mr Tarnopol is considered by Dr. Spielvogel to be among the nation's top young narcissists in the arts*' (p. 100). In fact, Tarnopol, writing from 'Quahsay, Vt.', authors this send-up of the author's reference, thus creating a fitting prologue to the succession of texts through which the writer achieves a great deal besides, but not including, self-definition.

In the five numbered and titled sections of 'My True Story', Tarnopol tells the story of his marriage to Maureen and his affair with Susan, hints at his childhood, describes in detail the lives of his brother, Moe, and his sister, Joan, characterises Spielvogel, and reproduces the versions of himself inscribed by others in diaries, letters, professional articles, and stories. Reading these, we discover that the preceding 'useful' fictions are prior renditions of Tarnopol as Zuckerman; thus, even these are not about 'Tarnopol himself'; rather, they have the same status of (and prefigure) other Tarnopol-fictions such as those engendered in Spielvogel's 'Creativity' or Maureen's diary-version of Tarnopol as artist bereft of muse. It may seem a strange claim to make for the autobiography of a narcissist, but 'My True Story' is least of all about the 'true' Tarnopol, since it is entirely made up of often conflicting fictions ('lies') about Tarnopol. Even these versions of the artist are not provided by Tarnopol in a project of self-assemblage; instead, most of them come from others, from without, so that Tarnopol's role in 'My True Story' is largely responsorial as he criticises the self-variation under scrutiny at any given time. When he responds negatively to Spielvogel's disguised version of Tarnopol in 'Creativity', the psychoanalyst catches him in a revealing logical error: 'First you complain that by disguising your identity I misrepresent you and badly distort the reality. You're a Jew, not an Italian-American. You're a novelist, not a poet. You came to me at twenty-nine, not at forty. Then in the next breath you complain that I fail to disguise your identity enough – rather, that I have *revealed* your identity by using this particular incident. This of course is your ambivalence again about your "specialness"' (p. 249). The revelation about an ambivalence regarding his 'specialness' is less important in this passage than the fact that it both conceals and reveals the primary anxiety suffered by the author of 'My True Story' – the fear that the 'I' may not exist at all except as a kind of co-operative fiction created by others.

The sources of this anxiety and its manifestations are portrayed in numerous ways here, as they are in the succession of Roth's novels since *My Life as a Man*. Tarnopol, who fears not just that the self might be a fiction, but one which is not self-authored, makes assertions such as that which declares Maureen 'was not a character out of a play by Strindberg or a novel by Hardy, but someone with whom I'd been living on the Lower East Side of Manhattan, sixty minutes by subway and bus from Yonkers, where I'd been born' (p. 192), as if simply saying so guaranteed the existence of his own non-fictional being. Yet even here, a form of self-assertion ('being born') hinges upon the positioning of another as 'real' in relation to the self. Tarnopol desires to locate some authorised version of the self, some single, objective, empirically verifiable rendition of his story so that, symbolically, he as an 'I' can 'be born', though the whole of *My Life as a Man* works against this tendency from the outset by providing, as prior or founding fictions, two fragmentary spin-offs of Tarnopol in the Zuckerman stories. Complaining, again, to Spielvogel about his article, Tarnopol cries out at the felt injustice of the portrayal/betrayal. 'Why should it matter so much to you?', Spielvogel queries, and Tarnopol responds: 'Because, among other things, I am the subject of that writing! I am the one your imprecise language has misrepresented! Because I come here each day and turn over the day's receipts, every last item out of my most personal life, and in return I expect an accurate accounting! . . . You were my friend, and I told the truth. I told you everything' (p. 252). Tarnopol assumes (or wishes) that there could be an accurate 'accounting' of the self, that it is possible for the subject of a 'writing' to be precisely represented in language and, more largely, that this accurate, precise self can come into being by means of that writing. His sense of betrayal is magnified by the fact that he regards Spielvogel as an author in many senses – of the article in question, of Tarnopol-as-narcissist, of the son creating a father by means of transference. About conversations with his ghostly real father, Tarnopol writes that 'whatever he read of mine he could never really associate with our real life; just as I on the other hand could no longer have a real conversation with him that did not seem to me to be a reading from my fiction' (p. 271). Thus, the author of *A Jewish Father* (Tarnopol's first novel) is implicitly forced in his auto-biography to come to terms with the notion that the self as the 'subject of writing' is multiple and unauthorised, lacking a 'real' father who will provide the proper evidence regarding the origins and validity of the self. To the contrary, in conversations with his father, Tarnopol is put in the paradoxical position of feeling as if he had authored his own father's words. In writing his own true story, Tarnopol is not able to say that the self authors itself, for he inscribes himself as a character in many fictions by other hands over which he has no control.

One could stop here and say that Roth has written in *My Life as a Man* an absurdist autobiography that takes 'manhood' as the subject of a play where six or many 'I's are in search of an author. Viewed in this way, the novel presents a variation on what Said defines as a classic novelistic practice and corresponding anxiety, the attempt upon the part of 'writing itself' to establish its own beginnings, origins, and authority.[9] In a more straightforward Freudian context (the kind of reading Spielvogel would endorse), Tarnopol might be seen as a fragmented being in search of a father, though this quest is buried in his anxiety-ridden sexual life where he is unable to satisfactorily discover or reveal his 'manhood'. Another way of putting this would be to say that Tarnopol has not survived the 'castration threat'. He is still dominated by alternatively threatening and nurturing mothers whom, according to the Freudian model, he has not symbolically castrated ('seen as women'), so that he has neither 'found' his own phallus, nor that of his father. Thus he lacks identity, wholeness, and 'manhood'. In the translated terms of his 'true story', he is an assemblage of partial selves (characters) in search of the father (author). Indeed, the novel is filled with so many images of mutilation that it might be thought of as a kind of male nightmare where primary fears are displaced on to several characters, and where the protagonist suffers from his own symbolic dismemberment as he 'remembers' the past. Yet to accept 'Tarnopol' within the limitations of this superficial analysis would be, on the one hand, to ignore Roth's careful framing of Tarnopol's self-presentation and, on the other, to simply create one more Tarnopol version to add to the list. Tarnopol's 'problem' runs much deeper, as does Roth's novel which goes beyond the idea that the 'self' is a collection of its different versions to a questioning of what, if anything, defines these as variations of some single entry or subject.

What I have suggested the 'typical' reader experiences in the delayed beginnings of *My Life as a Man*, particularly when these are placed within the contexts provided by other Roth novels where Zuckerman becomes an authorised protagonist, is an exaggerated sense of Tarnopol's fictiveness, or the fact that he is 'just' another in a succession of imagined creations. If we read this novel alongside *Zuckerman Unbound*, we are compelled to think that Tarnopol is no more 'real' than Zuckerman, and that Zuckerman is the imagined stand-in for this 'Tarnopol' who, now, has no status as the original of his fictional double. Since Tarnopol consistently defines himself in terms of others, his framing as a fictional character encourages our sense of him not as a traditionally defined self, or character, but as a linguistic operation. He appears to be an 'ego', indeed, at times, as an egomaniac, but his story reveals him to be an ego-projection 'in whose apparent unity the subject misrecognizes himself'.[10] In other words, Tarnopol might be said to be looking for the wrong thing: he seeks definition, manhood, or selfhood, a 'thingness' to which he can attach the label 'Tarnopol'. But as the 'subject' of a fiction, and as a narrative function which tells stories by creating networks of reference that pertain to the positioning of 'Tarnopol' within these stories, the narrator of 'My True Story' misrecognises himself in seeking out his manhood as the sign of his identity.

One way in which the novel critiques identity is to assign various definitions to words such as 'manhood' and 'manly'. For Maureen and in the eyes of society, 'manliness' is an activity of conscience whereby Tarnopol will honourably accept the responsibilities of husband and father, even though his marriage is based on a lie. For Tarnopol himself, achieving manhood runs the gamut from violent maturation ('if my future as a man required me to sever at long last the reverential bonds of childhood, then the brutal and bloody surgery on the emotions would have to proceed' – p. 219), to guiltless promiscuity ('As a matter of fact Dr Spielvogel, those two Italian whores and my colleague's wife back of the shopping center, and Karen, constituted the only praiseworthy, the only manly, the only *moral* . . . oh, the hell with it' – p. 256). Conversely, a form of moral responsibility appears to be at the source of Tarnopol's autobiography. Declaring 'Salad Days' to be 'something like a comic idyll honoring a Pannish (and as yet unpunished) id', and 'Courting Disaster' a 'legend composed at the behest and under the influence of the superego', Tarnopol defines 'the nonfiction narrative that I'm currently working on' to be evidence of 'the "I" owning up to its role as ringleader of the plot' (p. 113). Like the versions of 'Tarnopol', these contradictory versions of his desired manhood suggest that it is a fiction which, imposed upon him, is transformed into an image of what he should 'really' be.

More literally, 'manhood' is the subject of Tarnopol's unfinished manuscript which, like his being, lies in a state of utter disrepair:

> *That* book, based upon my misadventures in manhood, I still, of course, spent maddening hours on every day, and I had some two thousand pages of manuscript in the liquor carton to prove it. By now the various abandoned drafts had gotten so shuffled together and interwoven, the pages so defaced with X's and arrows of a hundred different intensities of pen and pencil, the margins so tattooed with comments, reminders, with schemes for pagination (Roman numerals, Arabic numerals, letters of the alphabet in complex combinations that even I, the cryptographer, could no longer decode) that what impressed one upon attempting to penetrate that prose was not the imaginary world it depicted, but the condition of the person who'd been doing the imagining; the manuscript was the message, and the message was Turmoil.   (p. 238)

Here, Tarnopol's 'self' and 'manhood' are represented as a series of rough drafts or false starts, as skewed codes and schemes for alphabetisation, as impenetrable prose. Manhood, then, as a sign of identity, is undermined by these representations which suggest, first, that it is a social construction or a fiction, and second, an unfinished, indecipherable text. 'It' (manhood, identity) cannot be signified simply; it exists as a palimpsest of directions, defacements, and intensities that defines the writing subject in a continuous process of (self)-erasure and (self)-inscription that never comes to unity or completion.

Tarnopol may sense at some level that this is what his quest for manhood and his failed attempt to write down 'his life as a man' will come to, though he resists the recognition by means of his comic, at times, grotesque sexual exertions. The thinly-veiled sexual violence he inflicts on Maureen, his exhausting labours over Susan's unresponsive body, his habit of leaving his sperm in public places, all testify to Tarnopol's obsession with the phallus as the thing which, if nothing else will, signifies his identity.[11] So great is the importance Tarnopol places on the phallus both as object of desire and that which confers identity that he can say, comparing what Maureen 'wants' to what Susan 'wants': 'for where Maureen generally seemed to want to have something largely because someone else was able to have it (if I had been impotent, there is no doubt she would have been content to be frigid), Susan now wanted what she wanted in order to rid herself of the woman she had been' (p. 137). Spielvogel might suggest that in such thoughts resides further evidence of Tarnopol's narcissism (he has what all women want). More to the point, Tarnopol implicitly makes the connection between the phallus and Susan's identity in suggesting that she wants his phallus, and the ensuing orgasm, because she wants to get rid of her old self and discover a new one. Tarnopol confesses of his sperm-leavings to Spielvogel that they are his 'signature' (p. 211). As vulnerability is the 'mark' of women, so it seems that in the life-writings of Peter Tarnopol, the mark of manhood is the phallus, and the sign of the self its disseminations.

Yet within these terms, Tarnopol is neither a successful 'man' nor a successful writer: his affairs end in disaster, and his 'work in progress' lies in a box, though the Zuckerman variations emerge as minor works. (The status of 'My True Story' is unclear – is *it* the unfinished manuscript lying in tatters? Does it have the status of a text? Is the voice who speaks in the novel talking to himself, to Spielvogel, or to some implicit confessor-audience?) Tarnopol is, to be sure, the subject of his own 'true story', but through that story, the subject has been dismantled to such an extent that in the end, speaking about himself, Tarnopol can only speak in tautologies: 'Oh, my God, I thought – now you. You being you! And *me*! This me who is me being me and none other! (p. 330). At this point,

Tarnopol is facing Susan soon after the death of Maureen, but the 'you' and 'me' of his final phrases appear to be interchangeable. Even though he says the 'me' is 'none other', the reader may well ask 'none other than who?' since the 'me' of 'My True Story' has been almost totally defined in terms of otherness, expression, and phallic extension. We are left with the question at the end of *My Life as a Man* of 'who is this I who speaks'? Even though, as I have often done here, it is possible at times to discuss 'Tarnopol' as a character who has a history, personality, and motives, this version of the self, the novel convinces us, is simply one more 'useful fiction' which allows us to discuss the subject. The subject, itself, of *My Life as a Man*, upon whom Philip Roth has conferred the name of 'Peter Tarnopol', is more a process than a character – a process of self-inscription that leads to an awareness of the subject as multiple and as represented by its positioning in relation to those references (other characters, events, conversations, etc.) that define it as such. In one telling scene, Tarnopol wanders through a bookstore and has the eerie experience of locating 'himself' (his first book, *A Jewish Father*) in the 'T' section. This discovery takes place in a section of the bookstore Tarnopol refers to as 'Schulte's crypt' (p. 236); moments later, he figures his unfinished manuscript as a 'corpse' which he cannot bring himself to 'remove . . . from the autopsy room to the grave' (p. 238). The implication is that these remnants, book and manuscript, are dead selves, that the 'life' or true subjects of Tarnopol's autobiography is protean, always in motion, though only 'known' by what it leaves behind as the dead traces of writing. This writing is the corpse left behind by the 'me' who composes it as the design of a still-life that graphs the cluster of stories, relations, and versions of the self which make up 'Tarnopol'.

In *My Life as a Man* as in much of Roth's major fiction, the self is not solitary, but social. If Tarnopol's disease is narcissism, his cure is some recognition on our part, if not his, that to gaze in the mirror of self-reflection is to acknowledge the least true version of the 'self' which, as a subject of 'useful fictions', is construed by relation, not reflection. In this ignored novel, Roth provides a significant critique of the subject of fiction – a critique which, for David Carroll, resides in all fiction that attempts to seriously consider the representation of the self:

> Representation derives its force on the one hand from a desire to solidify and unify the traces constituting experience, as if to

constitute a unified image of oneself . . . and at the same time, on the other hand, from a desire to expunge from oneself the unformed, unpresentable violence of experience, the work of time and death, and to produce not a metaphorical equivalent of oneself or the sense of one's experience but the irreducible and repetitive loss of this unity.[12]

The pathos of *My Life as a Man* resides precisely in the tension between Tarnopol's attempts to signify himself, and the recognition that 'himself', the subject of all the novel's true stories, is irreducible and unrepresentable save as partial, somewhat falsified, 'dead' fictions. If the self is a prison, and selfhood or 'manhood' a form of penance, then *My Life as a Man* indirectly represents the escape and consolation provided by the thought that 'self' is only a dead husk left behind by the writing subject's transgressions of its limits, yet still, always, defined in the form of a posited relation to the past and the fictions made by others. These become 'true stories' in that moment when the 'self' is defined both as a resistance to these constructions and the result of their confabulations.

NOTES

1. Philip Roth, *My Life as a Man* (1974; rpt. New York: Penguin Books, 1985) front matter. All future references will be to this edition and will be noted parenthetically in the text.
2. Patrick O'Donnell, 'The Disappearing Text: Philip Roth's *The Ghost Writer*', *Contemporary Literature*, 24 (1983) pp. 365–78.
3. Roth makes the distinction between Roth (the living American novelist) and 'Roth' (the critical fictions supposedly based on Roth) in 'Document Dated July 27, 1969', one of the essays in Philip Roth, *Reading Myself and Others* (New York: Farrar, Straus & Giroux, 1975) pp. 23–31.
4. The reviews of *My Life as a Man* were generally unsympathetic, and many of them found the novel to be as narcissistic as its protagonist, or 'too close' to Roth's own life. For examples, see the reviews by J. W. Aldridge, *Commentary*, 58 (September 1974) p. 82, and Morris Dickstein, *New York Times Book Review*, 2 June 1974, p. 1.
5. The reference to 'pasteboard masks' is, of course, to Ahab's speech in *Moby-Dick*, where he articulates the desire to strike through the façade of appearances to the essential self or reality. Hermione Lee, in *Philip Roth* (New York: Methuen, 1982) p. 20, glosses this passage as revelatory of Roth's own concern with versions of the constricted, social self (Ishmael), or the liberated, boundless self who may be self-destructive (Ahab).

6. John Ashbery, *Self-Portrait in a Convex Mirror: Poems by John Ashbery* (1975; rpt. New York: Penguin Books, 1976) p. 68.

7. Edward Said, *Beginnings: Intention and Method* (Baltimore, Md: Johns Hopkins University Press, 1975) p. 22.

8. Sigmund Freud, 'On Narcissism: An Introduction (1914)', in *Collected Papers*, trs. Joan Riviere (New York: Basic Books, 1959) vol. 4, p. 50.

9. These large concerns are discussed throughout, *Beginnings*, but for an extended analysis of the relation between writing, the novel, and the concept of authority, see ch. 3, 'The Novel as Beginning Intention', pp. 79–188.

10. Rosalind Coward and John Ellis, *Language and Materialism: Developments in Semiology and the Theory of the Subject* (London: Routledge & Kegan Paul, 1977) p. 110. The quote appears as part of Coward and Ellis's discussion of the subject; here, clearly, I am indebted to their re-interpretation of the subject in psychoanalytic theory. For some recent developments on the uses of Lacan for an understanding of narrative texts and subjects, see Robert Con Davis (ed.), *Lacan and Narration: The Psychoanalytic Difference in Narrative Theory* (Baltimore, Md: Johns Hopkins University Press, 1983).

11. Coward and Ellis note the crucial difference in Lacan's psychoanalytic theory between the penis, the physical organ of male reproduction, and the phallus, which is 'the sign around which the dialectic of identification of the subject is made' (p. 57). It is this second notion of the phallus that I use in discussing Tarnopol's quest for the sign of his identity, expressed through his sexuality.

12. David Carroll, *The Subject in Question: The Languages of Theory and the Strategies of Fiction* (Chicago, Ill.: University of Chicago Press, 1982) p. 116.

11

Some Notes on Roth's *My Life as a Man* and *The Professor of Desire*

MILAN KUNDERA

I. ON *MY LIFE AS A MAN*

Twelve years have gone by since Philip Roth visited Prague for the last time. The night before, I had reserved a table at a restaurant in the Old Town. When we arrived, the little table next to ours was already occupied by a man immersed in a book. We ate and drank, and, throughout, the man continually glanced over at us. To make his continuing solitude seem natural, he kept up a pretence of waiting vainly for a woman. This role became harder and harder for him to keep up since we lingered in the restaurant for more than four hours. Once, he rose and went to search for his imaginary friend in the street outside. At that moment, Philip placed a pack of cigarettes on his table as a reward for the man's efforts and, when the lover returned, smiled broadly at him.

A visitor to Prague, under close surveillance, Philip had come at first only in search of traces of Kafka. Seeking one thing, he found another: Kafka forbidden in a country whose culture had been massacred by the Russian occupation. He wrote about this in his novel *The Professor of Desire*, in one of the book's most beautiful and lucid chapters: Kepesh, an American Kafka specialist, meets a Czech professor, a Kafka specialist as well, who had been dismissed from his university by the Russians. Here is the confrontation of two existences, of two worlds, of two 'professors of Kafka' but also of two readings of Kafka. For the Czech scholar, Kafka speaks of the impotent solitude of a man confronted by implacable political power. To Kepesh, Kafka speaks of the solitude of an impotent man confronted by the implacable power of his own body.

The profound meaning of this confrontation is this: these two

160

interpretations do not contradict each other, they are comp-
lementary, marking two opposing faces of man's essential
impotence. For political and private life both have their roots in the
same metaphysics of man. The hell of intimate life is no more
bearable than that of political life. In both cases, the infernal
machinery is set in motion by the same, terribly human force: the
will to power. We know this will to power when it is disguised as
ideological argument or sentimental discourse; we never see it as it
truly is; we can only guess at its real nature beneath its rational
disguise. It was Kafka who described those situations which seem
absurd only because, in his work, the will to power is stripped of all
its ideological garments and surges forward completely naked. The
court and the castle do not present arguments, nor do they even
justify their behaviour on the basis of their material interest: the only
thing that guides them is the simple desire to dominate – a desire
wholly disinterested, unmotivated, and absolutely arbitrary since it
is so purely irrational.

Everything that Maureen, the heroine of *My Life as a Man*, does is
undertaken against her interests, against her happiness, against her
pleasure, against her sexuality. Even the alimony payment for
which she fights so passionately is only a pretext through which her
will to power can affirm itself, impose itself upon Peter, *manifest*
itself, make itself visible.

The intensity of the panic and rage evoked by the alimony
problem, the ferocity evinced by otherwise reasonably rational and
civilised people, shows well, I think, what a shocking and
humiliating conception of the fundamental role that each of them
plays in the other's life is held by the couple as they appear before
the divorce court. 'So, we've come to this', say the exasperated
adversaries, looking balefully at one another. But even these words
are only an attempt to continue to dissimulate the most humiliating
fact of all: 'that they were always there, from the beginning'.

But yes, behind the emotions, moods, lovers' quarrels, behind the
endless conversations – seemingly so rational, so logical – there was
hidden something immutable: the old *polemos* of Heraclitus,
aggressiveness. 'They have always been there, from the beginning.'
Once the will to power is stripped naked, things appear at once in all
their terrible *vulgarity*. It is important to understand this word which
refers neither to aesthetics or morality, but, rather, is an *ontological*
category – that is to say, it designates an aspect of being. We can be
scandalised by Maureen, but her vulgarity will not cease to exist; it

embodies that part of being which, freed from everything spiritual, removed from every achievement of history and of culture, belongs to the eternal interests of our bodies and of our animality. It is thus inseparable from man, an indestructible part of our condition; it is also our shame, which is why it was more or less banished from literature (James Joyce, it seems to me, was first to unveil it) and also why it still awaits its explorers and analysers.

If one wants to understand it one must go to the end, to descend to the depths as Dante descended to the very foundations of Hell. And if Roth's Dante is named Tarnopol, if he is a man of letters, a sensitive, even a beautiful soul – a *Schöngeist*, as Hegel called it – if he descends into Hell because he feels guilty and seeks his penance, then vulgarity loses its banal, everyday aspect (that is to say, its Joycean side) and becomes painful and heartrending: it becomes *drama*.

Maureen, this queen of vulgarity, no matter how frankly monstrous and repugnant she may appear, never seems like a caricature or a simplification. She is real, 'more real than reality', and if I say that she is real, that does not mean that she resembles such and such a woman. Novels do not speak of the real but of the possible. Novelists draw the map of human possibilities: the points of orientation on this map are these outermost limits, that is to say possibility pushed to its extreme – and that is what Maureen is. She seems true to us not because she exists in reality, but rather because we fear her and pay our respects to her potentiality. I know her by heart through my nightmares; from the time I was eighteen I have feared one day becoming her victim, and all my life I have constantly been defending myself against her dreaded attacks.

Maureen's aggressiveness resides in her weakness; this is the paradox around which her character is constructed – she has understood how to transform her weakness into a weapon, into artillery. All that disfigures this woman – ugliness, age, the inability to have an orgasm, the short legs, the sad childhood – becomes the ammunition for her terrible 'artillery of weakness'. The unforgettable scene in which she shits in front of Tarnopol during an hysterical quarrel represents a magnificent ontological metaphor: in order to attack Tarnopol, Maureen willingly assumes the posture of a victim. Metaphorically speaking, she lays down before him and, from below, from the depths of her misery, she hurls her accusation at him, she holds him responsible for everything – for her frigidity, for her unhappy childhood, for the bad lovers she had before him.

Yes, she holds him responsible for her entire being; and her being, which is just misery, is incarnated in her shit. Thus Tarnopol stands accused by his wife's shit. The shit accuses Tarnopol and condemns him!

And how does he react? Does he oppose her with the same virulence? No. He yields. He gives in from beginning to end. And because he yields, he constantly empowers her aggressiveness. If he is therefore guilty, he is guilty because of his sense of being guilty, because of his weakness – and this makes me think once more of the writer who drew Roth to Prague and thus allowed me to meet one of my dearest friends. In effect, *The Trial* contains the archtypal situation: the Court accuses K. without any reason, through the absolute arbitrariness of its will to power, and K., instead of rebelling, accepts the accusation, indeed manifests a genuine desire to confess his crime even though he has no idea of the offence of which he is guilty. These zealous efforts to feel guilty constitute the comic side of the terrible story of *The Trial*. Tarnopol is like K.: he gives ground before Maureen (he mobilises all his writer's imagination to justify his behaviour), and his weakness (which never transforms itself into any sort of artillery) renders him admirably ridiculous. Yes, he is ridiculous, he is not in any sense 'the philosophical axis' of the novel, or its 'truth'. He is not a projection of Roth himself, and if there is something of Roth in him, it is a slaughtered, demolished, ridiculed Roth.

What has been massacred (albeit discreetly, subtly, so subtly that a naïve reader may not even notice) is the activity of writing itself, this activity so absurdly regarded as sacred in an era deserted by culture and dominated by graphomaniacs. In effect, Tarnopol is much more graphomaniac than writer, which simply means that what impels him to write is not an aesthetic design, a passion for form, or the need to discover what no one has discovered before, but rather the imperative to talk about oneself, to confess, to settle scores through one's writing, to enlarge the 'I' beyond the 'I'. In this sense, Tarnopol mirrors Maureen: she too had 'lived to tell the story, to write the story', she too had 'entertained the idea of a literary career', she too had wanted to settle her accounts and avenge herself through writing. Graphomania, that most impotent and comic version of the will to power, dressed up in the noble drag of art, creates the ironic backdrop to this comedy of vulgarity.

The ironic backdrop. Yes, irony, the word is out. Irony without which I cannot imagine any novel being great. Irony signifies that truth (what the author himself thinks) is never glued to its enunciation (that is to say, that sentence in the novel that can be identified with an author's own thinking). The truth of the novel is located elsewhere, beyond the phrases themselves. In the struggle between Maureen and Tarnopol, it is not good and evil, truth and falsity, which confront each other, but rather the ridiculous artillery of weakness and the equally ridiculous weakness of a beautiful spirit. This noble, beautiful spirit knows toward the end of the novel its only moment of happiness, of catharsis (and how well we understand him!) when he learns of his wife's death. This is the moment when Roth's irony, without being any less discreet and enigmatic, reaches its diabolical paroxysm.

Roth is infinitely sincere in his desire to tell all, to say everything he has in his heart and to say it openly, 'naïvely', like someone who at confession wants to hold nothing back. Infinitely vulnerable in his sincerity, Roth is infinitely ungraspable in his irony.

II. ON *THE PROFESSOR OF DESIRE*

Did Karenin make love with Anna? Did Vronsky know how to make her come? Wasn't Anna frigid? Did they make love in the dark, in the light, in bed, on the carpet, for three minutes, for three hours? We don't know anything. Love, in the novels of that time, occupied that vast territory which stretched from the first meeting to the threshold of coitus; that threshold constituted an impassable frontier.

The discovery of sexuality belongs to the novels of our own century; heralding and accompanying that unbelievable transformation of morals, which, in America, took place with such vertiginous speed. In the 1950s one stifled under a merciless puritanism, but in a single decade one had arrived (to quote Roth) in the era of *total abandon*.

From that moment, the wide space between the first flirtation and the act of love disappears. Man is no longer protected from sex by a sentimental No Man's Land. He is confronted directly, implacably, by his own body.

The conquest of sexual freedom leads, in D. H. Lawrence, to a dramatic and tragic revolt. A little later, in Henry Miller, it is transformed into a lyric euphoria. Thirty years later, in Philip Roth, sexual freedom is nothing more than something given, acquired, universal, banal, codified: not dramatic, tragic, or lyrical.

We arrive at the limit we cannot cross. No 'further' exists. Man no longer finds himself in opposition to laws, parents, and conventions. Everything is allowed – the only remaining adversary is our own body, stripped, demystified, unmasked. Philip Roth is a great historian of American eroticism. He is also the poet of that strange solitude of the man, abandoned, face to face with his own body.

The solitude of a man confronted by sex might be called an *eroticism* without love. It would be ridiculous to accuse Roth of cynicism simply for having unmasked a real aspect of our condition.

Nevertheless, history has moved so quickly during the last decades that one can still remember clearly that earlier time, the era of our parents who lived their loves more in the manner of Tolstoy than of Roth.

The unbearable nostalgia which takes over in *The Professor of Desire* whenever Kepesh's mother or father appear is not simply the nostalgia for one's parents; rather, it is the nostalgia for love itself, for that moving and old-fashioned love of which the modern world has been deprived.

This nostalgia for our parents' world imparts to Roth's 'cynicism' not only an aura of tenderness but an entire novelistic background: the background of another era.

The acceleration of history has profoundly changed our existence: in past centuries a human life unfolded over the course of one given era; today it may straddle two or more. The rapidity with which history unfolds has reached the point where the links with the past are in danger of being broken for good. This fact confronts a novelist with a quite new task: to preserve that sense of continuity which is being lost, to capture that fugitive sense of historical time, and to indirectly demonstrate the parallel between our way of living (of feeling, of thinking, of loving) with the half-forgotten ways of our predecessors.

This is what I see as the profound meaning of the intellectuality of Roth's heroes – all professors and authors, constantly writing essays on Chekhov, on Henry James, or on Kafka. This is not the futile intellectual exhibitionism of that type of literature which narcissistically refers back to itself. Rather, it is a way to preserve the past within the novel's horizons and not to abandon the characters of fiction to an empty void in which ancestral voices will no longer be audible.

In reading and rereading Roth, I have come to appreciate more and more the artistry of his dialogue. I can recall only two other novelists for whom dialogue represents, as it does for him, the *principal pillar* of the narrative: Diderot and Hemingway. Here are three completely different ways of understanding what a character's own voice is meant to be.

In *Jacques the Fatalist,* each of the stories is presented in the form of a dialogue, a dialogue told by one person to another and in which the interlocutor not only listens but intervenes. Thus one piece of the dialogue is boxed inside another so that finally everything becomes dialogue: it is the most *theatrical* novel I know.

Hemingway's dialogue is *lyrical*: the repetition of words and a restricted, spare vocabulary give his work the melodic, magical charm of a litany. In Hemingway, men speak but one does not know what they are thinking. Dialogue is an accoustic screen which hides an undiscoverable meaning.

Roth's dialogue is *epic*. Like Venus rising from the waves, each character is born through his own words and in words reveals himself. Discreetly outlined to begin with, a Claire, a Helen, a Maureen (that unforgettable monster from *My Life as a Man*) become crushing presences once they begin to speak, to speak at length, like an unstoppable torrent, presences that can no more be stifled than the internal voices of Joyce's characters.

The art of each of these writers is divided between two tendencies: that of order (architecture, reason, discipline) and that of the irrational (the unconscious, disorder). In Roth's work, the demon of order goes under the name of ironic reason. It finds its fullest expression in *The Ghost Writer*, that masterpiece of concision. The demon of the irrational appears in the character's voice and dominates *My Life as a Man*, that masterpiece of the baroque.

Kepesh's romantic itinerary involves three women: the vicious Birgitta; the terrible Helen; the idyllic Claire. These three characters are derived from bad literature: Birgitta is the heroine of a pornographic tale; Helen, a *femme fatale* out of some exotic/erotic detective fiction; Claire (virtuous and lovable, who saves our unhappy hero) is a fairy out of the purest kitsch.

But it is precisely here that one can learn what it really means to 'give to the smallest situation to entire richness of the world'; these three one-dimensional figures are lifted out of the simple images from which they are derived and acquire an indomitable vivacity: three outlines become suddenly complex, indecipherable, ambiguous.

The last chapter of the book recounts a day Kepesh spends with Claire basking under the blue sky of their love. Their beatitude is heightened by the arrival of his beloved father. And so that there can be even more happiness, the father is accompanied by another old man, a survivor of genocide. What quadruple felicity! And yet it is at that moment that Roth with his tender irony begins to make these colours decompose: the blue of the sky becomes spectral gray; behind all this happiness, one perceives the fear of death; behind the fear of death, insouciance; behind insouciance, the precariousness of love; behind that, pity; behind pity, the ridiculous, and so on, and so on.

In *The Professor of Desire* there is a marvellous portrait of a seducer, Baumgarten, who gives Kepesh an invaluable piece of advice. If one goes up to an unknown woman whom one is trying to pick up, one must never try to be witty but rather one must ask obvious, banal questions and then to affect astonishment at the answers one receives. 'I beg you, no irony! Your problem is that you scare them off with your marvelous predeliction for the complexity of things.'

In other words, to succeed as a seducer one is obliged to play the 'game of kitsch'. The game of kitsch consists of refusing all irony. Let's stay with literature: the spirit of kitsch may tolerate, if it must, cynicism (which is often just moralising in reverse, a wounded sentimentality), it can accommodate itself to modernist sophistication ('modernist' kitsch is more and more widespread), and it can even adopt the provocative gestures of protest ('the kitsch of rebellion'), but it can never make peace with irony.

It is irony which is at the opposite pole from that rosy, didactic, and sentimental vision which we call kitsch. Irony does not simply contradict one certainty on behalf of another. Guided by its 'marvelous predeliction for the complexity of things', irony calls into question *all* certainties, and certainty itself. This inimitable, ironic freedom is what renders the work of Philip Roth – to use the wonderful, untranslatable French word – completely *irrécupérable*.

12

The Son is Father to the Man

CLIVE SINCLAIR

Let's begin at the horse's mouth. Here's Philip Roth himself (in conversation with the author) describing his reaction to the hostility *Portnoy's Complaint* engendered in some quarters.

'I think it's one of the oddest misreadings, if I may say, that any contemporary writer has run into. But it's also given me a subject. After all, it's the subject of the Zuckerman books, though I'd just as soon it weren't. But I couldn't have avoided it, it was just too big . . .'. At which point there was a verbal leap, a transferance, and Roth was no longer speaking of himself, but a fictional *alter ego*. 'Some Gentile critics can't understand why Zuckerman responds so to these swipes. They don't understand why comparisons to Goebbels and Streicher hurt. Perhaps I haven't made them understand that its in the very nature of being a Jewish writer to be pretty open and unguarded in the face of those kind of accusations. They don't understand the historical magnitude of this thing. Updike has said that by the time a writer's fifty certain reviews shouldn't matter to him any more. But these aren't reviews, this is history, in which Zuckerman is up to his knees.' Then it was back to autobiography.

'Part of me wishes the misreading had never happened, but I also know that it's been my good luck; that the opposition has allowed me to become the strongest writer I could possibly have been. In fact the Jews insisted on my being a Jewish writer by their opposition. I'm rather surprised that I've spent these last six years of my life, from forty-four to fifty, which is really the *filet mignon*, writing these three books. I'd much rather have had fun.'

Since that exchange a fourth volume has been added – *The Prague Orgy* – and the entire corpus published together as *Zuckerman Bound*. The *Encyclopaedia Britannica* (ninth edition) describes Prometheus thus, 'As a culture-hero or inventor and teacher of the arts of life, he

168

belongs to a wide and well-known category of imaginary beings.' Zuckerman also, it should be emphasised before we go any further, is an imaginary being. It follows, therefore, that when I call *Zuckerman Bound* a passionate defence of a career it is Zuckerman's not Roth's to which I am referring. The irony being that Zuckerman is unaware of his powerful advocacy. Of course Zuckerman's career has much in common with his creator's but they are by no means the same. Zuckerman has nothing like *When She Was Good* to his credit. He is, in a sense, the Semite-obsessed writer Roth's Jewish detractors imagine him to be. If I were really as they say, Roth seems to be thinking, what kind of mess would I be in?

Prometheus's punishment for stealing fire, you'll recall, was to become the open-all-hours deli of ravenous vultures. Poor Prometheus, but poorer Zuckerman, for he is in a double bind; bound, as in bondage, but also bound within the confines of literature. Punished for the fruits of his labours, as if his vocation weren't punishment enough! Or so it seems to Zuckerman. 'The way I found to spring myself from everything that held me captive as a boy, and it's simply extended the imprisonment to my fortieth year' goes a lament in *The Anatomy Lesson*. 'Enough of my writing, enough of their scolding. Rebellion, obedience – discipline, explosion – injunction, resistance – accusation, denial – defiance, shame – no, the whole God damn thing has been a colossal mistake. This is not the position in life that I had hoped to fill' (pp. 508–9).[1]

The position belongs (or belonged: he dies in 1961 of a bone-marrow disease) to Emanuel Isidore Lonoff, artist, to whom the green Zuckerman goes in search of a spiritual father, his own having been found wanting. Some years before describing this visitation, Roth published a piece entitled 'Looking at Kafka' in which he speculated upon the possibility that Franz had survived his consumption and the Nazis, and had emigrated to America to become the writer's Hebrew teacher. He supposed that Kafka had, above all, shaken off the influence of his father. Needless to say, he never did, as the most famous unposted letter ever written testifies. Later, in the same article, Roth writes how he or his fictional counterpart found his own way blocked by his father's love, how he felt compelled to demolish his family 'in the name of this tyrannical need that I call my "independence"'.[2]

In *The Ghost Writer* Zuckerman also begins to write his father a letter, concerning a family row precipitated by one of his stories, itself based upon an earlier incidence of family feuding. However, he is interrupted by a discussion, both clandestine and nocturnal, between his host, Lonoff, and his doting student, Amy Bellette. As a consequence Zuckerman revives Roth's aforementioned fantasy; only this time it is Anne Frank not Kafka who has made it to America. Anne Frank who actually experienced what Kafka only imagined; Anne Frank who did, despite her predicament, declare herself independent of her parent. 'I have now reached the stage that I can live entirely on my own. . . . I don't have to give an account of my deeds to anyone but myself' (p. 140). Zuckerman further imagines himself betrothed to this ghost, in the hope that such an engagement will finally placate the father who considers himself and his people betrayed.

Anne Frank (as will Zuckerman) fed off her experience when she wrote; whereas Lonoff, the maestro, presents the Jamesian ideal of a quiet life devoted to the madness of art. Lonoff is the Jew who got away; escaped from Europe, Palestine, and the family, though he has been bruised by all three. In particular he remains married to Hope, his wife of over thirty years; though, in another way, he lives without illusion or hope, and is consequently able to resist the temptation of Amy. Reason enough why Zuckerman could never really take his place.

The Ghost Writer begins with a mixture of precision and vagueness that characterises the ghost story (which is what it is, in part): 'It was the last daylight hour of a December afternoon more than twenty years ago . . .' (p. 3). Darkness and December, words to make you catch your breath, as any reader of *The Turn of the Screw* will know. It is some pages later that we learn, in passing, that the year is 1956. However, by 1976 when *The Prague Orgy* commences (very precisely on 11 January), Zuckerman has become firmly rooted in history (up to his knees) and its concomitant moral concerns; primarily his own and those of his family, but also those of the Jews, America, and Czechoslovakia. Since *The Ghost Writer* takes place in December 1956 and was composed more than twenty years later, it is clear that Zuckerman must have written it some months after the eponymous visit to Prague (only *The Ghost Writer* and *The Prague Orgy* are narrated in the first person, in a voice that introduces a Jamesian concern for precision and plot to a Kafkaesque sense of self), presumably in early 1977. The Epilogue thereby becomes a Prologue. In a way Zuckerman has fulfilled his own prophesy, made in *The Anatomy Lesson*, and disappeared up his own asshole. But, if so, it turns out to be a triumphant exit, as we shall see.

As Lonoff was to Zuckerman, so is Zuckerman to Sisovsky. It is to

Zuckerman that Prague emigré Zdenek Sisovsky comes on that January day in 1976 with the words, 'Your novel . . . is absolutely one of the five or six books of my life' (p. 701). The novel in question being the infamous *Carnovsky* (the title owing more to its meaty sound than I. J. Singer's family saga), which changed Zuckerman's life as surely as *Portnoy's Complaint* changed Roth's. Art draws upon life and then, as if dissatisfied with that minor role, seeks to influence the subsequent lives of the artist and his subjects in completely unexpected ways, so that real people are forced to act out sequels to fictions. Zuckerman's brother Henry is consequently able to blame Nathan and his scandalous book for the death of their father, the same father poor, guilty Zuckerman wanted to replace with Lonoff anyway. Thus he is a soft touch for honey-tongued Sisovsky, who tells the sad story of his own father's death at the hands of the Nazis. A death that may yet be redeemed if only Zuckerman would go to Prague and rescue his father's manuscripts, now in the hands of Sisovsky's ex-wife. 'I'm obsessed now with this great Jewish writer that he might have been' (p. 720). That Zuckerman now is. What a temptation! To save a Jewish father's soul, to be a good son and, in the bargain, a father to Sisovsky.

Sisovsky, aged thirty, is accompanied by forty-year-old Eva Kalinova, formerly Czechoslovakia's greatest Chekhovian interpreter, *formerly* because of an even greater predilection for Jews. The fact that she once played Anne Frank on the stage is given as evidence of this unhealthy philosemitism by the Vice-Minister of Culture. As a matter of interest it was in 1956 that she undertook this role, and was probably impersonating Anne Frank on the very December evening when the young Nathan Zuckerman became convinced that Lonoff's protégée, Amy Bellette, was not only Anne Frank herself but also his future wife. On the same subject, it is worth noting that Caesara O'Shea, Nathan's superstar lay in *Zuckerman Unbound*, in her turn had half of Dublin tearful over her rendition of the same Anne Frank. Like Eva she was just nineteen.

Having failed Anne Frank in *The Ghost Writer* Zuckerman makes amends when she reappears as Caesara 'in a dress of veils and beads and cockatoo feathers' (p. 258). As he wryly notes, 'life has its own flippant ideas about how to handle serious fellows like Zuckerman. All you have to do is wait and it teaches you all there is to know about the art of mockery' (p. 270). How can Zuckerman resist when he is rewarded, in the shape of Eva Kalinova, with a third visitation? And yet at the same time he knows that the blandishments are mirages; Eva is not Anne Frank, actress, as was Caesara before her. Nevertheless, Zuckerman swallows the bait. Why? Because Eva, like him, is a victim of the 'unforeseen consequences of art'. The ghost of Anne Frank has returned to haunt her, has been used by her enemies to drive her from the stage. Later, in Prague, Zuckerman muses,

> Had Eva Kalinova been born in New Jersey she too would have wished that Anne Frank had never died as she did; but coming, like Anne Frank, from the wrong continent at the wrong time, she could only wish that the Jewish girl and her little diary had never even existed. Mightier than the *sword*? This place is proof that a book isn't as mighty as the mind of its most benighted reader. (p. 759)

Zuckerman is echoing a remark made by Sisovsky, to the effect that misinterpretations of *Carnovsky* have become a part of the book itself, have created 'another grotesque dimension' not dreamt of by the author.

Actually what gives Sisovsky and Kalinova most credibility in Zuckerman's eyes is the mere detail that Prague was once their home. Prague is a revelatory city; a city in which the human struggle for freedom against repression, long waged by Zuckerman, is played out not in the head or on the shrink's couch but in cafés, streets and prisons. It is a place where all the demons that plague Zuckerman's conscience are alive and kicking. It is a metropolis where the consequences of art are neither psychological nor ambiguous but crystal clear; break the rules and you don't get a ticking off in *Commentary*, oh no, it's the pokey for you. As a result the intelligentsia, unable to put pen to paper, act out what Zuckerman has only imagined: the Prague Orgy. Life without the moral salvation of the written word. Compared to them Zuckerman is indeed a regular Henry James. Having edited that awe inspiring series 'Writers from the Other Europe' for American Penguin, Roth knows better than anybody what marvellous literature such circumstances can provoke, but he also knows that it is not *his* material. Speaking of *Writing on the Wall*, an anthology of recent Czech literature collected by Tony Liehm, Roth said, 'There's nothing you know that they don't know, and there's no way of doing it they haven't thought of, from the most surreal to the most realistic. So, the thing is, how the hell do you use it?' With the help of the aforementioned Henry he has found the answer to that question. It would not do, amid all this talk of Jewishness, to forget Roth's nationality and its *literary* inheritance.

Besides, Roth has been to Prague before. In 1977 he sent David Kepesh there in search of Kafka, the visit being wonderfully described in *The Professor of Desire*. Well, Kepesh found Kafka's tomb and that of his barber and also, most memorably (although, alas, only in a dream), Kafka's whore. All this ancient trollop can remember is that Kafka didn't beat her and that, like all the other good Jewish boys, he was fastidiously clean. In the interests of literature she is prepared to let Kepesh see her pussy, since she is convinced of his seriousness of purpose. Kepesh looks but declines to touch. Even for Kafka the Professor cannot summon up the necessary desire.

Zuckerman, in his turn, rejects a similar offer from Olga (the ex-Mrs Sisovsky), guardian of the manuscripts, who also habitually (*pace The Aspern Papers*) displays her pussy. It is the old exchange; life for art, a not-so-heroic sacrifice. Yet Zuckerman, like Kepesh, declines with less reason, for Olga is still voluptuous. She is also sharp. Any man may see her secret flesh, but she in turn can see through every man. She knows better than Zuckerman why he wants Sisovsky's father's stories. 'The marvelous Zuckerman brings from behind the Iron Curtain two hundred unpublished Yiddish stories written by the victim of a Nazi bullet. You will be a hero to the Jews and to literature and to all of the Free World. On top of all your millions of dollars and millions of girls, you will win the American Prize for Idealism about Literature' (p. 770). The same reason, of course, why his younger self so fancied being the groom of Anne Frank. Worse, she sees through Sisovsky. Did Zuckerman really believe that he was concerned about his father's memory? Oh no, says Olga, he wants to publish the stories under his own name and claim the credit for himself. Even worse, the tale of Sisovsky Senior's demise is a falsehood. According to Olga he sat out the war in hiding and was killed, not by the Nazis, but by a bus. In the end, however, it all becomes irrelevant. The stories, retrieved from Olga by Zuckerman, are taken into custody minutes thereafter by cops belonging to the Ministry of Culture.

There is no redemption for the Sisovskys, father and son; no lives are changed by publication in America. Sisovsky Senior, finding no Brod, will receive none of Kafka's posthumous fame. Yet again Zuckerman has failed, both as father and son. In *The Professor of Desire*, Roth quoted from Kafka's 'Letter to His Father': 'My writing is all about you . . . yet it did take its course in the direction determined by me.' Following on from that, the whole of *Zuckerman Bound* can be seen as a search for 'patriarchal validation' to counterbalance familial and critical vituperation. Not that Zuckerman could have done anything but the latter in Prague. Indeed, even as the Minister of Culture is expelling him personally, he cannot resist mythologising his own father, the salt of the earth, 'yet another fabricated father manufactured to serve the purposes of a storytelling son', notes Zuckerman (p. 783).

Has he learned at last that no patriarchal validation is possible for a post-Freudian son? Fathers, even Kafka's father, are filial constructions. To be sure, the guilt they engender is real enough, but it is in such stories that our most acute moral dilemmas are most finely articulated. Even as he is kicked out of Prague, presumed guilty (cf. Kafka's K.), and returned in humiliation to his 'little world around the corner', Zuckerman can still manage this valediction, a triumph of sorts: 'No, one's story isn't a skin to be shed; it's inescapable, one's body and blood. You go on pumping it out till you die, the story veined with the themes of your life, the ever-recurring story that's at once your invention and the invention of you' (p. 782).

In fact Nathan Zuckerman made his debut in *My Life as a Man*, some years before his appearance in *The Ghost Writer*, Peter Tarnopol, that book's protagonist, having been his creator. At the end of Tarnopol's first sketch, 'Salad Days', Zuckerman is bouyant, but the author sees pain ahead for his precocious invention.

> The story of Zuckerman's suffering calls for an approach far more *serious* than that which seems appropriate to the tale of his easeful salad days. To narrate with fidelity the misfortunes of Zuckerman's twenties would require deeper dredging, a darker sense of irony, a grave and pensive voice to replace the amused, Olympian point of view . . . or maybe what that story requires is neither gravity nor complexity, but just another author.[3]

Tarnopol did have a shot at it in 'Courting Disaster', wherein his *alter ego* was tortured by inexplicable migraines, but it took a decade for that other author to come along with the necessary qualifications to turn *Zuckerman Agonistes* into a comedy.

Roth, it should be noted, considers himself *less* not *more* serious these days. '*The Anatomy Lesson* is a book about comic writing,' he told me. 'Zuckerman is always compromised by a laugh. Tarnopol was on fire. He's like a flame thrower, he sees Zuckerman is really burning himself up.' When shown the coincidences detailed above he replied, 'All I can say is that I had forgotten those references, nor did I go back and look at that book when I began these. The choice of name was far less determined than you may think. The only sly part about it was my saying, this Zuckerman will stand in the same relation to me as that Zuckerman stood to Tarnopol. These books exist by themselves and don't rely, connect, or need *My Life as a Man*. My notes are visible, that's all. However, the paragraph you read about the pain is strangely relevant.' It seems to me that Roth's present tone is Jacobean; cruel and unforgiving, in the post-Shakespearean manner, but also sly, self-protective, intellectual, and Jewish, like the Jacob who outwitted Esau. Roth will wrestle with angels, but he'll also revenge himself upon critics who have wronged him. As for the latter, suffice it to say that Milton Appel's attack upon Zuckerman, reproduced in *The Anatomy Lesson*, bears more than a passing resemblance to Irving Howe's commentary upon Roth.

Prague puts such scraps into perspective, enabling Zuckerman to feel comfortable at least in his 'little world around the corner'. Isaac Bashevis Singer once said, 'As a matter of fact in all my writing I tell the story of my life. . . . Only the dilettantes try to be universal; a real writer knows that he's connected with a certain people, a certain time, a certain environment, and there he stays. There he stays put, I would say, and he doesn't mind it because there is enough to investigate and to learn even from a small world.' Singer, in the perverse way that one man's poison is another man's story, has benefited from having lived through more interesting times than Roth. And his own biography, not surprisingly, illuminates his main preoccupation; the conflict between the pull of his imagination and the course of Jewish history, the requirements of the first being constantly undermined by the tragic denouements of the second. This is personalised into a dispute between rabbi-father and writer-son, the traditionalist against the enlightened one. The very enlightenment, Singer now believes, that led inevitably to the Holocaust. In espousing it he was therefore, albeit unconsciously, guilty of patricide.

Zuckerman bears a similar guilt and, moreover, carries his father's curse, 'Bastard' being the last word the old man utters. Thus Zuckerman Senior's demise, which should have let his son off the parental hook, is actually (*pace* the book in which it was described) his binding. The ropes are invisible, but they hurt none the less. At the end of *God's Grace*, Bernard Malamud reverses this Abraham-Isaac relationship and has the monkey/son burn the teacher/father, a representative sacrifice on behalf of all those other followers of the Father who were murdered by disciples of the Son. Biblical imagery, no less than that of the Holocaust, informs Jewish-American writing. With Singer the hyphenated bridge between those two adjectives is no real problem. Though a long-time resident of 86th Street, he writes about the ghettos and shtetlach of Poland and his dead family without need of ironic distance for only luck (and an older brother) saved him. Being a Jewish writer Roth shares the same bag of images, the difference being that when Zuckerman sees jackboots as threatening, it is a symptom of paranoia rather than the world's murderous intent. Bathos, not tragedy, seems to be Zuckerman's lot, being part of a dislocated age.

The world is out of joint, as is Zuckerman in *The Anatomy Lesson*. This erstwhile prince of letters may now be king but, like Oedipus, he doesn't much enjoy it. Having bumped off his father (perhaps), he doesn't get into his mother's bed until after her death. Not only is Zuckerman by now physically incapable of writing, being incapacitated by a pain that branches down from his neck like an upturned menorah (suggesting an excommunicant), he is also without inspiration. 'Without a father and a mother and a homeland, he was no longer a novelist. No longer a son, no longer a writer. Everything that galvanized him had been extinguished, leaving nothing unmistakably his and nobody else's to claim, exploit, enlarge, and reconstruct' (p. 446). Why the problem? Singer has no trouble reconstructing Warsaw. But that resurrection is a triumph of memory over forgetting, and if not necessarily courageous it is at least part political; whereas the rebuilding of Newark, Roth's home turf, could only be sentimental regression.

Not that Zuckerman doesn't have well-documented infantile tendencies, occasioned in *The Anatomy Lesson* by the onset of pain. 'When he is sick,' that book begins, 'every man wants his mother' (p. 409). To ease his aches Zuckerman purchases a playmat in a children's furniture store upon which he reclines, sometimes with one of four replacement mothers, who take care of his sexual needs by lowering their various orifices upon his supine body. Consequently he would seem a sucker for the panacea offered by Dr Kotler. This suggestively named medic (note the first syllable) offers to cure Zuckerman for free out of gratitude for *Carnovsky*, which he reads, not as a pornographic handbook, but as a guide to Newark that was. All Zuckerman has to do is sleep upon his patented pillow. In effect, Zuckerman is being offered the opportunity to lose himself in the mock intimacy of collective nostalgia.

A more persuasive voice is that of Jaga, one of his playmates, who appeals, not to his hometown instincts, but to his out-of-town ambitions to be a writer of significance. For Jaga, assistant to his trichologist (Zuckerman is losing his hair, in addition to everything else), is Polish. Enraptured by one of Jaga's monologues, delivered during lovemaking, Zuckerman transcribes it from memory immediately thereafter. Excited, he even considers making her the subject of his text book, provisionally entitled *The Sorrows of Jaga*. Some hopes!

> Hopeless – and not only because of the grass and the vodka. If you get out of yourself you can't be a writer because the personal ingredient is what gets you going, and if you hang onto the personal ingredient any longer you'll disappear right up your ass-hole. Dante got out of hell easier than you'll escape Zuckerman-Carnovsky. You don't want to represent her Warsaw – it's what her Warsaw represents that you want: suffering that isn't semicomical, the world of massive historical pain instead of this pain in the neck. War, destruction, anti-Semitism, totalitarianism, literature in which the fate of a culture hinges, writing at the very heart of the upheaval, a martyrdom more to the point – some point, *any* point – than bearing the cocktail party chitchat as a guest on Dick Cavett. Chained to selfconsciousness. Chained to retrospection. Chained to my dwarf drama till I die.   (pp. 550–1)

Zuckerman unbound, indeed!

Yet Zuckerman never becomes a solipsist. Hence he rejects the offer of Jenny, another of the quartet, to share her woodland sanctuary (thereby inheriting Lonoff's hermit-like fate). Yes, everyone from Milton Appel to his brother knows what is best for him; Herzog had his Reality Instructors, Zuckerman had his prescribers. Diana, youngest of his mistresses, cannot understand why he should have been so pricked by his father's opposition and Appel's strictures. Being a Gentile she does not grasp that the arguments are historical as much as personal. A subtle difference, illuminated by his mother's last word, which happens to be

'Holocaust'. Dying she scribbles the word on a scrap of paper which her son (*pace* Appel) cannot bring himself to throw away, though he doesn't know what to do with it either. Neatly summing up Roth's own attitude to the Jewish tradition, encapsulated latterly by that word. His mother, on her death bed, thinks of the six million; Zuckerman, in pain, thinks only of himself. 'This is not the position in life that I had hoped to fill,' groans Zuckerman, 'you'll recall, I want to be an obstetrician' (p. 509).

He flies to Chicago intending to become the Jewish Schweitzer, incidentally relinquishing the painful burden of self, but once there finds himself impersonating a pornographer. This is the nub of the trilogy. The drugs and drink with which he tries to suppress his pain only succeed in releasing his inner self, no saint. In Milton Appel, pornographer, Zuckerman creates his most successful literary impersonation for years, taking in all he meets. Like it or not, his great talent consists of being able to dream up moral outlaws, Jewish heroes of the future, genuine Jacobean wits who call brothels Adult Day Care Centers. The book's comic pace accelerates as Zuckerman, swinging from one moral extreme to the other, heads for his inevitable comedown. It occurs in a Chicago graveyard where he attacks his friend's father (defending the latter's worthless adopted grandson) only to have his 'filthy' mouth shattered by a dead Jew's headstone. Later the uninjured party, on learning that Zuckerman is an orphan, forgives him.

In hospital, on the mend, Zuckerman, growing a white beard, considers himself reborn as a father-figure. But there is no escaping his future as a man apart or from the 'corpus that was his'. Lonoff he will never be.

Long ago, on that unforgettable evening, Lonoff himself had remarked that 'an unruly personal life will probably better serve a writer like Nathan than walking in the woods'. It was a prophetic remark, as we have seen. At the finale of *The Ghost Writer* there is a dramatic confrontation between Lonoff, his wife and his would-be mistress, which ends with Hope on the run. As he makes ready to follow her, Lonoff administers Zuckerman's rites of confirmation with the following remarks, 'I'll be curious to see how we all come out someday. It could be an interesting story. You're not so nice and polite in your fiction . . . You're a different person' (p. 180). By now it should be clear that Zuckerman, despite all his best and worst efforts, will never be anyone but himself – a self that has become so bounded by literature that Lonoff's distinction no longer holds true, as the Prague valediction confirms. Zuckerman is what he writes, because his readers mistook him for what he wrote; the son is father to the man.

NOTES

1. All references to the three novels and epilogue comprising *Zuckerman Bound* are to the Farrar, Straus & Giroux edition (New York, 1985) and will be included in the text.
2. Philip Roth, *Reading Myself and Others* (New York: Farrar, Straus & Giroux, 1975) p. 87.
3. Philip Roth, *My Life as a Man* (New York: Bantam, 1975 [1974]) pp. 31–2.

13

The Unspeakable Self: Philip Roth and the Imagination

JONATHAN BRENT

O, What a world of profit and delight,
Of power, of honour, of omnipotence,
Is promised to the studious artisan!
(Christopher Marlowe, *Doctor Faustus*)

'Only my "self" . . . happens not to exist in the
everyday sense of the word.'
(E. I. Lonoff to his wife; Philip Roth, *The Ghost Writer*)

At the outset of his brief visit to E. I. Lonoff, the 'great man' and
short story writer, Nathan Zuckerman thinks:

Purity. Serenity. Simplicity. Seclusion. All one's concentration
and flamboyance and originality reserved for the gruelling,
exalted, transcendent calling. I looked around and I thought, This
is how I will live.   (p. 5)

To a great extent, the entire trilogy of *Zuckerman Bound* develops
from this simple reflection. Nathan finds a model in Lonoff because
he does not *know* how to live, and the question of how to live one's
life is at the centre of his endless self-interrogations and the
interrogations he is subjected to by others. The question comes up
again over the brandy Nathan and Lonoff sip together in the
Master's study.

'How else am I to conduct my life?'
'How else would you like to?'

. . .

180

'How else might I like to?'

It thrilled me to see him standing there taking altogether seriously what I had asked. 'Yes. How would you live now, if you had your way?' (p. 68)

It is difficult for either Zuckerman or Lonoff to propose a suitable alternative to Lonoff's present life, but it is precisely the possibilities contained in the original question that haunts Zuckerman until *The Prague Orgy*, when the Czech official smiles 'the smile of power being benign' and ushers Zuckerman through the airport checkpoint with the words 'Zuckerman the Zionist agent. . . . An honor . . . to have entertained you here, sir. Now back to the little world around the corner' (p. 784).

Zuckerman the Zionist agent, the anti-Semitic Jew, the treacherous brother, the ungrateful son, the monkish artist, the celebrity star, the would-be doctor, the maniacal pornographer king. Identities pursued, identities pursuing him, identities spun out of thin air. How he lives and who he is are connected in the play of his imagination and that of others. 'But what do I know, other than what I can imagine?' he asks rhetorically at the end of *The Ghost Writer* (p. 180). By *The Prague Orgy*, it is clear that he cannot be anything either except through the mediation of his and, as he painfully learns, others' imaginations.

Coming upon Amy Bellette at Lonoff's house, his aroused body and mind do not lead Zuckerman toward inventing gratifying erotic encounters but toward constructing a life for the girl who incorporates his own suppressed longings and struggles for identity. It is part of what is appealing about Nathan that his imagination is freed from the gross weight of his daily experience. It purifies his conflicts and offers a remarkably open horizon of ethical and psychological possibilities.

In Nathan's dream of her, Amy rediscovers who she is by reading about herself in *Time*; she comes upon herself, so to speak, by chance in a dentist's office. Nathan endures a similarly dramatic self-encounter in *The Anatomy Lesson* while his own mouth is being inspected by doctors who finally wire it shut. Detached and controlled by others, Amy's identity as Anne Frank confronts her by accident. It hovers toward her from the page. It is contained in the language she reads and in the copies of *Het Achterhuis* she eventually purchases from the Dutch publisher. In Roth, the self is always a

literary construction, containing both the author's intentions and
the intentions of those who read it.

The irony of Amy's discovery that her father still lives and that she
herself has become famous – a celebrity such as Nathan will become –
is the permanent suppression of her identity. After the scene in the
New York theatre, Amy realises that she can never again be who she
is: it would destroy too much in the minds of other people (p. 124).
Like Nathan, she possesses a hidden identity, or more precisely a
forbidden identity, the identity of a dead person. First, she is taken
for dead among the heaps of corpses at Auschwitz; then later the
whole world believes her dead as *The Diary of Anne Frank* is read and
performed. Her death is a necessary part of *their* experience. She
remains permanently severed from herself. In the world Roth has
created there can be no resurrections.

Lonoff is the hero of this unspeakable (in Nathan's case) or
unspoken (in Amy's) self. Ironic, without illusions, frighteningly
self-conscious, meticulously attuned to the needs and limitations of
this self, which, as he informs his wife, 'happens not to exist in the
everyday sense of the word' (p. 41), Lonoff is exquisitely
imprisoned in and by the sentences he endlessly turns around. He is
isolated from the world in his Berkshire retreat, from his Eastern
European past, from the traditions of his people, from his own wife
and children; he requires no resurrections. He knows no 'second
chance' at life, no second life awaits him or is possible or even
desirable. He has achieved the great condition of renunciation
reserved in James's *The Middle Years* for the novelist Dencombe
whose words Nathan finds pinned above Lonoff's writing desk, 'A
second chance – *that's* the delusion. There never was to be but one.
We work in the dark – we do what we can – we give what we have.
Our doubt is our passion and our passion is our task. The rest is the
madness of art', Nathan reads late that night (p. 116).

It is a condition Nathan will never be able to achieve. Nathan
imagines that Amy reads her book on a park bench much as
Dencombe reads his in *The Middle Years*. Nathan likewise is
alienated from the images of himself he finds in the eyes of other
people, newspaper clippings, the essays of murderous critics. He is
obsessed with the problem of bringing these objective constructions
of himself into line with his own inner evaluations. This is the source
of his great bitterness toward Milton Appel. Appel takes, in
Nathan's view, everything out of context and deprives *Carnovsky* of
all that Nathan thought he had put into it.

It's one thing to think you're pretending to your students when you tell them there's a difference between characters and the author, if that's the way you see it these days – but to strip the book of its tone, the plot of its circumstances, the action of its momentum, to disregard totally the context that gives to a theme its spirit, its flavor, its life . . . .   (pp. 570–1)

To Appel, Nathan is as 'dead' as Amy Bellette was to her adoring readers. Nathan burns to be reborn in Appel's eyes. Impossible. He cannot accept this death and runs off to Chicago to become a doctor: 'I want a second life. It's as ordinary as that', Nathan informs Bobby Freytag when he arrives (p. 601). But what Nathan wants, Roth denies. Dencombe's words reverberate with increasingly sinister irony and the 'madness of art' becomes ever more perilously akin to mere anger and self-hatred as Nathan pursues his chosen task.

Like Lonoff, Zuckerman is isolated from his family, his people, and ordinary human contact (first in his Quahsay retreat, then in his New York 'Ward'). His inner self feels no immediate allegiances. It is detached, ironic, self-parodying, gravityless. He seems strangely without even erotic passion, something he exposes in his relationship with Betsy toward whom his disloyalty is as unmotivated by antipathy as his outburst of lust for her friend on the kitchen floor is unmotivated by desire (pp. 34–5). Lonoff recognises the weight of his accumulated experience and accepts that he will never quite be who he is. Zuckerman cannot. He lives in a kind of existential outer space. At his father's bedside, he tells the nearly dead old man about the creation of the universe, the original egg of energy and matter exploding into nothingness. He could not formulate, as Henry angrily points out, the simple concrete statement, 'I love you' (p. 397).

In Zuckerman we find not the portrait of the artist brought up to date since Stephen Dedalus, but the portrait of the imagination severed from any world except that contained in the artist's mind. While it acts to purify and dramatise its own self-creating conflicts, Zuckerman's imagination is not chastened by any moral, social, political, religious, or even artistic objectives, aside from the requirements of the well-made story. Stephen Dedalus could write: 'O life! I go to encounter for the millionth time the reality of experience and to forge in the smithy of my soul the uncreated conscience of my race.' Zuckerman's experience possesses no such reality; his soul contains no such smithy. Even in *The Ghost Writer*, the 'uncreated conscience' of his race was hardly a concern.

What his soul does contain, however, is exceptional imaginative force. Blocked from a satisfying harmony with the world, this force subverts the meaning of ordinary experience and sets Zuckerman's inner image of himself in irresolvable conflict with the world of 'facts': those his father adduces about his family history, those his brother points out about the consequences of art, those Milton Appel finds substantiated in *Carnovsky*, those insisted upon by Alvin Pepler, those authorised by the Czech government for whom the 'true Czech spirit' is embodied in people who 'understand what *necessity* is. People who do not sneer at order and see only the worst in everything' (p. 780) – essentially the same criticism Nathan's father makes about the story 'Higher Education', when he says, 'Well, Nathan . . . you certainly didn't leave anything out . . . I mean . . . you didn't leave anything disgusting out' (pp. 85–6).

In this anti-world of the imagination everything eventually becomes possible as Nathan's identity oscillates wildly between that of a socially useful doctor and Milton Appel, the 'wildest antisocial desperado of them all, the embodiment of crudity, the Castro of cock, the personification of orgasmic mania, commander in chief of the American pornocracy . . .' (p. 631).

Nietzsche defined nihilism as the situation in which everything is permitted, and the wild freedom of Zuckerman's inner world by the end of *The Anatomy Lesson* possesses a dimension of this nihilism. This side to Zuckerman originates in his condition of being a 'superfluous man' in the tradition of Lermontov's Pechorin, Turgenev's Rudin, and Dostoyevsky's underground man. Like them he has no place in the intellectual or social structure of his society. In contrast, however, they possess a kind of sincerity of which Zuckerman is incapable. He is consumed with 'ironic paranoia' which, as he notes, leaves him unable even to take himself seriously.

Violent, crude, sentimental, egoistic, altruistic, scatological, polite, self-pitying – by the end of *The Anatomy Lesson* Zuckerman is all these things. He is not simply a 'complex' character out of a nineteenth-century novel; he is a character with no centre at all, a vortex of energy producing a vacuum within. But Zuckerman's nihilism is dressed in the ordinary attire of the middle class and must be understood in a way entirely different from that of any of his fictive predecessors. He does not oppose society from the standpoint of an alternative social or ethical or economic norm. This opposition arises from the very constitution of the self he inhabits.

This self is a product of both psychological and ethical relationships and the evolution of a particular literary tradition. Zuckerman suggests this when he and Lonoff discuss their literary lineage.

> 'And what about you?'
>
> 'Me?'
>
> 'Yes. You haven't finished. Aren't you a New World cousin in the Babel clan, too? What is Zuckerman in all of this?'
>
> 'Why – nothing. I've only published the four stories that I sent you. My relationship is nonexistent. I think I'm still at the point where my relationship to my own work is practically nonexistent.'
>
> So I said, and quickly reached for my glass so as to duck my disingenuous face and take a bitter drop of brandy on my tongue. But Lonoff had read my designing mind, all right; for when I came upon Babel's description of the Jewish writer as a man with autumn in his heart and spectacles on his nose, I had been inspired to add, 'and blood in his penis,' and had then recorded the words like a challenge – a flaming Dedalian formula to ignite my soul's smithy.   (p. 49)

Just as Nathan wants to be a doctor but becomes a pornographer when he flies out to Chicago, here he wants to strike up this relationship with Babel but ends up with rather different literary connections. His inheritance from Babel is adulterated with a sensibility possessing alien impulses. The subversive humour of Rabelais and the cynical negation of Sade have fused oddly with Babel's Jewish perspective. Zuckerman does not stand in awe of the Cossacks of life; he does not dream of a ruined past. His artistic purpose and his code as a man seem to be to expose the unworthiness of all Cossacks and to explode the possibility of dreams. No one stands a chance against Zuckerman's brutal laughter – not even, finally, Zuckerman himself. Babel was related to a world of values, intentions, and dreams with which he could sympathise if he could not enter it directly. Zuckerman has no such relation either with the Cossacks or the shtetl he has left behind. The situation of Zuckerman's life may be the American equivalent to

Babel's, but Zuckerman challenges this situation with the comedy of Rabelais and the cruel delight of Sade.

What is both confusing and novel about Zuckerman's nihilism is that it is directed almost exclusively toward himself. To the outside world, Zuckerman is for the most part only polite, helpful, kind, and attentive, something which Lonoff observes and Nathan's father finds utterly baffling:

> 'Is there anybody who came into the house today whose face didn't light up when they laid eyes on you? And you couldn't have been kinder, you couldn't have been a sweeter boy. I watched you with your family and with all our old dear friends, and I thought to myself, Then what is this story all about? Why is he going on like this about ancient history?'   (p. 86)

For Babel such ancient history was the source of his dreaming. For Zuckerman it is the source of laughter, but only in his fiction. The energy of Zuckerman's imagination is rarely turned upon the world, and the quality of his opposition is rarely demonstrated in action. He resists Judge Wapter's views not by arguing with him, but by not arguing at all. He does not disrupt his father's funeral, or embarrass his sister-in-law, or confont the rabbi, or even attack his brother in return for his damning judgement. His father argues with him and he defends himself. He initiates nothing. He expresses his anger and resentment of Appel but only after he has practically immobilised himself with frustration and then in a telephone conversation which achieves nothing. Finally, his inner rage spins completely out of control when he attacks Bobby Freytag's father in the cemetery. But here, too, it is an attack that fails and has no real purpose. Zuckerman is a centaur-like creature – Babel from the shoulders up, but Sade and Rabelais down below.

Setting Zuckerman within the full spectrum of his literary context, it is possible to see how complex his character as a superfluous man is and how curious the nature of his inward opposition. 'Who are you?' is the question asked again and again of Zuckerman throughout Roth's trilogy. It is the question Lonoff poses when he presses Nathan about his literary kinship; it is the question the black man asks at the end of *Zuckerman Unbound* and the question raised by the little girls at the beginning; it is the question shouted at him by Olivia in *The Anatomy Lesson* (p. 459) and that dominates his psyche throughout; it is the question raised at the very end of *The Prague*

Orgy when the Czech official accuses him of being 'Zuckerman the Zionist agent'. It is a question that has as much of a literary as an ethical and psychological component.

Zuckerman is part Babel, part Rabelias and Sade, but he also shares literary affiliations with Camus's Stranger and Kafka's K. It is partly the richness and complexity of his literary forebears that makes this question so difficult to answer. Like the Stranger and K., Zuckerman is inwardly dispossessed. Like them, he is judged and condemned: Judge Wapter, his father, Milton Appel, the Czech Minister of Culture, all level verdicts against him. Like K. and the Stranger, Zuckerman finds the accusations incomprehensible or absurd. He exists in a magic world in which all reason fails and what is absurd is his persistent belief, much like K.'s, that through logical presentation of the facts he can clear his name. Impossible.

However, just as the Babel/Sade/Rabelais paradigms do not entirely explain Zuckerman, neither does that of the Stranger or K. He is not simply their American cousin. The Stranger commits a murder he *knows* to be absurd; Zuckerman could never pull a trigger, and his attack on Mr Freytag is both unsuccessful and motivated, however nonsensically, by his need to preserve the rights of sons against fathers. K. must die like a dog, executed by thugs; Zuckerman will die surrounded by doctors, mistresses, or adoring fans. Whereas the Stranger and K. exist in conditions of moral absurdity, alienated from a human community, Zuckerman is surrounded by concerned people: father, mother, doctors, lovers, critics, fans, even his chauffeur Ricky comes to take an interest in the well-being of his putative son. Zuckerman wants to be good, moral, truthful. He doesn't understand the outrage with which some people greet his efforts. He is immersed in the human community. He is not the Stranger whose anomie causes him to commit a senseless murder. He does not turn into a ghastly bug – and if he did he could count on a Diana or a Jaga or a Gloria – or his mother – to tend his every need. Though he is judged by those who do not understand him, they have no real power over him. In addition to his critics, Zuckerman has his Dianas, Dr Kotlers, and his mother.

Zuckerman, then, is something more than simply the 'New World cousin' of Babel, Sade, Rabelais, the Stranger or K. What he represents, I believe, is the very impossibility of the kinship he appears to possess. Who is Zuckerman? Raised on the great works of Western Civilization, devoted to the artistic ideals of the Great Tradition, imbued through this literature with the spirit of contemporary thought and feeling, his self is the product of these texts which in the world he actually inhabits, first in Newark and then in literary Manhattan, are woefully out of context.

Zuckerman is a uniquely American type. His nihilism is a peculiarly American strain. In a way, what Appel has done to *Carnovsky* (having disregarded, in Nathan's view, the 'context that gives to a theme its spirit, its flavor, its life . . .'), Nathan has done to these literary templates for his self. Zuckerman's demonic inner whirlpool is modulated through a wholly average middle-class persona. He takes K. or the Stranger or Sade and seats him 'sipping coffee . . . at a counter around the corner from the office of the investment specialist – studying, for the first time in his life, the business page of the morning paper' (p. 189). The first time for Nathan, but the first time for these strange European literary emigrés as well. The context does not make sense, and it is precisely this out-of-context quality that distinguishes Zuckerman from the line of lost Romantic heroes, on the one hand, and alienated modern anti-heroes, on the other. His nihilism is disguised in an enveloping everydayness.

Zuckerman is in many ways a terrifying creation. His opposition to the world does not have the quality of ethical or even passionate commitment. It is, rather, the product of a strange imaginative displacement. He is exiled, but not simply from Newark or immigrant fathers, as he himself supposes. His exile is from a landscape of the imagination as well. It is a literary phenomenon as much as it is historical or psychological. It is for this reason that, as with the Amy Bellette of his imagination, his inner identity is dead and cannot be regained. Beneath the polite, sincere, truthful, comic, angry Zuckerman is a negated self. Detached from all social or historical realities, unable to achieve a love relationship with another human being, without productive or useful work, and without faith in his own chosen vocation, Zuckerman achieves a degree of negativity reserved for the great demons of history.

Zuckerman had lost his subject. His health, his hair, and his subject. . . . What he'd made his fiction from was gone – his birthplace the burnt-out landscape of a racial war and the people who'd been the giants to him dead. . . . Without a father and a mother and a homeland, he was no longer a novelist. No longer a son, no longer a writer. Everything that galvanized him had been extinguished, leaving nothing unmistakably his and nobody else's to claim, exploit, enlarge, and reconstruct. (pp. 445–6)

This is what life has done to Zuckerman. By the end of *The Anatomy Lesson*, we find what Zuckerman has done to himself:

> 'My life as cud, that's what I'm running out on. Swallow as experience, then up from the gut for a second go as art. Chewing on everything, seeking connections – too much inward-dwelling . . . too much burrowing back. Too much doubt if it's even worth the effort. Am I wrong to assume that in anaesthesiology doubt isn't half of your life?' (p. 602)

The passion and task charged to him by his imagination have done to him what race riots have done to Newark.

The negating consequences of his imagination are similar to those Lonoff's wife complains of: '*Not* living is what he makes his beautiful fiction *out* of!' (pp. 174–5). Zuckerman's art likewise requires the rejection of life:

> He was seventeen and thought continuously about his courses, his cock, and his pals. . . . Talk to him about medical school in those days and he would have laughed in your face. . . . His life was too big for that . . . his life was *enormous*. (p. 571)

> He had the highest possible conception of the gigantic capacities of literature to engulf and purify life. He would write more, publish more, and life would become colossal. But what became colossal was the next page. He thought he had chosen life but what he had chosen was the next page. Stealing time to write stories, he never thought to wonder what time might be stealing from him. Only gradually did the perfecting of a writer's iron will begin to feel like the evasion of experience, and the means to imaginative release, to the exposure, revelation, and invention of life, like the sternest form of incarceration. He thought he'd chosen the intensification of everything and he'd chosen monasticism and retreat instead. (p. 586)

Nathan enacts Dr Faustus's dream of a life of 'profit and delight, / Of power, of honour, of omnipotence' but finds only impotence and undiagnosable pain at the end. The pain itself which afflicts him in *The Anatomy Lesson* has no meaning, no significance other than itself: 'it's the *opposite* of interesting, and nothing, *nothing* made it worth it. . . . Nothing made it worth the doctors' offices and the hospitals. . . . Nothing made it worth the depression and the humiliation and the helplessness. . . . Nothing made it worth not being able to make your own bed in the morning . . .' (p. 606). Nothing. The word rings ominously in this passage. When Zuckerman rides out to the cemetery with Bobby's father, high on drugs and vodka, this nothing invades his own being. When the old man pulls on Nathan's sleeve, 'Nathan wasn't there' (p. 643).

Zuckerman and Lonoff share a professional rejection of life, but in Lonoff it remains a form of ironic, if infuriating, detachment, while in Nathan it becomes nihilistic. Lonoff's detachment accepts the reality of his daily experience; Zuckerman's nihilism seeks to destroy it. Lonoff is the one who says 'no' to Amy's pleas that they go off together to Italy. It is Diana who says 'no' to Zuckerman's scheme of escaping to Chicago.

But despite this rejection and negation, the truly frightening thing about Nathan is that he is *not* a demon, because even demons, finally, have some discernible shape, locatable abode, and definable character.

For all his negating monasticism and self-denial, Zuckerman does not actively subvert ordinary notions of decency or social conduct. Nor does he objectively appear to deny himself anything. The wives he abandons for his art exert no passionate hold on him. Leaving them is no great act of self-denial. He indulges his anger toward Milton Appel, then calls him to discharge his fury. No self-denial there. His hair is falling out, so he goes to a trichological institute and then seduces his clinician. When the moment comes to part with Caesara O'Shea in *Zuckerman Unbound*, he sheds the demeanour ('cuts the crap', as he puts it – p. 262) of the serious man of letters and spends the night with her. Again, without particular passion or conflict. He thinks back on Caesara with neither remorse nor regret. He appears even to transgress his own artistic values when he pleads with Bobby in *The Anatomy Lesson* that all he wants is a 'second life' – that dream which Dencombe finally refuses and which Lonoff too rejects, but which Alvin Pepler, a grotesquely caricatured anti-self of Zuckerman, demands in *Zuckerman Unbound*: 'The truth! This is my *life* we're talking about, my chance at a second chance. I must have the truth!' (p. 333). By the end of *The Anatomy Lesson*, Zuckerman is weary and defeated, a caricature of himself: a Lonoff with a Pepler inside.

But hardly an incarnation of Mephistopheles, the self-proclaimed 'spirit that negates', of Goethe's *Faust*. Zuckerman's isolation and absurdity can be associated with Camus and Kafka, his Jewishness with Babel, his devastating humour with Rabelais, his carnality with Sade, but none of these correspondences defines him. Each is only a guise, a mask. He wants to be a doctor, but Faustus *is* a doctor. He impersonates a latter-day Sade, but Sade *is* a libertine for whom pleasure justifies everything.

> It was still Sade, and not the publisher of *Lickety Split*, who could carry that argument to the bottom of the bottom and dispense with every moral pretext. . . . Of course, he was a Jew and anti-Semitically speaking, if a Jew wants to make money running a brothel, he'll make it sound like an adult day-care center. Philo-Semitically speaking, what poor Ricky had endured in that bar was a saint in the line of the great healer Jews – do-gooding Dr Appel, easing suffering mankind of its psychic tensions. (p. 640)

The Marquis de Sade debauched young girls and measured the depths of pleasure. The women – even the girls – come to Zuckerman already debauched, ready for anything. Gloria debauchs *him*. Dr Faustus is torn limb from limb at the end of Marlowe's play. Zuckerman admits to being 'physically unfit for being torn apart' at the end of *The Anatomy Lesson* (p. 645). Camus's Stranger pulls a trigger. Zuckerman writes a book. Kafka's K. dies like a dog. Zuckerman has a pain in the neck. To a great extent, Zuckerman's self is symbolic, a collection of images reflected from different sources. He is a man who hardly exists; a nihilist whose object of aggression is himself – but not even physically as with Rimbaud (despite his Percodan and vodka excesses which, after all, are motivated by medical considerations), or even mentally or spiritually as with so many self-flagellating 1960s artists.

Zuckerman's nihilism is directed toward the self. Part literary convention, part social/psychological invention, the self remains a visible and potent force in contemporary American cultural parlance, while in European discourse it has practically ceased to denominate a discernible entity. It is through this preoccupation with the self that Roth maintains his connection with the tradition of literary realism. But one of the remarkable achievements of *Zuckerman Bound* is that by wedding this preoccupation to an inner sensibility of cynicism and absurdity which fundamentally attacks the notion of selfhood, Roth questions the premises of realism itself. *Zuckerman Bound* is as much about the situation of contemporary literature as it is about the self which has made this literature possible.

In its ordinary usage, the self appears as a collage of social rights, expectations, and assumptions about politics, family life, sex, and that lingering dream of the American way of life: happiness. And in one way or another it is the pursuit of happiness – not the Sadean drive toward pleasure – that characterises Nathan Zuckerman. When Nathan interrogates his brother after their father's funeral, he asks: 'How unhappy are you at home, Henry?' (p. 394). Nathan advises him to stop playing the obedient son and get on with his life. It is the American question and the American answer. Not pleasure, not power, not even sex or money is capable of justifying one's way of life to the degree that the pursuit of happiness can.

Zuckerman's brotherly counsel discloses the inner character of his point of view: give up your role-playing (as *he*, Nathan, supposedly has done) and be yourself. In that, you will find happiness and authentic life. And if you cannot necessarily always find happiness, at least you will pursue it honestly. Good enough advice to a younger brother with a stifling marriage and an over-zealous conscience, but not so easy for Zuckerman himself to follow.

The Anatomy Lesson in particular and *Zuckerman Bound* as a whole brutally analyse this naïve quest for happiness through authenticity. What Zuckerman finds is that at the centre of this authentic selfhood is nothing but images, an empty, gravityless void – a hole, a mouth, an orifice: 'He had turned from a neck and shoulders and arms into a mouth. In that hole was his being' (p. 672). It had been there all along. From the point when Lonoff remarks about Nathan's 'voice' to the surgical wiring of his jaw, he is all mouth.

The ideal of happiness is never explicitly acknowledged by Zuckerman. Rather, he thinks about how 'big' his life was becoming during his undergraduate years:

> He became a large, hearty American six-footer and a contemptuous bohemian all at once, and returned home twelve pounds heavier for his first Christmas vacation, ready to pick a fight with the nearest philistine. In his first year at Chicago he'd go down to the lake and make noises there alone on starry nights – the Gantian goat cry he'd read about in *Of Time and the River*. He

carried *The Waste Land* with him on the El, reading away until Clark Street, where girls no older than himself were taking their clothes off in the striptease bars. If you bought them a drink when they came down off the runway, they did you a favor and put a hand on your cock. He wrote people letters about this . . . he met geniuses sixteen years old. . . . He met girls who never changed their clothes. . . . He had a roommate who wore a cape . . . he'd study from six till ten every night, then head off to Jimmy's where he waited with his friends for the racier members of the faculty to show up. . . . He learned German. He read Galileo, St. Augustine, Freud. He protested the underpaying of the Negroes. . . . He read Croce, he ordered onion soup, he put a candle in a Chianti bottle and threw a party. He discovered Charlie Chaplin . . . he went up to the Near North Side to look down his nose at the advertising types and the tourists. He swam off the Point with a logical positivist, he savagely reviewed beat novels for *The Maroon*, he bought his first classical records . . . from a homosexual salesman at the co-op . . . he began in conversation to call himself 'one.' Oh, everything was wonderful, as big and exciting a life as could be imagined . . . (pp. 581–5)

What stands out in this recollection is the feeling that this was a time of incredible activity, of action. He became, he carried, he'd go down, he wrote letters, he bought girls' drinks, he met geniuses, he studied, he read, he put a candle in a bottle, he threw a party, he discovered, he swam off the Point, he reviewed books; and finally he wrote a story which eventually caused all this wonderful action to end. Zuckerman's Rabelaisian catalogue of deeds does not discriminate between buying a girl a drink so that she would put her hand on your cock and reading *The Waste Land*, between throwing a party and reading Galileo. All is equally wonderful. He has no overriding moral or intellectual attachments. What interests him is not knowledge, beauty, or truth for their own sakes, but rather something like the feeling of life, of being alive. It is a sensation of abundance akin, perhaps, to that 'sentiment of being' which Rousseau believed to be the *sine qua non* condition for happiness and virtue. Zuckerman's instinct for life is extraordinary. Fed initially by literature, literature finally defeats it.

No religious, social, political, or moral identification could provide this 'sentiment of being'; in the end, literature itself deprives him of it. Neither authentic selfhood nor happiness are

possible for Zuckerman after a certain point, and he realises that his
life itself is without justification. All he can do henceforth is 'drift':

> Yet if that really was the psyche's enjoinder, to what end? To no
> end? To the end of ends? To escape completely the clutches of
> self-justification? To learn to lead a wholly indefensible,
> unjustifiable life – and to learn to like it?　(pp. 443–4)

A wholly indefensible, unjustifiable life may well be for Zuckerman
'the character test to top them all', but it is not terribly unlike the real
moral, psychological, and social test to which many of those in our
society who, like Zuckerman, have 'made it' are daily put. Expelled
from the possibility of real happiness, Zuckerman is propelled into
the life which, with some qualifications, any member of the
upper-middle class might well consider happy.

　　In his imaginative escape from the mind-ghetto of the middle
class – looking down his nose at advertising types, picking fights
with philistines – Zuckerman has re-entered it through a back door.
He recognises as much: 'Chicago had sprung him from Jewish New
Jersey, then fiction took over and boomeranged him right back'
(p. 586). Indeed, the whole narrative structure of *Zuckerman Bound* is
that of a rondo. Anne Frank haunts Zuckerman's dreams of Amy
Bellette, but then appears in the guise of Caesara O'Shea, who had
half of Dublin in tears over her youthful performance, then in
the guise of Eva Kalinova, the Czech actress whose stirring
performances won the heart of Prague but also the government's
slanderous accusation that she herself was Jewish – another case of
mistaken identity. What is imagined in *The Ghost Writer* becomes a
fact of the State in *The Prague Orgy*. Similarly, Judge Wapter's ten
questions for Nathan Zuckerman are posed somewhat differently
by the college staff of the *Chicago Maroon* in their attempted
interview in *The Anatomy Lesson*. Dencombe's avowal of doubt,
passion, and madness in James's *The Middle Years* becomes the
leitmotif of Zuckerman's struggle against his own vocation in *The
Anatomy Lesson* and is the theme of Sisovsky's personality ('tell him
about your doubt, Zdenek!' Eva urges) in *The Prague Orgy*.

　　The most brutally ironic repetition, however, is in Zuckerman's
own enactment of the life he attempts through art to escape. What
objectively characterises Zuckerman at the end? Certainly not an
overtly adversarial relationship to his world. True, he is in conflict
with his family – a 'conflict of integrities', as he puts it – but even his

is localised in his relationships to his father and brother. He criticises the US government, but here, as well, the disdain is localised to certain key figures (Nixon and Johnson) and does not encompass the system as a whole. So, too, with the 'culture' itself. Gone, by *The Anatomy Lesson*, is the contempt for the advertising types and philistines. Pepler fascinates him; he willingly submits to the care of his agents and the financial advice of his accountant; nor has he any apparent animus toward the ordinary, philistine businessmen and doctors he meets along the way. Zuckerman has none of the ironic acerbity of a Bellow, the outrage of a Ginsburg, or the moral weight of an Arthur Miller. The only member of society toward whom he evinces any passion is his fellow intellectual, Milton Appel.

Zuckerman is entirely middle class in his ambivalences, frustrations, and commitments. Even his relationship to his family is defined by a certain decorous intimacy – none of the open warfare of a Stephen Dedalus, for instance. His brother won't see him; he would welcome a reconciliation. At heart, Zuckerman appears to be a bit of a sentimentalist, as well. Over his mother's houseplants and clothes, he finds himself swept up in nostalgia. 'How are Things in Gloca Mora, this fine day . . . ?' brings on a 'spasm of emotion' when he accidentally tunes it in on the radio (p. 456).

No existential Stranger, Kafkaesque K., or Sadean libertine could ever touch this vein of ordinary 'human' sentiment. No Sartrean Roquentin could return to these sentiments as though they were givens of experience, rather than willed constructs of inauthentic consciousness. Zuckerman could never utter Sade's radical perception that 'moral science is simply geography misconstrued', though he could be imagined agreeing with it. Roth takes pains to show just how deeply a part of the moral geography Zuckerman is: his high-priced accountant weans him away from his Triple-A bonds and the accountant's wife weans him back to triple-x sex; his celebrity literary agents supervise his personal life and arrange liaisons for Zuckerman with other suitable celebrities. He is successful, rich, self-indulgent, surrounded by pliable, helpful, well-intentioned women, concerned doctors, loving parents, numerous fans and admirers. He is written up in gossip columns and fawned upon by the staff at Billings. While Zuckerman's name recalls the idea of 'sucker', it also contains it in the German word for 'sugar' – *zucker*. And, indeed, the two words are intimately connected. The final act of assimilation occurs in *The Prague Orgy* as, to the stifled artists of Czechoslovakia, he literally becomes an

ambassador of the United States. He teaches Olga about American
girls, how Americans speak and act; he is summed up by Bolotka
who tries on his herringbone tweed suit 'to see how it feels to be a
rich American writer' (p. 737).

These identities are created for him by others, but the key to
Zuckerman's identity is that he does nothing to reject them. He
offers no resistance. And even in the brilliant last chapters of *The
Anatomy Lesson* when his 'inner self' erupts in opposition to the
world of ordinary values, it is as a caricature, a transformation of
himself, a self-reflexive monster. Here, too, it must be noted he is
created out of a text – not *Carnovsky*, 'Higher Education', or *The Diary
of Anne Frank*, but *Lickety Split*, the greatest porno magazine of them
all. Zuckerman cannot resist these identities because there is
nothing to resist with. There is, finally, no inner self, no self at all
except that which emerges in relationship with the world.

What Nathan hopes to leave behind in Newark confronts him in
Czechoslovakia. His father's point of view has become that of the
state. Roth's intention seems to be not simply to suggest a facile
equivalence between the situation of writers in the West with those
in the East. Rather, by adding *The Prague Orgy* to the trilogy, Roth
cancels the possibility of escape. Nathan cannot get outside himself
– even by going to Czechoslovakia, even by wanting to become a
doctor, even through imagining the worst debauchery of the flesh
and most extreme violation of the soul. Nathan's imagination
enforces its own reality regardless of social, cultural, or political
circumstances. The idea of escape implies the idea of definite
location. Nathan's self is constantly reconstituted by his
circumstances, the projections of others, and his own inner
energies; it does not exist *within* him but between himself and the
strangely transmogrifying world around him. This is what Roth
makes so abundantly clear in *The Prague Orgy* where Zuckerman
becomes the straight man to the carnal shenanigans of others. There
is, finally, nowhere for Nathan to escape from. The Devil resides in
Hell, even if Hell is other people. The demonic quality of Nathan's
interior has no such definable zone.

Nathan's exile and disenfranchisement are unique in literary
history. He is no hero of conscience, art, morality, politics, or social
utopia. He has no plan that puts him at odds with his world. He is
menaced from within by his own insubstantiality. His imagination
serves no purpose and at the end no longer even produces stories
(though Nathan notices the onset of this strange sterility in himself

in *Zuckerman Bound* – p. 345). It has a life of its own shut off from the innumerable personas of his ordinary existence.

The picture of the imagination's life and purpose as it emerges from Roth's trilogy is bleak. Through the imagination the Romantics hoped to discover Universal Truth and the pantheistic spirit of Nature. For Henry James the educated imagination, if it did not lead to anything so grand, constituted the means by which one could 'guess the unseen from the seen' and enlarge one's sense of the truth of daily experience and ultimately the truth about oneself. Whether satisfying or not, happy or not, the truth produced or discovered by the imagination has generally been represented, since the nineteenth century at least, as an end to be pursued. In *Zuckerman Bound*, it is an end Zuckerman cannot prevent himself from pursuing. Nathan's imaginative power is his Mephistopheles, promising at first untold delights and a ravishing vision of the world, but delivering merely a series of trivialising expeditions into sensuality which lead to emotional exhaustion and intellectual sterility.

Zuckerman's consciousness of the contradictions ruling his life brings neither peace nor moral awakening nor happiness nor even that one prized possession, self-knowledge. While his imagination – that power of mind out of which he constructs the texts of himself and others – leads him to recognise and purify these contradictions, it also urges him to escape from them: to become a doctor or Milton Appel, porno tzar with a mission. It is only as these fictional selves that Zuckerman can find any constructive purpose or activity. His imagination has destroyed his ability to be a human being 'in the everyday sense of the word', as Lonoff might put it. But it is not clear from *Zuckerman Bound* that the non-everyday sense of self Zuckerman acquires, his non-everyday humanity is in any way superior to that which he has left behind. He may have fewer illusions than his brother, father, or Judge Wapter; he has, it is true an incomparable sense of humour and can laugh in a way the real Milton Appel cannot. But his laughter becomes hysterical and neither his store of moral virtue nor his sheer human vitality is increased by these attributes. The value of the knowledge and being provided him through the imagination is fundamentally questioned in these novels.

At the close of Dostoyevsky's 'Notes from Underground', the underground man can claim: 'I have only in my life carried to an extreme what you have not dared to carry half-way, and what's more, you have taken your cowardice for good sense, and have found comfort in deceiving yourselves. So that perhaps, after all, there is more life in me than in you. Look into it more carefully!' Nathan Zuckerman cannot end on this note of triumph; he does not have more life in him; nor has he become a man 'of the imagination' whose every thought and act are determined by the requirements of art. Rather, he is a man whose imagination is utterly cut off from the daily requirements of his life. It exists in a kind of mental pressure cooker until it finally explodes in the last scenes of *The Anatomy Lesson*. *Zuckerman Bound* is a work testifying not to the power, force, and redemptive virtue of imagination, but to its status as a kind of Grendl-like monster, detached, unassimilated, and unintegrated into the whole of consciousness.

As a figure of the writer in the last quarter of our century, Zuckerman calls attention to a situation not at all uncommon. In the absence of a true literary culture or tradition, in which Zuckerman's texts of himself could find an appropriate context, the imaginative life of the mind does not have a normal place in our society, nor does the writer himself have a specific or discernible role. The underground man could ally himself with a conception of truth given to him by a still vital Christian tradition; Wordsworth could rebel against the state of English society and letters by connecting himself to a tradition that linked Milton to the Bible and a specific conception of nature; Henry James was sustained by a model of culture developed by Matthew Arnold and others. Zuckerman, like most contemporary American writers, has no artistic, conceptual, or even political alternative to the fragmentary world into which he was born. He cannot link himself to a master text that would give unity and purpose to his life.

Cut off from such a master text, only individual readings of his life are possible, only fragmentary allusions, incomplete analogies, inconsistent and contradictory intentions, multiple, overlapping, centreless selves. In this situation, the imagination can no longer be a redemptive agent and becomes nihilistic instead, a tool, finally, of advertising, mass media, 'creative' writing classes, and spiritual self-help programmes, the honorific, if cynical, badge of virtue of the middle class. *Zuckerman Bound* takes us to the heart of his nihilism.

In the world Roth has created, the imagination has no particular affiliations, no mission to accomplish, and it causes only inestimable pain. By the end of *Zuckerman Bound*, Nathan's problems have become considerably larger than himself. 'That writing is an act of the imagination seems to perplex and infuriate everyone' (p. 450), he thinks in *The Anatomy Lesson*: fathers, brothers, critics, judges, governments, and finally Zuckerman himself in his desperate and futile struggle to 'unchain himself from a future as a man apart and escape the corpus that was his' (p. 697).

And yet for all the inner demise of Zuckerman's self, the defeat, weariness, and impotence, there is something not wholly defeated about him or entirely negative. It has to do with the quality of resistance he demonstrates in the face of all the meanings and varieties of significance placed upon the pain he suffers. He does not and cannot resist the selves constructed for him by others, but he does resist the essential process of meaning itself. Like Faust, his greatness consists in his *not* repenting, in his not relenting to the pressure to find meaning in the pain, not succumbing to the need of the imagination to make meaning out of that which is inherently meaningless. He remains open to a fundamental experience of reality to which others with their terrible, sometimes violent, need for meaning remain closed. The refusal to invent, to supply what should be there even if it isn't, marks him with that 'moral stubbornness, the passionate otherness' which he admires about his own incarnation as Milton Appel (p. 640). It is to this principle of rejection that Roth finally purifies Nathan Zuckerman's life. He doesn't buy the meanings supplied by others – whether for his pain, for his hair loss, for his father's death, or his own lack of productivity:

But perhaps, the analyst suggested, the Zuckerman who was getting paid off wasn't the self he perceived as himself but the ineradicable infant, the atoning penitent, the guilty pariah – perhaps it was the remorseful son of the dead parents, the author of *Carnovsky*.

It had taken three weeks for the doctor to say this out loud. It might be months before he broke the news of the hysterical conversion symptom.

'Expiation through suffering?' Zuckerman said. 'The pain being my judgment on myself and that book?'

'Is it?' the analyst asked.

'No,' Zuckerman replied, and three weeks after it had begun, he terminated the therapy by walking out.   (p. 430)

The doctors, fans, judges, relatives, mistresses, government officials are all somehow 'in the know', but their knowledge obfuscates a deeper undecidability, indeterminacy, and impermanence. Finally, their knowledge is at best an arbitrary construction (such as the Czech government official's accusation that Eva Kalinova is Jewish because she appeared as Anne Frank), or at worst a means of pushing back a perception, which Nathan refuses to relinquish, of the absent centre of all meaning (such as his psychoanalyst's assumption that his physical pain provides vast unconscious 'pay offs'). 'But what do I know, other than what I can imagine?' Nathan had asked. He decides to know nothing. This decision is what sets Nathan 'apart' despite all the camouflage of middle class success; and it is to this principle of refusal that Roth has distilled the artistic will.

Index

201